Applying Multicultural and Global Concepts in the Classroom and Beyond

Susan C. Brown
University of Portland

Marcella L. Kysilka
University of Central Florida

Allyn and Bacon

Boston ■ London ■ Toronto ■ Sydney ■ Tokyo ■ Singapore

Series Editor: Traci Mueller
Series Editorial Assistant: Bridget Keane
Marketing Managers: Brad Parkins and Kathleen Morgan
Production Editor: Annette Pagliaro
Editorial Production: Walsh & Associates, Inc.
Composition Buyer: Linda Cox
Manufacturing Buyer: Chris Marson
Cover Administrator: Kristina Mose-Libon
Electronic Composition: Peggy Cabot, Cabot Computer Services

Library of Congress Cataloging-in-Publication Data

Brown, Susan C.
　　Applying multicultural and global concepts in the classroom and beyond /
Susan C. Brown, Marcella L. Kysilka.
　　　　p.　cm.
　　Includes bibliographical references and index.
　　ISBN 0-321-05398-2
　　　　1. Multicultural education—United States.　2. International education—
United States.　I. Kysilka, Marcella L.　II. Title.

LC1099.3 B75 2002
370.117—dc21   2001034134

Printed in the United States of America

10   9   8   7   6   5   4   3   05   04

To the memory of my husband, Robert J. Brown,
whose love of life and care for others needed no translation,
and to our children—Bill, and his wife Tammy, and Jennifer.
SCB

To those students, colleagues, friends, and families
who constantly remind me of their individuality.
MLK

CONTENTS

v

PREFACE

The primary concern of preservice and practicing teachers must be the students in their care. This text is designed for caring teachers because it is about helping these teachers to help their students succeed in the institutions that hold them captive six hours a day, five days a week, and twelve school years of a lifetime. Caring teachers surely hope that the institutions are welcoming and supportive, encouraging all students to succeed. These teachers know, however, that classroom and school environments far too often are suffocating and even threatening, discouraging students in many ways. Fortunately, the application of concepts from multicultural education and global education can provide teachers and other educators with practical possibilities, backed by theoretical foundations, for helping all their students.

Unless teachers truly understand themselves in relationship to the many cultural influences they have had over their lifetimes, they will have trouble understanding their students' cultural backgrounds and experiences, whether these are similar or different from their own. Teachers, in effect, must recognize their individual cultural identities in order to recognize and honor those of their students. Several authors discuss the difficulty of this task for White middle-class teachers, especially for White men who have never experienced personal and/or institutional discrimination (Alquist, 1992; Banks, 1994; Howard, 1999; Nieto, 2000). Those individuals whose behavior has always been considered the norm often do not recognize or do not give credit to other ways of knowing and doing. Even those individuals who have experienced discrimination in one form, for instance, might not have generalized their understanding to include acknowledgment of biases and discriminatory practices against other cultural groups such as those of class, language, religion, or ableness.

This text encourages caring preservice and practicing teachers to take the first step toward providing a welcoming and supportive learning environment for all of their students by providing initial exercises to examine personal cultural influences, beliefs, and attitudes. Without this necessary step, individuals cannot confront their ethnocentric biases and behaviors. The text then leads teachers to acknowledge and confront their deep-seated ethnocentric beliefs and biases so they can begin to develop multicultural and global perspectives. Once they have begun to develop these perspectives, teachers must in turn enable their students to live productive and contributive lives in the global society. Students themselves will need multicultural and global perspectives that give them the knowledge, skills, and attitudes to become active participants in their global world. This whole process is, of course, a monumental undertaking for even the most caring and concerned preservice and practicing teachers. The reward is the transformative knowledge, skills, and dispositions that teachers who are empowered pass on to students who then become empowered. Change can be made, and teachers can be the leaders in change making. This text hopes to offer a support and guideline to those who accept the challenge of the never-ending journey knowing that they and their students will benefit greatly from the experiences and enlightenment along the way.

Text Purpose and Design

This text will provide some theoretical background about multicultural and global concepts, but its main emphasis is on practical applications. The text assumes that preservice teachers and practicing teachers who plan to use the text have had or are presently taking a course or in-depth training in multicultural or global education. If readers do not have this necessary background knowledge, we the authors suggest reading one or more of the standard texts in the fields. This text is, in fact, designed to be a supplementary text or a guidebook for preservice and practicing teachers already familiar with multicultural and global concepts. As such, it deliberately emphasizes the practical application of concepts rather than the theoretical grounding these applications are based on.

The design of the text makes it possible to use later chapters out of sequence. We highly recommend, however, that anyone using the text start with Chapters 1 and 2. Chapter 1 gives background information and Chapter 2 centers on the teacher, the first major critical element in any teaching–learning situation. Without self-assessment, a reader will have difficulty assessing any other critical element in the classroom. Chapters 3 through 7 focus on the other five essential classroom elements: students, environment, curriculum, instruction, and assessment. Finally, Chapters 8 and 9 go beyond the classroom into the school and the community.

In many ways, the chapter divisions are artificial. For example, curriculum, instruction, and assessment often become interwoven, particularly when curricular outcomes such as specific process skills call for authentic tasks and authentic assessment. A less obvious example might be how certain classroom arrangements make cooperative learning activities possible while other arrangements prohibit such student–student interaction. Still, we feel that the divisions allow readers to focus on one element at a time, providing a closer and more in-depth analysis.

The text does not attempt to provide a fully comprehensive coverage of everything preservice and practicing teachers could do in a classroom, school, or community to promote multicultural and global education and to apply the concepts described. It does, however, give a starting point for teachers in classroom, school, and community arenas. It also encourages teachers to go beyond superficial levels of understanding that often result in lack of change by recommending simple modifications that can lead to more complex, involved transformations. For instance, the examples given in the curriculum chapter describe a variety of possibilities for teachers willing to work on curriculum development but do not offer complex lesson plans to be implemented. Other texts that focus on curriculum alone have lessons and even units with multicultural concepts and themes. In turn, they say little about teacher–student interaction or the classroom environment. The benefit of this text is its holistic approach, realizing that all classroom elements are affected by teacher changes in behavior while appreciating that sometimes seemingly small steps are all that can be managed by overburdened preservice and practicing teachers. Small steps in the case of multicultural and global concept application can cover a lot of territory and make a huge difference if they are taken continuously and consistently.

Use of "Think and Act" Boxes

The activities in the "Think and Act" boxes have been designed for both preservice and practicing teachers. For activities needing classrooms, preservice teachers can use college classrooms, their field experience classrooms, or even hypothetical classrooms. For those activities needing individual students, preservice teachers can use their peers if younger students are not available. Lesson plans and units can be developed or modified from practicing teachers, teacher textbook guides, or Internet sites. Texts, journals, and articles can be obtained from most teacher education media centers. The development of excellent scrounging abilities is a hallmark of an inventive teacher, so preservice teachers will do well to start practicing.

The closer the students, colleagues, materials, and teaching–learning situations replicate regular classroom and school elements, the better the learning experiences are likely to be. Practicing teachers, of course, have their own classrooms and their students who will benefit from the proposed applications of multicultural and global concepts. In a university course with a field placement component, preservice teachers can work with practicing teachers. Sharing classrooms for these activities can be enriching for cooperating teachers and preservice teachers alike.

The "Think and Act" activities are meant to be done in pairs, triads, or small groups. The combination of dialogue and reflection is a vital part of rich learning experiences, in our opinion. As advocates for multicultural and global education, we the authors strongly urge that multiple perspectives be presented, analyzed, and discussed. Unless different perspectives are made explicit, many beliefs or assumptions that deeply influence attitudes and behaviors will remain unexamined. U.S. demographic studies show that the preservice and practicing teacher populations have very little of the diversity found in student populations. Bringing out alternative perspectives while discussing multicultural and global concepts with colleagues becomes even more important when other viewpoints are not there to be heard.

Emotional Considerations

Attempting to apply multicultural and global concepts without first examining personal beliefs, values, assumptions, and attitudes is very risky because of the emotional impact of many of the issues. Instructors and students are cautioned to establish a safe and secure classroom environment before multicultural and global education discussions that can be painful are begun. Individuals who have never confronted their own biases before will often resist, either acting out angrily or withdrawing from the conversation or even the course (Ahlquist, 1992). These discussions must not be avoided, however, since the heart and soul of the essential concepts touch also the heart and soul of humans everywhere.

As continuous discussion and reflection about multicultural and global issues causes cognitive dissonance, individuals need to find ways to cope with the emotional stress. One way is through the use of a learning log or diary in addition to the usual notebook of classroom discussions and activities. The learning log, contrary to typical professional journals, should focus on the affective aspects of learning about multicultural and global perspectives and application. Preservice and practicing teachers can gain a better understanding of their own deep-seated beliefs and values by expressing their reactions to specific issues on paper. The specific triggers and the personal reactions can be recorded for future reference. This type of learning log must be private in order for the individual to feel comfortable about revealing feelings. It should therefore be separate and apart from all other written work such as observation journals or research notes.

Even with serious self-assessment, preservice and practicing teachers will find that applying the concepts is hard work that requires the patience and dedication of a lifetime. Again, the authors recommend strongly that all readers work in cooperative and collaborative groups. Group members can act as a support team while offering their individual perspectives on the same issues. Group members can also cheer successful efforts and, even more important, empathize and offer alternative approaches when plans or activities do not go so well. As in most teaching–learning endeavors, cooperation and collaboration keep teachers from feeling isolated and overwhelmed. Besides, this work is too valuable not to be shared with others who can benefit from participation. The reward of enriching the lives of students as well as enriching one's own personal life is worth the extra hours of thought, research, and preparation.

Terminology

Terminology changes over the years, and what was politically correct at one time might not be acceptable at another time. Terminology also changes over distance so what might be used in one place might not be used in another. Nieto (2000) suggests that terminology used to describe people be based on two criteria: (1) what the people themselves want to be called and (2) what is the most precise term. This text will therefore use the following:

1. African American rather than Black unless race is the specific issue
2. American Indian or Native American
3. Asian American
4. European American rather than White unless race is the specific issue
5. Latino or Hispanic

6. People of color as a collective term for people of African American, Latino, Asian American, and American Indian backgrounds rather than non-Whites or minorities
7. United States rather than America for the country; United States or U.S. instead of American

In cases where a specific group within these larger categories is being discussed, that term will be used. For example, Puerto Rican or Cuban American will be chosen over Latino or Hispanic if either of those more specific groups is discussed.

The terms "culture" and "cultural group" have different definitions depending upon the various authors' viewpoints. The definition of culture given by Nieto (2000) is used in this text:

> Culture consists of the values, traditions, social and political relationships, and worldview created, shared, and transformed by a group of people bound together by a common history, geographic location, language, social class, and/or religion, and how these are transformed by those who share them. (p. 138)

Thus, a cultural group is a group of people who share a common culture. In this text, the following cultural groups and their issues are discussed: race/ethnicity, class, religion, gender, sexual orientation, ableness, age, geographic location, and nationality.

In this text, race and ethnicity are grouped together for the discussion of issues, although they are not synonymous terms. Race does not have biological or genetic meaning, but historically the concept of race has been used to categorize people for purposes of discrimination and oppression. Like race, ethnicity has served as a form of group identification. An ethnic group as defined by Banks (1994b) is "an involuntary collectivity of people with a shared feeling of common identity, a sense of peoplehood, and a shared sense of interdependence of fate" (p. 71). Although membership in an ethnic group is involuntary, individual identification with the group is optional. Federal and state forms use combinations of racial, ethnic, and linguistic classifications to identify individuals for a variety of purposes including funding, but any forced labeling of people becomes problematic at best. The richness of cultural diversity in the United States cannot be captured in little boxes. Yet the terms must be considered precisely because of their historical, political, social, and economic implications.

About the Authors

Susan C. Brown has lived and worked in Australia, Canada, Indonesia, Italy, Lebanon, the Philippines, and the United States. Her educational experiences range from second grade teacher in Canada, to Pakistan Embassy School Principal in Indonesia, and to Parents Advisory Board Chair of the International School of Milan in Italy.

Her research interests have focused primarily on multicultural education and global education. In addition to presentations, articles, and book chapters in these areas, Brown has published and presented work in reflective thinking and innovative university teaching. She is Assistant Professor of Education at the University of Portland, Oregon.

Marcella L. Kysilka has traveled extensively and has consulted on educational issues in Australia, the Czech Republic, England, Lithuania, and Taiwan. She is currently engaged in an Urban Teacher Residency Program for new teachers. Kysilka has written and/or edited books on teaching of thinking, educational foundations, adjunct teaching, and honor in teaching. She has published over sixty articles on educational issues and has presented over 100 papers at professional organizations. She is Coordinator of the Doctoral Curriculum and Instruction Program at the University of Central Florida.

Acknowledgments

Our thanks to all who have helped with ideas, suggestions, and thoughtful critiques. Our special thanks to Alex Casareno, Associate Professor of Education at the University of Portland, whose careful review of early and later versions of the manuscript contributed greatly to the final product. Our thanks also to the following reviewers for their time and input: Janet S. Arndt, Gordon College; Mahmoud Suleiman, California State University, Bakersfield; Jaime Romo, National University; and Connie Titone, The College of New Jersey.

PART ONE

Understanding Essential Multicultural and Global Concepts

The twenty-first century will be one of increasing diversity among the peoples of the United States. People of color, one-fourth of the population in 1990, will soon be one-third of the population. In two states, California and Texas, and in many of the major cities, students of color are over half of the public school population.

The immigrant population, from as geographically and culturally diverse groups as Hispanics, Filipinos, Vietnamese, and Russians, will continue to grow in the twenty-first century. The majority of these immigrants are school-aged children, some with little or no experience with schooling.

Linguistic diversity is also increasing in the United States. Although English continues to be the language of economic and social advance, 14 percent of the school population speaks another language at home. In many schools today, over fifty different languages are spoken by the students. For instance, students in one high school in Orange County, Florida, have fifty-two different Latino, Asian, and Eastern European first languages. In addition, numerous other schoolchildren speak some form of dialect or nonstandard English.

Another increasing area of diversity is class as the U.S. population continues to show a widening disparity between the rich and the poor. According to federal government standards, about 20 percent of the population lives below the poverty line. Families in poverty are often headed by single parents, usually women, and have school-aged children.

From these statistics and others, including those for religion and exceptionality, comes the obvious prediction that teachers will continue to work with students of ever-increasing diversity. Yet the teacher population at the turn of twenty-first century is still primarily European American, middle class, Christian, and female. Efforts to attract qualified people from diverse ethnic and racial backgrounds into teaching have met with limited success. Thus the large majority of teachers, in the beginning of the twenty-first century at least, do not have the same cultural heritage and experiences as a large percentage of their students.

How teachers work in classrooms, schools, and communities to teach, honor, and empower all students to be successful is the essence of multicultural and global education as applied in teachers' lives. Chapter 1 introduces the concepts of multicultural education and global education, describes how they can be combined into a cohesive philosophy of multicultural and global education using six major principles, and then discusses the application of these principles in the classroom.

1 Essential Multicultural and Global Concepts

Controversy has surrounded the concepts of multiculturalism and multicultural education from the start (de Anda, 1997; Sleeter, 1995). Many people, including educators like Ravitch (1990), see any approach that emphasizes individual and group differences as being divisive. Others are worried that multiculturalism ultimately means cultural relativism, the acceptance of all beliefs and values as equal. While some wonder what the fuss is all about since there are laws to protect individuals against discrimination, others see laws such as affirmative action legislature as a chance for less-qualified individuals to take away positions from those who rightfully earned them. On the other hand, the radical left critics, such as Giroux (1996), complain that multicultural education is more interested in obtaining justice for students in schools than in confronting the larger societal structure and institutions that oppress groups.

Controversial elements of multicultural education are initially divisive, especially when individuals are forced to confront their own biases and prejudices. Yet no thoughtful educator can ignore the weight of statistics about the students we fail to educate in our school systems. Authors such as Kozol (1991) and Delpit (1995) remind us that student populations that are poor, live in urban settings, have limited English proficiency, and belong to cultural groups of color have high percentages of academic failure. If advocates of multicultural education see the application of its principles as a hopeful way to reach all schoolchildren, then teachers have an obligation to investigate what multicultural education has to offer them.

Global education has had a very different reception from multicultural education. For the most part, global education has been ignored until the contextual circumstances of a school, district, or state have forced some sort of reluctant acknowledgment of its necessity (Diaz, Massialas, & Xanthopoulos, 1999; Merryfield, Jarchow, & Pickert, 1997). Although economic fears drive much of this concern, the reality of global interdependence confronts us in daily issues and events such as global warming predictions and international terrorism. As the new millennium starts, the global economy and the international communication network are forcing educators and policymakers alike to reevaluate their positions.

Being a part of the economically and politically powerful United States has affected the viewpoints of many Americans towards other countries and continents.

Because of their privileged positions as U.S. citizens, they tend to be insular and poorly informed about issues elsewhere. In a sense, they have attitudes found commonly in a dominant cultural group: "It's their problem; let them solve it." The lack of knowledge and understanding about realities in other parts of the world give U.S. citizens, especially those who have not lived or traveled extensively in other countries, less chance for comparisons and contrasts and less possibility of seeing other perspectives. This insular approach also leads some critics to feel that it is somehow un-American to find fault in the international policies and practices of U.S. companies and the government. Stressing global perspectives in the classroom, however, does not lead to a diminishing of national pride but a heightening awareness of citizen duties, responsibilities, and positive global attitudes (Diaz et al., 1999). Teachers need to be aware of international concerns and controversies, especially those involving the United States, so they can act as informed citizens and participants in the global society.

This chapter deals with how the two fields of multicultural education and global education can be combined to produce a cohesive philosophy for caring teachers. Further, it provides essential concepts that establish a foundation for classroom practice.

Defining Multicultural Education

Multicultural Education Approaches

Multicultural education has taken several forms over the last thirty or forty years. In the 1960s three different approaches emerged, according to Sleeter and Grant (1988). The first was teaching the exceptional and the culturally different. This was primarily seen as a way to help students of color, students in poverty, students with limited English proficiency, and students who had special educational needs succeed in mainstream education. The second was the human relations approach, an attempt to help people with differing backgrounds—especially race, gender, and handicap—communicate and work together better. The third was the single group studies, especially ethnic and women's studies, which tried to raise consciousness about that group's oppression and to take social action.

By the 1970s, two more approaches were emerging. The first one, multicultural education, is described by Sleeter and Grant (1988) as an approach that "links race, language, culture, gender, handicap, and, to a lesser extent, social class, working toward making the entire school celebrate human diversity and equal opportunity" (p. 28). The second approach, education that is multicultural and social reconstructionist, extends the multicultural education approach to social action and the restructuring of teaching–learning contexts and society itself. This approach emphasizes the process and context as well as the content, and leads students to be decision makers and change makers for social good.

Think and Act

■ Make a note of your first awareness of the term "multicultural education." Was it in public school, university, teacher training, or in practice?

■ Describe your first impressions of multicultural education. Did you relate it to your personal life and/or your teaching? Did you relate it to a particular cultural group, a specific content, an experience, and/or a philosophy?

■ Research past issues of your local newspaper for mention of the terms "multicultural," "multiculturalism," and "diversity." How are the terms used? In what contexts?

Multicultural Education as a Process

Although Sleeter and Grant's (1988) terminology for this approach, "education that is multicultural and social reconstructivist," has not been adopted by most authors in the field, the concept of change making or transformation is basic to most definitions. In this text, multicultural education is seen as a combination of definitions by Geneva Gay (1994) and Sonia Nieto (2000). Gay (1994) sees multicultural education as

> the policies, programs, and practices employed in schools to celebrate cultural diversity. It builds on the assumption that teaching and learning are invariably cultural processes. Since schools are composed of students and teachers from a wide variety of cultural backgrounds, the best way for the educational process to be most effective for the greatest number of students is for it to be multicultural. (p. 3)

Although this definition sounds as if any policy, program, or practice used to mention diversity would qualify as multicultural education, Gay is very careful to define "celebrate" as incorporating the appropriate knowledge, skills, attitudes, and behavior needed. Events such as international festivals are often considered community celebrations, but they would not fit Gay's definition of celebrating cultural diversity in the truest sense.

Nieto's (2000) definition puts more emphasis than Gay's on the dynamic process component of multicultural education. In her text, *Affirming Diversity,* Nieto (2000) states:

> Multicultural education is a process of comprehensive school reform and basic education for all students. It challenges and rejects racism and other forms of discrimination in schools and society and accepts and affirms the pluralism (ethnic, racial, linguistic, religious, economic, and gender, among others) that students, their communities, and teachers reflect. Multicultural education permeates the schools' curriculum and instructional strategies, as well as the interactions among teachers, students, and families, and the very way that schools conceptualize the nature of teaching and learning. Because it uses critical pedagogy as its underlying philosophy and focuses on

knowledge, reflection, and action *(praxis)* as the basis for social change, multicultural education promotes the democratic principles of social justice. (p. 305)

Although sexual orientation, age, and ableness are not explicitly stated, these cultural groups must also be included. Nieto's definition expects teachers, students, and other participants in multicultural education to play active roles in the ongoing process of promoting social justice. Also stressed is the complete involvement of every part in the educational system.

Multicultural education that calls for social action is similar to critical pedagogy in that "both refer to a particular ethico-political attitude or ideological stance that one constructs in order to confront and engage the world critically and challenge power relations" (Sleeter & McLaren, 1995, p. 7). Teachers who support these positions are not just actively working toward human rights, equality of opportunity, and so forth in their classrooms. They become "cultural workers" for social justice in that their context goes beyond the classrooms to schools and other public arenas such as community centers and social services (Freire, 1998; Sleeter & McLaren, 1995).

Recognizing multicultural education as a dynamic process that changes the teaching-learning contexts leads to the acknowledgement of the interaction of critical elements in the classroom, the school, and the community. The classroom elements, discussed in Part Two, are the teacher, the students, the classroom environment, the curriculum, the instruction, and the assessment. Critical elements beyond the classroom, discussed in Part Three, are the school and the community. The outcome of multicultural education would be students' having the knowledge, skills, attitudes, and behaviors to be active participants for a democratic and just society.

Think and Act

- What do you remember from your own schooling about issues related to multicultural education? Share in a group your most vivid impressions and analyze their effects.
- Why have many teachers centered on celebrating special cultural events as their approach to multicultural education? Why are topics like racism and sexism avoided or minimized?
- Describe what Nieto (2000) means by a process as it relates to you and your teaching. Where do you see yourself in this process now? Five years from now?

Defining Global Education

Global Education Content

Global education, sometimes associated with but distinct from multicultural education, can be seen as having multicultural concepts applied to the world community and emphasizing the planet, its natural resources, and all interconnections. The Hanvey (1976) model includes five interdisciplinary dimensions. The first, *perspective consciousness,* includes an awareness of and appreciation for other viewpoints of the world. The second, *state of the planet awareness,* emphasizes global issues and events. The third, *cross-cultural awareness,* is an understanding of world cultures, especially in light of similarities and differences. The fourth, *systemic awareness,* deals with the nature of global systems and their patterns of interrelationships and interdependence. The fifth, *options for participation,* presents possibilities for participating in local, national, and international settings.

Although earlier explanations of content for global education were expressed more as intellectual understandings (Hanvey, 1976; Kniep, 1986), more recent approaches have included social action as well as social thought and debate. Merryfield and colleagues' (1997) content list, for example, contains eight general elements: *human beliefs and values, global systems, global issues and problems, global history, cross-cultural understanding and interaction, awareness of human choices, development of analytical and evaluative skills,* and *strategies for participation and involvement.* Educators such as Kirkwood (1990), who implemented global education in Dade County, FL, would agree with viewing global education as an agent for social action and change.

Think and Act

- Make a note of your first awareness of the term "global education." Was it in public school, university, teacher training, or in practice?
- Describe your first impressions of global education. Did you relate it to your personal life and/or your teaching? Did you relate it to a particular national group or groups, a specific content, an experience and/or a philosophy?
- Research past issues of your local newspaper for mention of the terms "global education," "global competition," and "global village." How are the terms used? In what contexts?

Global Education as a Process

As global education has matured over the years, the definitions have also been refined. An early definition of global education used by the National Council for the Social Studies (NCSS, 1982) is:

> Global education is an effort to cultivate in young people a perspective of the world which emphasizes the interconnections among cultures, species, and the planet. The purpose of global education is to develop in youth the knowledge, skills, and attitudes needed to live effectively in a world possessing limited natural resources and

characterized by ethnic diversity, cultural pluralism, and increasing interdependence. (pp. 1–2)

Merryfield's 1994 definition, although very similar, differs in crucial ways:

Global education develops the knowledge, skills, and attitudes that are necessary for decision-making and effective participation in a world characterized by inter-connectedness, cultural pluralism, and increasing competition for resources. (p. 4)

Merryfield's substitution of "decision-making and effective participation" for "living effectively" gives a clearer image of a proactive person. The addition of the element of economic competition for the limited world resources and markets reflects the more modern concerns of the twenty-first century.

Teachers advocating global education would think in terms of the multicultural global village and its problems, rather than considering only the multicultural community of the immediate or national environment. Like multicultural education, however, global education is also seen as a process that transforms. Teachers who support global education also wish to enlighten and empower students for the social good.

Think and Act

■ What do you remember from your own schooling about issues related to global education? Share in a group your most vivid impressions and analyze their effects.

■ Why have many teachers centered on concepts and related activities like pollution and recycling? Why isn't there more emphasis on dangers of international conglomerates, for instance?

■ Describe what is meant by "a world characterized by cultural pluralism, interconnectedness, and international economic competition" as it relates to you and your teaching now and five years from now.

Combining Multicultural
Education and Global Education

As can be seen from the earlier discussions, multicultural education and global education have many commonalties but different emphases. Both involve a process whereby individuals develop knowledge, skills, attitudes, and behaviors for participating effectively in a culturally diverse society. While multicultural education stresses individuals and cultural groups within their local and national society, global education emphasizes world problems and interconnections within the global context. When combined, multicultural education and global education can be seen as two parts of the same theme of how individuals, groups, and institutions can work together to build a better world locally, nationally, and internationally (Brown, 1993).

The resulting definition for multicultural and global education used in this text is the following:

> Multicultural and global education can be seen as the educational process of acquiring certain knowledge, skills, and values to participate actively in a complex, pluralistic, and interconnected world society and to work together for change in individuals and institutions in order to make that world society more just and humane.

This definition includes student preparation to become knowledgeable, caring, and active citizens. Implied is the need to develop and practice the skills of citizenship. The focus is not only on the diversity of individuals and cultural groups but also on the interconnectedness of all individuals and groups and the need to work together for solving the world's problems.

Combining the Major Concepts of Multicultural Education and Global Education

In 1984, Donna Cole discussed common connections between multicultural education and global education that she could anticipate leading to a merger of "multiculturalized global education" (p. 153). Using Cole's ideas combined with references from multicultural education and global education, Brown (1993) listed five categories, which are discussed in the sections below.

- Understanding of social living in groups
- Understanding of the "other"
- Understanding of interrelatedness and interdependence
- Development of skills in living with diversity
- Adjustment to changes for the future

Social Living in Groups

This concept involves understanding oneself and how one fits into cultural groups and into larger macrocultures, such as the United States and Earth. Each person needs to understand himself or herself as an individual, a member of various cultural groups, and a member of humanity. One way to see this conceptually is to imagine each individual as a whole pie shape divided into three equal parts. The first third is composed of individual characteristics—what makes that person unique. The second third is composed of cultural group characteristics—what makes that person part of the specific culture or cultures relevant in that particular situation. The last third is composed of human characteristics—what makes that person part of humanity.

Keeping all three parts of any individual's characteristics in balance is an important part of the combined multicultural and global education. A heavy emphasis on any one of the parts affects the other two parts. If teachers look at only the individual characteristics of their students, the students' memberships in cultural groups might be ignored. For instance, one European American middle school male teacher demanded that a young Latino being disciplined look at him directly: "Look me in the eye. A man looks a man in the eye!" (Brown, personal experience). The teacher focused only on the individual and ignored, or was ignorant of, any possible differences in cultural behaviors. If that student's Latino relatives had taught him to stare at the ground to show his humility and lower status when being disciplined, for the student not to do that would be, in effect, an insult to the teacher according to his culture. Such cultural mismatches can leave students bewildered, embarrassed, or frustrated.

In an attempt to avoid uncomfortable issues, some European American teachers naively state that they see every student as an individual, not as a member of a race. According to Nieto (2000), these teachers are like most Whites, who have the advantage of seeing themselves as individuals—"an opportunity not generally afforded to those from dominated groups" (p. 79). In this case, the overemphasis on the individual reduces the importance of the cultural group of race, minimizing or ignoring real problems such as personal and institutional racism.

An overemphasis on the specific cultural group of an individual also affects the other two parts. When others acknowledge only the race or the religion of an outsider person, they are ignoring that person's individual characteristics and human characteristics. In this form, such an emphasis becomes the basis for "isms" such as racism and sexism. The Ku Klux Klan and neo-Nazi groups, for instance, foster extreme hatred by whipping up emotions around one salient group characteristic such as skin color. Groups themselves can overemphasize the group, forcing members to give up individual choices different from the group or friendships with others outside the group. Some religious groups like the Amish might not directly target other religions, but unity is achieved at the price of submitting to the group will. In the case of cults, submission is to the leaders as ultimate authorities.

Ethnic studies provide the positive benefits of supplementing cultural history and information too often lacking in the middle-class European American Christian curriculum that dominates most U.S. schools. One potential danger, however, is that an extreme emphasis on ethnicity could ignore individual differences within the group or ignore the commonalties found in humans. Examination of multicultural issues through the study of various cultural groups contains the same risks, since generalizations about groups can easily lead into stereotypes. For example, in interactions like the one mentioned above between the European American teacher and the Latino student, a rigid expectation that every European American man would demand eye-to-eye contact or that every Latino boy would feel conflict and embarrassment would be stereotyping both persons even if their respective cultural groups had tendencies to act in certain predictable ways. In any interaction, the individuals must be considered as well as their cultural groups.

Finally, an overemphasis on the similarities of people as humans can adversely affect the acceptance of individual and group characteristics of a person. Those people who wish to see multicultural and global education as only an acknowledgment of similarities between individuals and groups ignore the multitude of differences within the human race, both as individuals and as cultural groups. Yet the differences are at the center of cultural conflicts. Human history is full of such conflicts, whether caused by race, religion, class, or combinations of these and others. Personal biases, group discrimination, and institutional oppression can be witnessed throughout the world, whether "ethnic cleansing" as in Bosnia, homophobic murders as in the United States, or economic domination of "have not" countries by multinational corporations.

The strong emphasis put on commonalties of humans might leave individuals and groups isolated and frustrated because they do not match the norm model of the dominant society. Certainly their experiences of discrimination in the United States tell children and adults that females are not males, and people of color are not White, Jewish are not Christian, and so forth. Kim, a White student teacher, was heard comforting a Black second-grade girl in a predominantly White class. The girl had just said that nobody liked her because she was Black. The student teacher's comment was "It's because you're new here and the other children don't know you. I remember when I was new in school. . . ." The student teacher's attempt to comfort the little girl ignored the child's race and stressed only the similarities of the human experience of being in a new social situation. In a sense, she treated the girl's blackness as nothing, not worth bothering about, instead of acknowledging two crucial points: the reality of possible racism and the richness of diverse cultural heritages.

Think and Act

■ Describe briefly a childhood incident (one that you are willing to share) when you were discriminated against because of your membership in a cultural group. Explain your feelings at the time of the incident. Looking back, how do you feel now?

■ Observe a group of students talking among themselves. Note the power relationships. Who dominates and is listened to? Who is ignored or excluded?

■ Share stories told by children about acts of discrimination. Compare and contrast these stories to your own.

The "Other"

The combined multicultural and global education concept emphasizes multiple perspectives. If every individual is unique, carrying a unique combination of individual, group, and human characteristics that is "self," then each person's perspective or worldview is also unique. In dealing with ethnic identity issues, the difficulty comes in recognizing other perspectives as valid while maintaining a positive attitude and self-esteem about one's own ethnicity. Teachers will probably find this concept the most challenging, since it touches many core beliefs and values. Yet teachers and students must be open to other perspectives for any multicultural and global learning to happen.

An initial step to understanding can be gained by being aware of the growth process necessary. Banks (1991) describes stages that individuals can experience in his typology of ethnic identifications: Stage 1, ethnic psychological captivity; Stage 2, ethnic encapsulation; Stage 3, ethnic identity clarification; Stage 4, biethnicity; Stage 5, multiethnicity and reflective nationalism; and Stage 6, globalism and global competency. Banks suggests that these stages are developmental, although not strictly sequential, and that the stages are not distinctly separated.

The first two stages have serious negative implications. Stage 1, ethnic psychological captivity, describes the individuals who have low self-esteem and shame about their ethnicity as a result of internalizing the negative beliefs and ideologies about that ethnicity that are found in the dominant society. This would be typical of Blacks, for instance, who have internalized the White message of the lighter the skin, the better. Stage 2, ethnic encapsulation, describes the individuals who see only their ethnic position or viewpoint as the right or superior one as a result of living and working primarily within their own community and accepting the societal myths about their ethnic superiority. This would be typical of Whites who have not been forced to examine their privileged position in U.S. society or who have felt so threatened by confrontation with another ethnic group that they have reacted negatively.

Stage 3 of the typology by Banks (1991), ethnic identity clarification, is the beginning of a positive approach to ethnicity. It describes the individuals who have positive self-acceptance of their own ethnicity and are ready to respond positively to other ethnic groups. Stage 4, biethnicity, describes the individuals who are bicultural with positive ethnic identities and the skills to function successfully in two cultures. Stage 5, multiethnicity and reflective nationalism, describes the individuals who are able to function effectively within several ethnic and cultural groups. This stage, according to Banks (1991), represents "the idealized goal for citizenship identity within an ethnically pluralistic nation" (p. 66). As such, the fifth stage is the desired outcome of multicultural education.

Stage 6, globalism and global competency, describes the individuals who have achieved the highest level by being able to function effectively in ethnic cultures nationally and internationally. According to Banks (1991), these individuals "have internalized universalistic ethical values and principles of humankind and have the skills, competencies, and commitments needed to act on these values" (p. 66). This sixth stage represents the desired outcome of multicultural and global education and the goal of this text.

Although the typology by Banks (1991) refers specifically to ethnic identity, similar stages can be found with other cultural identifications. Sexual orientation, for instance, becomes extremely sensitive as children reach puberty. While adolescents of color may have special difficulties because of racist issues in the dominant society, all adolescents face struggles with finding their identities, including their sexuality (Santrock, 2001). Therefore, it is very understandable why middle school becomes the place for serious sexual harassment and why boys and girls who think they are gay, lesbian, bisexual, or transsexual feel so much at risk. Without a supportive environment at home and in school, they internalize the homophobic messages their peers and adults send.

Tied with multiple perspectives is the understanding of knowledge as a construction process, one of Banks's (1997) dimensions of multicultural education. Historical data and explanations in textbooks, for instance, can be seen as selected information reflecting the viewpoint of the dominant culture instead of as objective, accurate reports of past times and events. When viewed in this manner, all sources of information become open to examination for omissions, distortions, and biases. Multiple perspectives bring in the voices not heard when historical material has been processed through ethnocentric filters by the winners of any cultural conflicts.

Multiple perspectives affect cultural, national, and international viewpoints as well as individual ones. The concentration on Western civilization in high schools and universities to the marginalization or exclusion of world cultures has left U.S. students ignorant of much of the world's rich history. Presenting these from multiple perspectives adds a richness and wholeness not seen in the Eurocentric perspectives of most history textbooks in the United States. Global history or global studies, a content dimension of global education (Kniep, 1986; Merryfield et al., 1997), reminds teachers of global systems, global interconnectedness and interdependence, and global problems and issues in the past, present, and future. Unfortunately, the courses are too often taught from a European American perspective by teachers who are woefully lacking in world history and world studies content knowledge.

Think and Act

- Choose a recent local or TV event known by you and several others. Each person should jot down details of what happened. Compare results.
- Use a newspaper account of some educational issue as a starter. Put down as many perspectives as you can. Discuss who might hold each perspective and why.
- Make a collection of international news stories from your local newspaper. Discuss the perspectives presented. Note what U.S. interests are revealed. Why are these particular stories given space in the newspaper?

Interrelatedness and Interdependence

This aspect of multicultural and global education is particularly important in the information age. In the past few years, as the concept of a global village has become more of a reality to students and teachers everywhere, global education as a discipline has gained momentum and greater recognition, although multicultural education is still more widespread (Merryfield et al., 1997). Instant access to information about these individuals and institutions, even instant access to the people and groups themselves, has brought about a realization that isolation from the world and its problems is virtually impossible. Interrelatedness, or interconnectedness as used in much of global education literature, and interdependence are certainly realities as well as global concepts for the twenty-first century.

Global systems, according to Kniep (1986) and Merryfield and colleagues (1997), include economic, political, technological, and ecological elements and the ways they are interconnected and interdependent; a change in one part affects other parts. For instance, an example witnessed and explained to one of the authors involved a small settlement of Brazilian Indians. Years earlier a European-owned manufacturing plant built in the upper Amazon region attracted many impoverished people, some walking two hours each way to earn very low wages. Then in the early 1990s, a cruise line arranged with the settlement leaders to allow the passengers a tour of the village and its homes. The tourists with their dollars disrupted the village patterns again, making it more profitable for the villagers to sell handmade goods or to beg than to walk to work. Both the manufacturing plant and the cruise line provided much-needed wages and, in the case of the cruise line at least, extra funds for building and supplying an elementary school. Yet the two international corporations destroyed the traditional way of life without replacing it with a stable, self-sufficient economy. A small village, international corporations, several countries and their governments, and citizens from a multitude of nations all became interconnected and interdependent, creating one example of a global problem.

Think and Act

- Jot down two or three personal ties to people and organizations outside of your country. How were the ties established? How are they maintained? What purpose do they have in your life?
- Think of a recent world event that has had an impact on your life. Describe the circumstances and your reaction.

Living with Diversity

As the world becomes more and more interconnected and interdependent, the skills of working cooperatively with others for solutions to local, national, and international global problems become more and more important. At the local level, corporations and institutions have become more service oriented, demanding of their employees better interpersonal skills to deal with suppliers and customers. Businesses also expect the employees to be able to work on teams within the company to problem solve. As businesses expand nationally and internationally, executives are learning that their employees must have appropriate skills for living and working with diverse people. In international situations, company representatives stationed in foreign countries have found that corporate success often depends more upon the expatriate manager's personal skills of empathy, ability to remain nonjudgmental, and tolerance for ambiguity rather than his or her technical and managerial skills (Gregersen & Black, 1990; Hall & Gudykunst, 1989).

The Brazilian story highlights the question of responsibility for global problems and issues. The corporations were not the only participants in disrupting the village way of life. People who demanded cheaper goods and people who paid to see the Amazon and its inhabitants must also take responsibility. The governments that allowed the exploitation of labor must also be held responsible. Global problems and global issues then become everyone's responsibility. Learning about these concerns and what individuals can do is an initial step toward bringing about change.

Think and Act

- Describe briefly a childhood incident (one that you are willing to share) when you overcame a misunderstanding related to differences in cultural backgrounds. What responsibility did each person take for clearing up the misunderstanding?
- Investigate one of several issues associated with huge cruise ships: influx of foreign capital, pollution of the oceans, disruption of traditional ways and livelihoods, redistribution of land, or others. What perspectives do the various stakeholders take?
- Write letters to cruise lines or international entertainment groups such as Club Med about their policies and practices toward indigenous peoples in impoverished areas. Ask how they contribute to the welfare of the communities other than through salaries.

Changes for the Future

Adjustment to changes must be seen as active preparation for the future rather than a passive acceptance of what is to come. Part of this active participation is the use of knowledge and skills to work toward solutions to local, national, and international problems and issues. This combines the personal need to be flexible and open to multiple perspectives with the ability to act for social justice. Multicultural and global education is a positive approach and a process empowering students now for present and future action.

Think and Act

- Name one action you have taken outside the classroom for social justice. It can be something in your personal life such as a stand against racist or sexist jokes or a position in your professional life such as membership to an organization promoting multicultural or global concepts. Why did you do this? What type of personal courage did it take?
- Prepare and role play scenarios from these personal experiences of you and your teammates. Ask the audience to provide a variety of endings.

Applying Multicultural and Global Education in the Classroom

The six applications below come from the multicultural and global education concepts just discussed. If teachers truly support multicultural and global education, in our opinion, teachers must accept both the concepts and the process of empowering students. Belief in multicultural and global education must become part of teachers' core values and beliefs system. If the belief is not internalized, teachers will only bring superficial aspects of multicultural and global education into their classrooms. They will be unable to bring the kind of multicultural and global education that empowers students to participate actively as global citizens.

- Diversity must be celebrated.
- Human rights must be honored.
- Multiple perspectives must be sought.
- Interconnectedness and interdependence must be developed.
- Co-responsibility must be practiced.
- The global society must be experienced.

Diversity

Diversity of every sort makes up our planet Earth, providing infinite variety in so many ways. The richness of that diversity is something to enjoy, treasure, and protect. In a similar way, diversity of humans and human characteristics fills the classroom. The wide variety found in even a small handful of students offers exciting possibilities to the teacher who knows how to take advantage of these differences. In multicultural and global education, the diversity of humans is seen as a richness to be enjoyed, treasured, and protected. Teachers and students must not see diversity as a problem. The challenge is *not* the diversity itself but tapping into the diversity in a positive way. Given the global village of today with its interconnectedness and interdependence, students need regular and positive experiences with as many types of diversity as possible. Such experiences, with the guidance of the teacher, will help them to develop the lifelong skills needed to be a proactive citizen in the global society. Not providing students with tools to enjoy and benefit from diversity is a serious neglect on the part of any teacher.

Think and Act

- Why might a teacher be unwilling to see diversity as something to celebrate?
- Jot down three types of diversity that seem the most challenging in a classroom. Give a reason for each choice. Compare your results with two or three others.
- Attend an event or exhibit that highlights types of diversity in your community. Look beyond ethnic and racial diversity for examples.

Human Rights

Lynch (1992) advocates that multicultural and global education should start with human rights at its core. In the classroom, human rights must certainly be a main emphasis. Each student must feel safe, secure, and wanted as a member of the class. All students need to learn how to work with one another without resorting to bullying, name calling, or any painful tactics. For teachers, honoring human rights means not exploiting the power and position by using sarcasm or any other form of belittling. Beyond avoiding blatant behavior, however, is the subtler positive behavior of affirming students and their diverse cultural heritages and experiences.

In many U.S. schools, student harassment of other students is a common occurrence. Corridors and cafeterias have become hostile places for the targeted individuals or groups. Teachers and administrators have an obligation to prevent such behavior from continuing and to punish those who persist. Ignoring verbal and physical threats creates tolerance for discrimination, thereby destroying the foundations for any application of multicultural and global education. Schools and communities can work together to reduce racism, sexism, and classism in the schools. Programs such as those that stress conflict resolution can help students find alternatives to violence. Other programs—such as diversity training—can increase understanding and appreciation of cultural differences among all school members.

Nationally and internationally, human rights issues can be explored using a variety of sources including the Internet. For instance, the Universal Declaration of

Human Rights, adopted by the United Nations in 1948, and the Convention on the Rights of a Child, ratified in 1989 by all United Nations members except Somalia and the United States, can be studied. Of interest to older students can be the reasons given by the United States for not ratifying the latter. UNICEF information about the living and working conditions of women and children around the world can be found on numerous Internet sites, including www.unicef.org/aclabor.

Think and Act

- Remember an incident of name calling when you were a student. How did you feel? How did the teacher act? From each child's perspective, was the incident resolved successfully? From your adult perspective now, what should a teacher have done?
- Call the local school board to see what sort of diversity training is provided in the district for administrators, teachers, and staff. Ask for copies of the literature used.
- Check Internet sites for either women's rights or children's rights information. Research a particular issue such as sweat shops.

Multiple Perspectives

The acceptance of diversity of humans as a richness means also the acceptance of different ways of looking at the world, for each human in his or her uniqueness looks at the world through a unique perspective. Teachers have the huge responsibility of seeing and searching out other perspectives while helping students to do the same. They must model the openness and flexibility needed for empathizing with others. They must be able to walk in another's moccasins, truly understanding where that person is situated in the world. This openness and flexibility must be for their own students first, then for the other voices not ordinarily heard. Teachers and students together must actively seek out places and spaces in the critical classroom elements described later where one viewpoint only is represented and where other viewpoints are missing.

Think and Act

- How does the saying "walk in another's moccasins" demonstrate a universal idea while portraying specific Native American cultures? Research the origin of this saying.
- The saying is often stated as "walk *a mile* in another *man's* moccasins." What perspective does "a mile" imply? How do you know that this is an inaccurate perspective for the saying? What perspective does "man's" imply? What kind of research would be necessary to check the accuracy of this part?
- Discuss the full inclusion issue from the different perspectives of the full inclusion child, the other children, the teacher, and the parents.

Interconnectedness and Interdependence

The Internet has brought the world into the classroom and the classroom into the world in a very obvious way. Before the Internet, however, forces around the world daily affected the lives of teachers and students, either directly or indirectly. When OPEC decided to restrict the quantity of petroleum sold in the world, the cost of gas for cars went up in the United States. Higher gas prices made a greater demand for small- and medium-sized cars. When U.S.-based companies found new sources of cheap labor in countries such as Indonesia and China, less expensive clothing flooded the market. Companies continue to justify low wages to their workers, in the United States or elsewhere, by claiming international competition. Thousands and perhaps millions of examples can be found as more economic, social, and political ties are made every day.

In the classroom, teachers need to point out the fast-growing international as well as national aspects of students' own lives. Using the community's resources, students can make links to other people and places. Companies with national and international branches, families with relatives in other cities and countries, and social organizations with national and international affiliations are among the possibilities. Having students establish their own interconnected webs gives them realistic experiences and opportunities to practice skills for their global world.

Classes can also explore the ecological issues within the concept of interconnectedness. For example, the change in oceanic ecosystems caused by the dumping of ballast waters from tankers can be a research area. Land use can include the ongoing arguments about the destruction of forests such as the Amazon, which can be investigated. Studying the cycle of deforestation, and cultivation leading to depletion of the already poor soil and the probable creation of deserts can trigger questions about the livelihoods of poor Brazilians and the involvement of multinational companies.

Think and Act

- Have students work out the different possibilities for connections with other classmates. Suggestions include classes, cafeteria, sports, extracurricular clubs, transportation to school, friends outside school, neighbors, and relatives.
- Refer back to your notes about personal ties to people and organizations outside of your country. How can these be shared with your students? What benefits can you see for both groups of people?
- Select a water or land use issue that is debated globally. Present several positions on the issue, including those of the multinational companies and the indigenous peoples.
- Investigate a local water or land use issue and positions presented in the local newspapers and media.

Co-Responsibility

"If you are not part of the solution, you are part of the problem." Issues of racism, sexism, and classism, for example, are so complex and so buried in individuals and institutions that wholesale reform is needed to correct the injustices. For example, White teachers who say that they do not need multiculturalism in their classroom because they do not have any children of color have not yet acknowledged the position of favor they and their students have had by being White. They have also ignored all the other concerns that multicultural and global education addresses: ethnicity, class, gender, sexual orientation, and so on. These teachers, and others like them from all ethnic and cultural groups, need extensive, in-depth education to overcome their ignorance about these concepts and their reluctance to take responsibility for their application.

Teachers can and must be part of the solution by first being open to personal and professional growth and change. With growth and change, they can become change makers themselves, helping their students in turn to become change makers. Teachers and students everywhere have to work at the personal and institutional levels to overcome discrimination of any kind. Practice begins in the classroom where the teacher and students together learn about multicultural and global concepts and take the responsibility to apply them in their daily lives.

Think and Act

- How have you dealt with discriminatory comments or jokes in the past?
- What part of your class rules deals with co-responsibility to overcome discrimination of any kind? How is that made clear to the students?
- What does taking a passive role in solving multicultural and global problems imply?

Global Society

As the world is brought into the classroom, the students must go out into the world. Teachers have a responsibility to help their students prepare for the world in as many ways as possible. Part of this responsibility is to help students be actors rather than spectators in their world. Projects that involve change in local conditions, for instance, are ways to give students voices outside the classroom. This belief is expressed in "Think globally, act locally," with the understanding that action comes after reflective consideration. Students need to practice the skills of advocacy now in a safe context so that they will be able to use the skills throughout life.

Skills for a global society include appropriate application of the five concepts just discussed. Celebrating diversity, for instance, is a meaningless phrase unless it can be applied in students' lives. Skills for celebrating diversity include the ability to be open to other viewpoints and to withhold judgment until all perspectives are sought and examined. These skills are further discussed in Chapter 2. Other skills needed for a global society include being flexible and willing to accept change. Acceptance of change is not enough, however, because only empowered global citizens can participate in bringing about change.

The information age is forcing changes of all sorts at an ever-increasing pace. One crucial change in the past few years, the access to information through technology, has so radically affected human lives worldwide that individuals and institutions without technology are the "have-nots" of the twenty-first century. Teachers who are not computer literate are at risk because they cannot assist their students in developing essential skills of information collecting, sorting, and applying. Students with fewer opportunities to use computers in their classrooms and homes will be at a disadvantage in many ways, especially economically since virtually every business in the United States now depends upon computer-stored and manipulated information. Teachers have an obligation, therefore, to keep up with technological changes and to facilitate their students' learning in these areas. They also have an obligation to fight for the resources necessary to supply their students with these crucial tools.

Change-making skills include the ability to think critically and creatively; the ability to work collaboratively on complex, persistent human problems; and the ability to carry out long-term goals through action steps. Student practice in these skills comes through classroom activities that require higher-order thinking and affective involvement. These activities involve experiential learning that aligns curriculum, instruction, and assessment as closely as possible. In effect, the classroom is used as a microcosm of the global world. What is learned in the classroom about multicultural and global concepts is constantly applied there as well as in the world beyond.

Think and Act

■ Consider a local project such as a neighborhood clean up. Contact local citizens' groups for ongoing community activities.

■ Check for action groups on the Internet such as TreeLink (www.treelink.org).

■ How do you define a change maker? How are you a change maker in your profession?

Conclusion

Certain implications for classroom practices can be drawn from the definitions and concepts given in this chapter. Preservice teachers and practicing teachers who have truly understood and adopted multicultural and global concepts should demonstrate these qualities in all that they do as professionals and as caring people. They should apply these concepts in all interactions with their students. They should apply these concepts to the curriculum, texts, materials, and supplementary resources. They should apply these concepts to the teaching strategies and activities for the students. They should apply these concepts in evaluation methods of student achievement. They should apply these concepts in the classroom environment, both physical and emotional/social. These teachers should apply these concepts in the school context. Finally, these teachers should apply multicultural and global concepts in all their interactions in their communities—local, national, and international. Overall, in all the decisions and actions teachers make in their classrooms and communities, teachers themselves must act as role models for the application of multicultural and global concepts.

This text will act as a guide and suggestion book for teachers who wish to apply multicultural and global concepts in their classrooms and beyond. As a guide, it will only give possible directions to take. It cannot provide a complete blueprint for the journey because each person's journey is a unique adventure. But perhaps, like a good companion, it can offer support and encouragement along the way.

PART TWO

Applying Multicultural and Global Concepts in the Classroom

The classroom setting for teaching and learning is composed of six critical elements: teacher, students, environment, curriculum, instruction, and assessment. If any of these is altered, the teaching–learning situation is changed. An effective teacher regularly reflects on ways each of these elements and the interactions among them can be addressed to improve student learning. An effective teacher with awareness of multicultural and global concepts includes these concepts in the reflective thinking process.

Part Two, Chapters 2 through 7, examines each critical classroom element and how multicultural and global concepts can be applied. Because of the tremendous influence a teacher has over what happens in the classroom, the first element to be analyzed is the teacher. The teacher's beliefs, values, attitudes, and assumptions influence teacher and student behavior and help to determine the teaching and learning taking place. When examining multicultural and global concept application, therefore, starting with teachers and what they bring to their classrooms seems logical. Chapter 2 helps preservice and practicing teachers examine themselves as the first critical classroom element.

The second critical classroom element, the students, is equally as important if not more so because learners are at the heart of any teaching–learning situation. Teaching without knowing and understanding the students being taught can rarely if ever be good teaching. Good teaching implies solid learning by all students, and such learning does not happen when the heritages, experiences, interests, and needs of the individual students are not taken into account. After gaining a thorough understanding of themselves, effective teachers try to learn as much as possible about their students. Chapter 3 investigates students in regard to applying multicultural and global concepts.

The last four elements—environment, curriculum, instruction, and assess-ment—play important roles as they interact with the teacher, the students, and each other in the classroom. Chapter 4 discusses the importance of establishing a warm and welcoming environment physically, emotionally, and socially. Chapter 5 ana-lyzes various approaches to incorporating multicultural and global concepts into the curriculum. Chapter 6 looks at a variety of teaching strategies and how they relate to constructivism and multicultural and global concept application. Finally, Chapter 7 investigates types of assessment and evaluation in light of contemporary issues and multicultural and global concepts.

CHAPTER

2   The Teacher

An investigation of one's own personal beliefs, values, assumptions, and attitudes is a necessary first step towards applying multicultural and global concepts in the classroom. All teachers enter the teaching profession with beliefs, values, assumptions, and attitudes about teaching, learning, and education. Some of these relate directly to the classroom, such as how a "good teacher" should act. Others might be less obvious but still have an influence on the teacher. Religious beliefs, for instance, might not be part of the state-mandated or district-interpreted curriculum. Yet they certainly will have an influence on the curriculum delivered by the teacher and on the hidden curriculum, the part of the curriculum implied by each teacher's attitudes and actions in the classroom and by the school's culture.

Beliefs and values come from each person's unique experiences interpreted and reinterpreted over time. Getting back to those experiences, both external and internal, requires time-consuming and sometimes painful analysis and reflection. External experiences can be seen as interactions with people, things, and events. Internal experiences relate to inner understandings of these interactions and the schemata or relationships the mind and memory make of them. Powerful experiences, those involving deep emotions, leave memories that can be triggered any number of ways. Religious beliefs and values particularly are deep-seated in a combination of personal, family, community, and cultural experiences that contain high emotional impact. Because of the increased emotional pressures on individuals and families during religious holidays, unusually high incidents of violence, even suicide and murder, accompany charity and good will.

Assumptions and attitudes are closely tied to personal beliefs and values in that they are the interpretations of interactions with people, things, and events based on those personal beliefs or values. Teachers make necessary assumptions daily that help them manage their professional world. The difficulty comes not in an action itself but in the interpretation of the action by different individuals. For any college instructor to believe, for instance, that every student attending an education class was there because the course was so fascinating that no one wanted to miss it is foolhardy. Likewise, it would be inappropriate to assume that every student was there because the course was required, not because there was something worthwhile to be learned in class activities.

Like assumptions, attitudes are often unthinking responses in the present based on experiences in the past, but they involve the emotions. Time and again women in elementary education programs report that they do not like and cannot do mathematics. When asked about their negative attitudes toward mathematics, they often report specific incidents either in elementary or high school where they were made to feel mathematically stupid or incompetent. Studies about girls in school support this finding about gender biases, especially in connection with mathematics and science (Sadler & Sadler, 1994; Wellesley College Center for Research on Women, 1992). These preservice elementary teachers have developed negative attitudes based on emotionally charged past experiences. The attitudes and emotions remain to influence consciously and unconsciously present and future teaching and learning situations.

Throughout this chapter and the chapters to follow, readers are urged to use a variety of metacognitive techniques to examine their own beliefs, values, assumptions, and attitudes. Dialogue and debate offer chances for verbal interchanges and challenges of other perspectives. Reading and responding to books and articles about multicultural and global issues allow for a more solitary time for reflection and articulation. As mentioned in the preface, a personal journal in addition to a professional notebook provides a place for thoughts and feelings too sensitive to share with others. Emotional struggles can be recorded in the journal as a way of releasing the tension and of distancing oneself in order to examine the issue as critically and objectively as possible. Professional decisions resulting from such examinations can then be recorded in the notebook. The following exercises with cultural concept maps provide another way to look at beliefs, values, assumptions, and attitudes.

Using a Cultural Concept Map for Self-Investigation

One way to examine personal beliefs, values, assumptions, and attitudes is to use some sort of graphic organizer such as the cultural concept map in Figure 2.1. The name of the individual investigator is placed in the rectangle. Primary circles branched off the rectangle are that individual's cultural groups of race/ethnicity, class, religion, gender, sexual orientation, ableness, language, age, regionality, and nationality. Each person starts with all of these categories, writing down words and phrases that first define one's self-identification in each category. For instance, under "class" a phrase such as "middle-class" is a starting point. At the primary circle level, identifying words tend to be general rather than specific. Adding phrases such as "family can afford state university education" or "family owns suburban house" begin to define more closely what "middle-class" means to each individual.

When this exercise is done as a class assignment for preservice teachers, students must know in advance if they are expected to share all, part, or none of the personal writings because of the sensitivity of the material. The sexual orientation cultural group in particular presents the most difficulty because university campuses

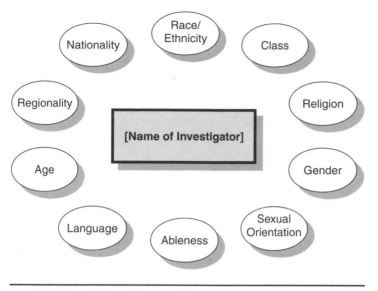

FIGURE 2.1   Cultural Concept Map

are usually not open enough for gays, lesbians, bisexual, and transgendered students to feel comfortable about revealing their orientation. Even when students have been asked not to write in their names because the forms would be collected afterwards, the sexual orientation group most often is left blank or filled in with "straight." Occasionally, a student writes "STRAIGHT!" in capital letters—which might be interpreted as a homophobic reaction.

Instructors facilitating the cultural concept mapping exercise can address the issue directly by discussing why some students feel the need to express themselves in such a fashion and why other students are not able to be open about their own positions on such a sensitive topic. Holding small-group discussions and then whole-class discussions about various aspects of the different primary circles can get individuals thinking about many other influences as well. Readers doing this exercise alone are urged to think of the repercussions of different answers, whether their own or others.

The next level of thought involves secondary circles that branch off each primary circle. Over time, all primary circles can be investigated more deeply by analyzing the separate influences noted for each circle. In the example shown in Figure 2.2, the primary circle being investigated is gender; secondary circles include family members, friends, and education experiences. Investigators going beyond the gender primary circle will find unique influences and other divisions that are personally more meaningful than those demonstrated here. From the secondary circles, tertiary circles branch off, such as mother, father, and perhaps stepmother and/or stepfather for family members.

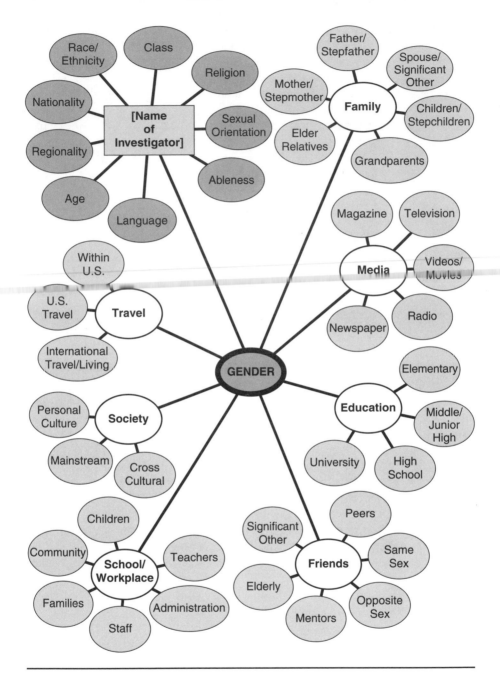

FIGURE 2.2   Cultural Concept Map: Gender Influences

The branches connecting the different circles can be used for words or phrases indicating the type of influence each person or situation had on the investigator. A woman looking at gender influences might consider the effects of her mother and other women relatives as role models for her own life, while a man might note such influences as role models for women friends and loved ones. The branches can include key words indicating answers to various questions: Did these women follow traditional roles for females or were they atypical? What were their own cultural heritages and how much did their heritages influence their choices? In-depth explanations can be put below or on another sheet. In Figure 2.3, some of the influences of educational settings on author Brown's personal life are explored. Obviously, these areas still have room for much more thorough development.

The cultural concept map becomes more complex with further extensions of branches and circles. Circles from one cultural group are often related to other cultural groups. For instance, any investigation of societal attitudes about gender would not only involve the dominant position but would concern the positions of other people in the investigator's ethnic, class, and religious cultural circles. Although the primary cultural groups overlap and interact, a thorough examination of each separately will uncover unsuspected beliefs, values, assumptions, and attitudes.

The cultural concept map also portrays dynamic relationships that are in many cases two-way influences. For example, the school/workplace circle includes children as an influence. Experienced teachers know that they are learning from children as the children are learning from them. Children's fresh eyes on gender issues in the classroom, for instance, help teachers see more clearly. When young boys say to a teacher, "You always pick the girls for those jobs," then the method of selection needs rethinking. Perhaps unconscious biases based on traditional gender roles influenced choices about classroom jobs.

Finally, the cultural concept map is very much a uniquely personal exercise. Depending upon the individual investigator and the cultural group being examined, each primary cultural circle will have its own selection of secondary, tertiary, and continuing circles with connecting branches and significant comments. It is expected in this chapter that each person completing the various parts of the cultural concept map will think in terms of himself or herself through life from the earliest stages, recording significant influences recalled over the years. It is also hoped that each person will simultaneously be thinking about the implications of these influences for teaching. Chapter 3, The Students, will also look at cultural groups, but from the perspective of students and their personal influences.

Think and Act

■ Start your own cultural concept map, using the text examples as a starting point.
■ As you read each of the next sections, fill in the related primary cultural circle and develop several secondary and tertiary circles. You might use a piece of large blank chart

(continued)

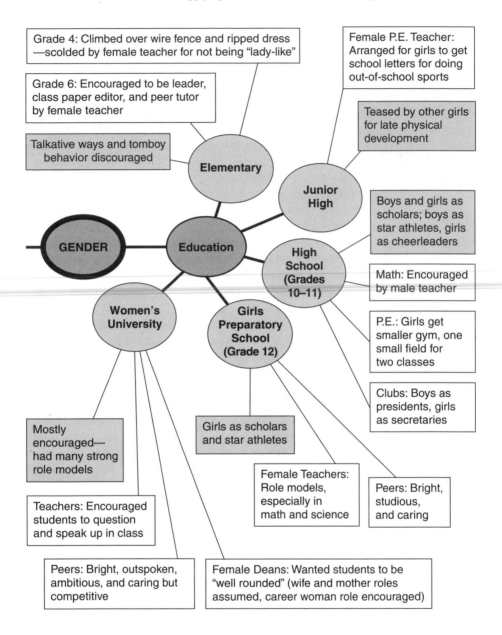

FIGURE 2.3   Gender Extension of Cultural Concept Map*

*This concept map is an incomplete example of education influences on the first author up to age 21.

paper for the whole map or separate sheets of regular paper for different secondary circles.
■ Which cultural circles do you predict will be the most comfortable for you to investigate? Which will be the most uncomfortable? How will you overcome any negative feelings you might have in order to prevent avoidance of the topics?

Race/Ethnicity

The race/ethnicity cultural group in particular brings up issues of power and privilege. European American teachers especially have a responsibility to examine ways that they have been favored (Howard, 1999; Sleeter & McLaren, 1995). Discriminatory practices against people of color still remain as legacies of hundreds of years of slavery and group oppression. Partially because the majority of teachers and preservice teachers are White, societal privileges for Whites have often been extended into the classrooms and schools. Disproportionate numbers of students of color labeled as special needs, more disciplinary incidents, and higher suspension and dropout rates are strong indicators that school is not as welcoming for them as for their White peers (Bennett, 1999; Irvine, 1990; Rossi, 1994).

As classroom leaders, teachers have the responsibility to promote an open forum for defusing tensions that might explode into words or acts of racial prejudice. Teachers cannot afford to be naive about this task, however. They must look for underlying causes of tension, including their own unconscious assumptions and attitudes that lead to inappropriate behavior on their part. As mentioned in Chapter 1, teachers, usually White teachers, who claim to be colorblind when working with students who are racially diverse are ignoring a vital part of those students' heritages and experiences (Howard, 1999; Irvine, 1990). In the United States color is a defining term and resulting condition that affects the daily lives of groups of people. This societal influence cannot be ignored. The denial of the importance of race is a refusal to accept responsibility to deal with issues surrounding race, issues that come into the school and the classroom. Certainly, students of color realize people are not really colorblind; at an early age many have already experienced some form of discrimination in school or elsewhere.

European Americans are not always aware of their own ethnicity, in part because numerous ancestors made a determined effort to become assimilated in dominant Anglo-Saxon influence in European American society. Names were Anglicized, English was spoken in the homes, and cultural customs were dropped. In his book *We Can't Teach What We Don't Know,* Gary Howard (1999) speaks to developing cultural awareness and racial identity as one of two goals for White educators. The other, an "examination of the role White educators can and must play in understanding, decoding, and dismantling the dynamics of White dominance," becomes the outward social action after the inward personal transformation (p. 5).

For European American teachers, rediscovering family roots can be a valuable although possibly painful exercise, providing learning experiences beyond discovering where certain family traditions started. One preservice teacher of Italian heritage in upstate New York shared his shock at the discovery of a "for sale" document from the late 1800s. The document stated "Italians and Negroes need not apply." Everyone present was forced to think about this blatant discrimination and, even more, whether some of the class's shock came from having a specific ethnic group of Whites put in the same category as Blacks.

Teachers of color also need to examine their own beliefs, values, assumptions, and attitudes concerning these racial issues. Painful experiences of discrimination need to be analyzed rationally and overcome emotionally. This does not mean denying righteous anger and hurt but being able to put these in some sort of workable perspective in order to avoid taking on victim status and behavior. José, a Cuban American educator, lost his status as a nearly qualified lawyer when Castro came into power. His family lost its home and much of its wealth. When his family immigrated to the United States, he found that many people saw his family not as part of the elite class but as unworthy refugees. Instead of being judged by his former social and intellectual status, he was judged negatively by his strong accent and light brown skin color. This searing experience continues to influence his present perception of race and ethnicity issues both positively and negatively. On the positive side, he understands what individual and institutional discrimination means, especially to those whose first language is not English. On the negative side, he sees the Latino position in the United States as being the most difficult and most discriminated against. His emotional reactions interfere with his reasoning; he is often unable to see others' pain and suffering to be as valid as his. Georgia, an African American woman well-respected as a multicultural education leader in her community, advises everyone to talk not about whose suffering is greater but instead about what he or she is doing to help prevent such discrimination in the future.

Think and Act

- If you have experienced painful discrimination because of your color, how have those experiences affected you as a teacher?
- What role do you, either as a White or as a person of color, have as a teacher in preventing racism in the classroom and school?
- Investigate the past year's coverage of racial incidents or discussions in the local newspapers or in popular magazines such as *Time* or *Newsweek*. Look especially for connections to schools and education. What concerns are expressed and what solutions, if any, are suggested?

Class

The class cultural group is another area of concern for teachers. Teachers generally come from middle-class and working-class backgrounds. They and their families very often struggled and made financial sacrifices for the required education degrees and certification. Partly because of their success in spite of difficult circumstances, teachers as a whole unrealistically believe the American myth of "Anyone can make it if he/she just tries hard enough." Great success stories, after all, are part of the dominant U.S. historical perspectives taught in schools (Adams, Bell, & Griffin, 1997). The media supports this myth by portraying touching stories of the very few individuals who have overcome great odds rather than dwelling on the very many individuals who have not succeeded.

What most teachers have not experienced is a family life of deep poverty and parents or caregivers with limited skills and virtually no legal opportunities to improve their economic condition. The most common success stories of individuals getting out of deep poverty are sports and entertainment figures or criminals, especially drug dealers. Realistically, few children have a chance of becoming highly paid athletes or entertainers; far more can and do manage lives of crime. Day after day, children in poverty-stricken neighborhoods face strong evidence that the American myth of "Anyone can make it if . . ." is not their reality. Even education will not rescue them if the quality of the education available to them is so abysmal that it perpetuates poverty.

Most teachers have certain middle-class standards that are based on their own sets of beliefs and values (Gollnick & Chinn, 1998; Sleeter & Grant, 1988). They expect students to come to school clean, tidy, and well fed. When a student appears dirty and hungry, far too often the teacher assumes that the parents do not care. A single mother might care tremendously but might not be able to supervise her children's preparation for school because of a nighttime or early morning job. Low-paying jobs provide little money for even basic necessities such as food. Families in poverty have hard choices to make each day; food and clothing for the children might mean not enough money for the rent. Limited job opportunities and no economic security result in precarious living circumstances like serious health problems, forced evacuations, constant home and school changes, and dangerous neighborhoods—threatening conditions beyond the experience of most preservice and practicing teachers.

From their middle-class perspectives, some teachers judge decisions of parents in poverty without taking into account the full context. Thus, student teacher Kristin, who reported seeing the parent of an assisted-lunch student buy "lots of lottery tickets," felt justified in criticizing the purchase. She, and others in the class, could see only that their tax dollars were "being wasted on tickets." They couldn't see other perspectives such as the deep need for hope or the desperate desire to escape poverty, however unrealistic the means of escape were. Furthermore, teachers use their middle-class perspectives when setting expectations for their students; for poor and working-class students the expectations are consistently lower even when the students' intelligence and achievement scores are similar to middle-class students (Nieto, 2000).

Think and Act

■ What assumptions are being made when someone believes in that American myth of "Anyone can make it . . ." ?
■ What barriers prevent individuals from breaking the cycle of poverty?
■ When faced with a similar scenario as the lottery ticket buying, how do each of these affect your thinking and behavior: beliefs, values, assumptions, and attitudes?

Religion

The cultural group of religion might relate to everything from separation of church and state issues to religious perspectives about abortion or homosexuality. Historically, since the arrival of the Europeans, the dominant society has been Christian and many of the values and beliefs implied in U.S. public schools reflect that influence (Gollnick & Chinn, 1998). School vacation breaks have been scheduled around Christmas in the winter and often Easter in the spring. At the same time, fundamentalist religious groups argue that schools teach secular humanism, a respect for human beings rather than a belief in God (Marzano, 1993–1994; Molnar, 1993–1994). They fight against texts, books, and curricula they see as undermining family beliefs and values and support teaching creationism in the schools.

Most teachers are Christian, and preservice and practicing teachers generally know little about other faiths and other special holy days. They are not aware of times, for instance, when older Muslim students might be fasting or when Jewish students might be absent. Traditionally, elementary teachers, especially in the primary grades, have developed curricula and activities around essentially Christian celebrations: Halloween, Thanksgiving Day, Christmas, Valentine's Day, and Easter (see Chapter 5, The Curriculum, for a further discussion). They tend to assume that not talking about the religious significance of holidays make all the decorations and partying acceptable to everyone. One preservice teacher recently complained about having only Hanukkah themes in her first-grade placement. At the same time, she did not comment about the many Christmas decorations located throughout the rest of the school. She also did not mention the lack of Kwanzaa symbols, even though there were many African American children in the school.

Think and Act

■ Choose the holy day you consider most important to your religion and discuss whether you have to make any special arrangements with your school or university if your family wishes to be together to celebrate this holy day? If so, what are those arrangements? If not, what arrangements would you anticipate people of other faiths have to make?

■ Interview someone who has had to make special arrangements. Compare your perspectives.

Gender

The gender cultural group presents both obvious and subtle differences for preservice and practicing teachers. Many social behaviors are determined very early by cultural mores about gender (Santrock, 1997). Rows and rows of shocking pink boxes in toy stores announce what toy manufacturers have determined are "girl" toys. Even the language of play has been influenced. Some parents, and sometimes the young children themselves, will protest if the boys play with dolls, yet buy a G.I. Joe for them since G.I. Joe is advertised as an action figure, not a doll—that is, not babyish or girlish. Children's early behaviors and interests affect their adult relationships and career choices. One reason that U.S. elementary teachers are mostly women is the traditional societal attitude that discourages men from choosing lower grades because teaching and caring for young children is seen as woman's work.

Other gender-related influences relate directly to classroom and school interactions. Traditional gender roles dictate that girls be dependent, caring, and uninterested in power while boys be more independent, aggressive, and power oriented (Santrock, 2001). Women teachers particularly, but all K–12 teachers in general, have traditionally been given low status partially because of the historic viewpoint of women being inferior intellectually (Cushner, McClelland, & Safford, 1992). Until recently they were not expected to be proactive in arenas outside the classroom. In addition, if they themselves were discouraged from speaking out or contributing in class as they were growing up, they might expect and encourage similar good girl behaviors of their female students but tolerate much more boisterous behaviors from boys (Sadler & Sadler, 1994). On the other hand, teachers and counselors might consciously or unconsciously discourage boys from participating in activities that are seen as feminine, such as ballet dancing or sewing, or condone other students' teasing remarks. Revisiting the preteen and teen years with adult insight can help preservice and practicing teachers understand their own positions on appropriate gender roles for young girls and boys and how these will affect their teaching.

Think and Act

■ What toys did you play with that were designated for the opposite gender? Do you remember anyone commenting on or criticizing your choices?

(continued)

- Check the Internet for information on Barbie dolls. Why is she so popular with young girls? How does her anatomically incorrect shape relate to media's image of an attractive woman?
- Read and discuss Pipher's (1994) book *Reviving Ophelia* about pressures on teenage girls. What topics would you include if you wrote a comparable book about teenage boys? about your own experiences?

Sexual Orientation

The sexual orientation cultural group can create a very difficult dilemma for some preservice and practicing teachers because of their religious beliefs. As mentioned before, beliefs are often based on cultural influences. In various Native American cultures, gay, lesbian, bisexual, and transgender people are respected as being two-spirited, possessing both masculine and feminine characteristics. Most teachers are European American, however, and have been raised in a culture that maintains homophobic attitudes (Gollnick & Chinn, 1998). Various religious organizations, including the Catholic Church and the Church of Latter Day Saints, have stated their opposition to homosexuality by labeling it a sin. It is still risky for teachers in many schools and districts to declare themselves gay.

Advocates for multicultural education include sexual orientation as a cultural group comparable to those of class and race (Adams et al., 1997; Gollnick & Chinn, 1998). Because of this position, multicultural education has been accused of having a gay agenda. Multicultural training sessions and workshops, especially those for youth, have been criticized for containing any material associated with gays, lesbians, and bisexuals. State sex education programs and practices have also been challenged by various interest groups. Measure 9, on Oregon's voting ballet in 2000 and narrowly defeated, would have prevented public schools from "instruction encouraging, promoting, and sanctioning homosexual and bisexual behaviors." Measure 9 supporters claimed the law would only prevent instruction in which adults encourage students to practice homosexuality. Opponents feared that virtually any lesson, information, or policy related to homosexuality would be eliminated from public schools. Under Measure 9, practices and policies making schools safer and more accommodating for gay students and staff along with any teachers supporting such policies and practices would certainly have been at risk. Clubs such as Gay/Straight Alliances or diversity clubs supporting gay students would most likely have been banned. Since gay students are often victims of harassment and at high risk for suicide, removal of support systems at school could have disastrous effects. Such legislated behavior also sends the message to all students that certain groups of people do not deserve the support and protection of the society.

All preservice and practicing teachers need to examine their position carefully because even if they are not gay themselves, they will be working with gay individuals. Gay teachers must decide whether they can risk being out or not and what the consequences are for either choice to themselves and to their students. Declared gays, for instance, can offer support and understanding and appropriate role modeling for students. Straight teachers with strong religious beliefs against homosexuality must be able to treat gay students, parents, and colleagues with dignity and respect. Bill, an elementary teacher, was once asked by a woman how he would react to discussing her son with her ex-husband and his male partner. His response was that all adults in influential relationships with the boy needed to be consulted. He further urged her to maintain ties with the father who cared for his son and wanted to play an active part in his life. Eventually, the mother, father, and father's partner learned to work together for the sake of the child.

Think and Act

- Check bookstores for literature on gays, lesbians, bisexuals, and transsexuals. Look for fiction and nonfiction books and magazines. How comfortable are you with looking at or buying the literature? What influences make you feel the way you do?
- Examine the sex education curriculum in your district. At what grade levels are sexual orientation issues presented? What resources are offered to the teachers and/or the students?
- Contact the Gay, Lesbian, and Straight Education Network bookstore (www. glsen.org) for resources on fighting anti-gay bias in schools.

Ableness

The ableness cultural group is another area where historically people with disabilities have faced "serious and persistent forms of discrimination, segregation, exclusion, and sometimes elimination" (Adams et al., 1997, p. 198). Until the legislation of All Handicapped Children Act, PL 94-142 of 1975, and the Individuals with Disabilities Education Act of 1990, children with significant disabilities were hidden away and educated separately from other students. Nowadays inclusion, providing education for students with a wide array of disabilities within the regular classroom, is becoming commonplace (Gonzalez, Brusca-Vega, Yawkey, 1997; Stainback & Stainback, 1996). Teachers, for the most part with no disabilities themselves, have the responsibility of knowing about the conditions of individual students and providing the modifications that must be made for optimal learning.

Individualized Education Programs (IEPs) are required by law for any students who have been labeled with handicapping conditions. What is carried out in practice is usually much less than what is mandated, however. For a variety of reasons—including inadequate funding, staffing, and training—accommodations by and large are left to the regular classroom teacher. Beyond that, each classroom usually has several more students who have not been labeled but also need accommodations that, if not provided, will result in poor achievement academically, socially, or emotionally. Close collaboration with the special education personnel is essential for developing specific strategies to use with students with different special needs. Also important is having high expectations for all students while learning as much as possible about individual student needs.

The ableness cultural group could have strong influences for preservice and practicing teachers if these are based on personal experiences with family members or friends. Extended experiences with persons who have had physical, mental, or emotional disabilities usually elicit in individuals a combination of positive and negative beliefs, values, assumptions, and attitudes. Sometimes people close to a student with disabilities or the individual himself or herself emphasizes the disability rather than the abilities, enabling the student to continue with inappropriate behaviors and preventing the student from achieving as much learning and self-sufficiency as possible. Teachers, with their sustained close contact with students, can also fall into this pattern; they have to guard against becoming enablers in the classroom. Examining past and present experiences for their effects on issues of ableness in general can lead to a more objective perspective.

Anyone considering a career in teaching must objectively examine his or her health and ability to withstand the strain mentally and physically. That teaching is a very stressful vocation cannot be emphasized enough. Chronic illnesses or conditions can wear on a teacher, perhaps triggering angry and exaggerated reactions to student misbehavior. Disabilities require a thoughtful and objective analysis of the distinction between mandated accommodations for students and those that would be provided for teachers. Preservice teachers must be able to speak to how they will perform the responsibilities of teachers, so appropriate and successful coping strategies are a necessity. People with learning disabilities, for instance, have to find ways to produce written work without flaws even if they have grammatical and spelling problems. Katrina, a secondary history student teacher, prepared her transparency notes in advance, using computer checks and her significant other for editing. For in-class writing on the board, she designated students as writers and editors. Thorough analysis and problem solving in advance can overcome many possible barriers to success.

In another example, two women who were legally blind have been students of the same teacher educator. The first student was very competent academically and well liked socially. She developed ways to handle required tasks, such as having a friend describe her body language in a video of herself teaching that had to be critiqued. When this woman decided to go into the human services field, the education faculty was disappointed to lose her. The second student was not as competent in her academic major. For student teaching, she was assigned a very enthusiastic and supportive teacher. She soon ran into difficulties, however, because she didn't have solid content knowledge to call upon when students asked her questions. Her removal from student teaching was caused by content knowledge problems, not her disability.

Think and Act

- In what ways have your past experiences influenced your attitude toward individuals with different levels of physical, mental, and/or emotional disabilities?
- If you have a disability, what coping skills have you developed? Where could you get additional information or assistance in continuing to improve these?
- If you have colleagues who have disabilities, in what ways have you empowered them without being intrusive?

Language

The language circle brings up historical questions, among others. The dominant English-speaking culture in the United States has a legacy of being intolerant toward speakers of other languages. Teachers usually come from an English-speaking background and rarely are fluent in another language. In the late 1980s, Zimpher (1989) found that only 5 percent of preservice teachers were fluent in another language, and nearly three-fifths were completely monolingual. The statistics have not changed drastically since then. In schools, teachers and students have too often discriminated against individuals who speak limited English or have a strong accent. The lack of linguistic abilities leave teachers much less prepared for working with students and parents who have diverse language experiences (Hernández, 1997).

Some preservice or practicing teachers whose immigrant parents or grandparents had to learn English see no reason why anyone else in the United States should not do the same. European Americans especially tend to feel that the practice of assimilation has worked historically because their ancestors succeeded in providing for their families while insuring even greater opportunities for the children. In the past, however, assimilation was in some ways easier for European immigrants because of the lack of need for higher-level education. Thus, craftsmen could use very limited English and still manage to succeed economically. Today, at least a high school degree and a mastery of basic English are needed for almost all occupations offering more than minimum wage.

Teachers who advocate assimilation have often overlooked the confounding issue of racism. People of color were never wholly assimilated into the European American dominant culture; their visual differences made them targets of discrimination over the years. Even if complete assimilation were possible now, this practice goes against multicultural and global concepts because it rejects the value of diversity and forces one perspective on a pluralistic society. The image of the salad bowl, with each ingredient contributing its own unique flavor, is more appropriate for teachers to advocate than the historical melting pot concept of all diverse groups blending into a monocultural society.

Hernández (1997) stresses the importance of context, process, and content for teaching effectively in multilingual classrooms. Teachers must have knowledge of the homes and communities of the English language learners so they can interact with the students and their families in appropriate, culturally sensitive ways. They must also understand how to provide content emphasizing multicultural and global perspectives and instruction emphasizing communication and interaction among all students. Even monolingual teachers can provide rich learning environments if they study the home and community contexts and incorporate that information into decisions involving the critical classroom elements.

The controversy surrounding African American Ebonics or Black English as a separate language from Standard English involves much more than district decisions and classroom practice. It also involves the recognition and importance of language as a reflection of culture (Gay, 2000). Teachers who declare that Standard English is the only correct language and insist on it at all times risk marginalizing and alienating African American students. Considering the controversy from a multicultural perspective of no one right version of a language but many ways to communicate will lead to the recognition of each form as being appropriate under certain circumstances.

Teachers will need to analyze their own assumptions and attitudes towards language and language usage to see if they hold biases against others who do have accents or do not speak Standard English. More subtle communication styles such as polite command forms used by middle-class speakers can, in fact, be barriers to student understanding. Chapter 3, The Students, discusses language and communication styles in more detail.

Think and Act

- What was your experience when you tried to learn a second language? How can you use that experience to understand your students with limited English proficiency?
- If English is your first language, do you have any close friends whose first language is not English? Do you know and use at least courtesy words in that language?
- How do you feel and react when people near you speak to each other in a language you do not understand? Do you assume they are talking about you?
- Listen to conversations in several public community areas like stores, cafés, and bus or metro stops. Note the variations of English and other languages spoken. Compare what you hear to a national broadcaster on television.

Age

The age cultural group is not always a category considered when discussing multicultural perspectives, but it certainly needs consideration by teachers. Whether young or middle-aged, teachers have an age gap between themselves and their students. Choices of music, videos, magazines, clothing, and language expressions demonstrate the obvious separation between adults and children or teenagers. Peer groups, even adult ones, have a strong influence on its members over the years. The baby boomers, for instance, have been documented so well that the research is being used to predict trends in the consumer markets. Teachers who read *Time* or *Newsweek* probably will find that their students rarely, if ever, do. In fact, these general magazines might not even be available at convenience stores or grocery stores where students shop. Older teachers will find their historical and literary references have little or no meaning to most of their students. Questions such as "Where were you when Kennedy was shot?" have no personal relationship to the generations of students (and young teachers) who had not yet been born at the time of that horrific event in U.S. history.

Think and Act

- Watch or listen to music targeted for a young audience for a week and compare it to your favorite type of music for common themes; treatment of cultural groups, especially females; ways to use the music or critiques of it in class.
- Observe the actions and interactions of children and teenagers in shopping malls. How do they compare to your own? What items are they purchasing and how much are they spending? What actions could be seen as threatening to store employers or employees?

Regionality

The next two cultural groups, regionality and nationality, are included by only a few authors. Cushner (1999) sees regionality or geographic location as culturally defined by the characteristics of the ecological environment in which a group of people live. The natural (mountains, deserts, plains, rivers) and man-made features (urban, suburban, rural communities) of the region are used by the inhabitants to describe themselves. New Englanders, for instance, often identify themselves and are identified by others as part of an "ethniclike group" with the same language expressions and accents, loyalties, and sense of belonging (Cushner, 1999, p. 49). Even with the increasing mobility of U.S. citizens, regional ties established in childhood may continue to influence individuals.

Teachers as a whole are a very stable population; most get their education and begin to teach within 100 miles of where they grew up (Cushner et al., 1992). Their experiences are limited geographically and they might have little understanding of diverse regional perspectives within the United States. Within a natural region, the man-made differences between urban, suburban, and rural attitudes and behaviors can cause problems. The student teacher from New York City who argued vehemently with his teammates about the research process they were going to use found himself being excluded from out-of-class discussions. He thought that he was just stating his opinion and working for a compromise while the other students, all from upstate New York, considered him rude and uncooperative. The instructor worked with the group to develop discussion methods that were acceptable to all the members.

Another concern for teachers is prejudice against or stereotyping of certain regions in the United States. The South, for instance, has been targeted as a place of "hicks" and "rednecks." People with southern accents are sometimes characterized as slow and lazy. Southern White women are often portrayed as being weak, compliant, and devious in their relationships with men, while southern Black women are labeled as strong matriarchs of the extended families. While historical conditions might have forced certain roles on many southern women in the past, any stereotyping of groups of individuals by region (and in this example, gender) must be addressed.

Think and Act

- List two or three characteristics usually attributed to people in your region. Discuss any stories or sayings from the region that support these attributes.
- Compare generalizations and stereotypes for different regions of the United States.
- Interview an immigrant about regional differences within the country of his or her origin.

Nationality

This cultural group expands multicultural perspectives beyond the national boundaries to include global perspectives. Because of the country's size, strength, and influence, most citizens of the United States have not been forced as yet to deal personally with global realities such as famine or war in their own homeland. Preservice and practicing teachers, like the majority of mainstream Americans, have little or no background knowledge and experience about international historical events and depend on shallow and often biased coverage by the U.S. media. Too many teachers seem unprepared to teach about international current events, global interdependence, or other countries from anything but an ethnocentric viewpoint.

Teachers, especially those in elementary grades, can easily fall into accepting stereotypical images of other nations and peoples in an attempt to simplify information for young learners. Most teachers, one would hope, would recognize and refute stereotypes of French men as excellent chefs and Latino men as romantic lovers. More subtle forms of ethnocentric and patronizing positions are harder to detect and counteract. Elementary textbooks talk about Canadians as "our good neighbors to the north," but often present a stereotypical last-frontier image of the country, forgetting to mention that it has a highly modernized superstructure and is the United States' largest trading partner. In fact, the Canadian government refused to sponsor the Canadian pavilion at EPCOT in Disney World because of Disney's emphasis on the natural sights for tourists approach rather than the high-technology image the Canadians favored.

Allowing seemingly benign photos such as Mexicans wearing sombreros to be the only or even main visual representations of a country creates for young students an understanding of foreigners as exotic "others." Yet few teachers have the experience and knowledge to go beyond these simplistic examples and stereotypes of other countries and cultures. Gaining an international knowledge base can be very challenging for teachers, especially when taking into account the within-group differences such as the distinctive historical, cultural, and linguistic characteristics of separate regions in the same foreign country. Teachers need cross-cultural experiential education. Living outside the United States can have a profound effect, but working cooperatively with international university students or other international adults to explore similarities and differences in countries and cultures can also be beneficial (Merryfield et al., 1997; Wilson, 1982).

For teachers working with immigrant students, Igoa (1995) recommends building a knowledge base and then consciously using a cultural, academic, and psychological model of intervention. The knowledge base includes the following: (1) cultural backgrounds of students, (2) cultural attitudes toward teachers, (3) teaching methods and educational systems of the countries, (4) how the United States discriminates against immigrants, (5) the importance of honoring and valuing immigrant students, and (6) how to be a model and an "educational parent" (p. 103) whom immigrant students can trust. Igoa's excellent book uses the students' words to explain her main points. Her intervention model is discussed in Chapter 6, The Instruction.

Trisha, a middle school math teacher in the Los Angeles area, uses a variety of ways to reach her many immigrant and bicultural students. She lived in Peru, speaks Spanish, and uses Spanish phrases regularly. She studied Japanese and traveled to Japan. She talks to her students about being a "dragon" in the Asian zodiac. She asks about their special holdays, favorite foods, special jewelry, or "anything that says I am interested in their culture and in them." Her students know that she eats salsa and sushi but "doesn't like kimchee yet." She attends East Indian dance recitals when "her girls" are performing and then is invited to other cultural events sponsored by various groups. She is very careful about preparing any assessment materials and has quizzes and tests translated or "spot" translated by her Korean, Chinese, and Japanese helpers. She uses the principles of specially designed academic instruction in English whenever possible (see www.catesol.org/shelter.html for more information). As she says, "And everything that helps my English language learners helps my regular students also" (Brown, 2001, personal e-mail correspondence).

Think and Act

■ What do you remember about the Gulf War? How did the media contribute to your emotional reactions? Do you recall any other nation's perspective being presented?

■ Find or create global maps that have other parts of the world in the center. Use Peters Projection Maps to get a more accurate perspective of relative sizes of land and water masses.

■ Interview someone who has lived in another country. Compare your knowledge of the country and its citizens with the other person's. How could that person's insights help you with teaching about the country or working with students from that country?

Cultural Heritage as Many-Faceted, Unique, and Influential

The worth of doing an in-depth cultural concept map comes in thinking about a personal heritage as having many different facets, some that immediately come to mind but others that require careful thought. Teachers might find it impossible to investigate so many cultural facets extensively at this time, but they can get started. All of these cultural groups concern teachers and their choices in their classrooms. If teachers do not realize their own beliefs, values, assumptions, and attitudes about each of these arenas of conflict, they will not see how these viewpoints differ from those of their students and they will not understand the sources of interpersonal problems in their workplaces. Less obvious but equally important, if teachers also do not realize how institutional favoritism and discrimination of all types have influenced their own lives, they will not understand how favoritism and discrimination continue to affect the real choices of students and their families in schools and beyond.

Applying Multicultural and Global Concepts to Teachers' Lives

Heightened Awareness

How can these new insights gained from the webbing exercise be applied in the classroom? First, a heightened awareness of personal beliefs, values, assumptions, and attitudes will prepare teachers for the probability that others will have different viewpoints or perspectives. Once teachers recognize multiple perspectives on issues, they can then work toward recognizing the importance of someone else's perspective to that person. This recognition does not mean unthinkingly giving equal value to every perspective. Rather, it means recognizing the power of that perspective for the person holding it and the right of that person to hold a different perspective. It means also recognizing that different perspectives lead to different behaviors in response to the same situation or event.

Conscious Openness

The next step is maintaining a conscious openness about different perspectives. Recognizing that everyone has his or her own set of beliefs and values that are of importance to that person should lead to honoring others' rights to have their own sets of beliefs and values. From personal research of cultural backgrounds and influences, every reader has probably realized how much beliefs and values were formed because of circumstances. If an individual were Jewish, for instance, the religion circle and its branches would have very different connections than if the teacher were Christian. Having accepted the various influences and their importance to who one is as a person and as a teacher, each reader must also acknowledge the importance of different influences upon others. Since different influences often lead to different perspectives on issues, acknowledging the different influences also means acknowledging the resulting different perspectives.

Both recognizing other perspectives and acknowledging the rights of individuals to different perspectives are huge accomplishments. Persons who have lived in other countries can cite different examples of confronting a cultural behavior that is the accepted norm in that place but would be considered unacceptable in the United States. The reverse situation is also true, of course, when Americans display behaviors inappropriate in another country. American preservice teachers in England, for example, might find that their outgoing, forthright manner is not valued very much. A British teacher's understated comment of "We certainly know where they are" warned the U.S. supervisor to inform the preservice teachers that their boisterous behavior was probably not welcomed by all in the schools.

In the United States, cultural differences can be more difficult to recognize. For example, some teachers do not realize that their polite form of a command could be interpreted by children as a question. "Would you please take out your books?" for middle and upper class European Americans is a nice way of saying "Get your books out." For children with more direct language experiences, this statement sounds like a question that can be answered with "OK" or "No, I am busy doing something else." The teacher's reaction to the latter answer from any child could be that the child is a troublemaker who cannot follow directions. These more subtle cultural conflicts are the cause of much anxiety, confusion, and even pain for the individuals involved.

Postponement of Judgment

Maintaining openness about other perspectives also involves withholding judgment until all perspectives are thoroughly examined. Ethnocentric people see the beliefs, values, assumptions, attitudes, and behaviors of their cultural groups as superior to those of other groups. Although they might be aware of other perspectives, they dismiss such viewpoints without reasoned analysis, insisting upon their "right" views and forcing other people to comply through persuasion or threat. According to Banks (1991), these people are at Stage 2, ethnic encapsulation, in his typology (see the discussion in Chapter 1).

Teachers sometimes act in an ethnocentric way through ignorance and/or lack of sensitivity to the situation and individuals involved. Andrea, a U.S. student teacher in a British school, struggled with a nutrition lesson in a Year Four class (ages 8 and 9) because she did not associate her pupils' puzzled looks or quiet repetitions of the word "vitamins" with the word itself. She hadn't realized that the British pronunciation of the word uses a "short i" sound for "vit" rather than the American "long i" sound. Still, her inability to pick up on the numerous cues given her by the pupils indicated an area that needed work. Stopping to find out why the students were not responding well to teacher questions probably would have revealed this simple misunderstanding. Unfortunately, most problems dealing with different cultural perspectives are more complex than this example and require a much more in-depth collection and analysis of data.

Ethnocentric beliefs are also revealed through thoughtless and insulting comments or gestures. One European American instructor speaking to Alex, a Filipino/Native American/Portuguese colleague, made a disparaging remark about people of color. When Alex commented, "What about me?" the reply was, "Well, you know what I mean, you're different, you're like us." Not so blatant, but certainly revealing, was another instructor's arm gesture toward Alex when the instructor mentioned diversity issues on campus. The received message was that diversity concerns were the person of color's problem, not all of the instructors' responsibilities.

Selection of Appropriate Behaviors

Maintaining a conscious openness while withholding judgment gives a teacher the opportunity to make choices. Simple situations such as the pronunciation difficulty can be easily resolved. In England, the preservice teacher would be wise to explain her U.S. pronunciation of "vitamins" and to use the British pronunciation. Better yet, she could ask her British pupils to remind her whenever she forgets again. In the United States, a teacher would help a student from England to learn the standard U.S. version, perhaps by expanding this teachable moment into a lesson about differences in words, spelling, and pronunciation in the same language. An extension of this might be differences seen in Spanish among Puerto Ricans, Cuban Americans, and Mexican Americans.

Even a seemingly simple example such as appropriate pronunciation and language usage presents complexities in a classroom, however. The controversy about Black English or Ebonics, mentioned earlier, is one example. Teachers need to put aside their middle-class lenses in order to make a decision that helps rather than hinders students. Constantly criticizing and correcting a student's spoken and written English will most likely silence the student instead of changing his or her communication patterns. Yet completely ignoring the social and economic power of standard English is to do a grave disservice to students. Explaining the purpose behind important teacher decisions such as this gives students understanding and perhaps appreciation of the teacher's desire to empower them.

In a number of circumstances, the approach needed is not so much one of teachers expecting students to learn their customary middle-class forms of language and language patterns that include etiquette but one of finding middle ground in which teachers and students can interact comfortably. Being open to compromise means willingness to share the classroom space in a more democratic manner. Openness has definite limits, however; student behaviors must honor core values of respect for individuals and for cultural groups. Teachers with multicultural and global perspectives cannot accept, for example, the use of derogatory terms such as "fags" or "retards" and cannot condone sexual harassment. Cultural relativism, when dealing with fundamental issues such as human rights and respect of others, is not an appropriate position for teachers to take.

Reexamination of Beliefs, Values, Assumptions, and Attitudes

After acceptance of multiple perspectives and the need to stay open to others' viewpoints, reexamination of personal beliefs and values is a logical next step. A few beliefs and values, made problematic by close analysis, can be modified or changed with sincere and conscious effort. Most individuals, however, find that there is a solid core of personal beliefs and values that determine who they are. This core might include certain basic religious tenets, a personal code of ethics, or a sense of place in relationship with significant others. When new choices collide with firmly held yet rarely analyzed core beliefs and values, a person could easily feel threatened and act out defensively or withdraw entirely from the conflict. Change at this level is extremely difficult.

Surrounding the core of beliefs and values are other beliefs and values as well as assumptions and attitudes developed from years of living. These nonessential elements could be modified more easily with knowledge or exposure to different experiences. The process is not an easy one, nor is it a nonreversible one. But falling back into old patterns of thoughtless assumptions and attitudes will not occur as easily once people have become more aware of such patterns. With reminders, the preservice teachers in England were able to tone down their exuberance in the schools. They also began to realize some of the advantages of watching and listening more closely rather than acting immediately. Their behavior changed and their attitude partially changed. Perhaps these modifications will transfer to situations in their teaching careers. These future teachers might not assume that outgoing exuberant behavior is needed in all teaching circumstances. They might also learn to back off at times in order to analyze certain situations more slowly and carefully.

Think and Act

- How do your essential beliefs and values affect your teaching? List three ways.
- What assumptions and attitudes do you carry with you into your classroom?
- Choose one attitude that you wish to modify. List at least three behaviors that will demonstrate this modification in the classroom.

Applying Multicultural and Global Strategies to the Classroom

Assessment of Self and the Classroom

After completing a cultural concept map and reflecting on how one's personal cultural heritage has affected beliefs, values, assumptions, and attitudes, every preservice or practicing teacher now needs to see how this self-knowledge relates to teaching. Using some kind of a self-assessment instrument is one way of trying to look at oneself in the classroom. Each person will need to guard against choosing the desired answers rather than the realistic ones. The Self-Assessment in Multicultural and Global Education Questionnaire (modified from Brown, 1993; Cooper, 1992) has partially provided for this concern by using a "What Is" and a "What Should Be" column (see Figure 2.4 on pages 52–53). Sections A and B deal with personal and professional development and awareness and sensitivity. Sections C through F deal with curriculum, instruction, parents, and the community. They will be discussed in later chapters. Assessment and classroom environment, not covered on this questionnaire, will be assessed separately.

Review of the Self-Assessment

A few days after the self-assessment has been completed, each person should return to it for as objective a look as possible at the results. Working with a partner who can play the role of a supportive but objective colleague is a good method to use. Partners could ask such questions as "What information did you use to evaluate yourself for each section?" "If you just reacted on emotional or 'gut feelings,' were you being accurate?" "What other sources of information are available?" The chapters following have more specific examples of ways to assess a classroom, but at this stage each person could review data such as classroom observations, teacher lesson plans, student work, and student conversations. Answers can be changed to give a more realistic picture.

The "What Should Be" category offers teachers a chance to look at their feelings about different aspects of multicultural and global education. If some answers were ranked less than "5," these areas must have been considered less important than others. With multicultural and global application, however, all areas are of great importance because they work together to improve the teaching–learning situation. Reflecting on personal choices and reasons behind them can lead to further analysis of beliefs and values.

No one should get discouraged if the Self-Assessment Questionnaire shows many areas that need improvement. This, in fact, might indicate a deeper awareness of the scope of multicultural and global education and its potential pervasive influence in classrooms and schools. A very high self-rating might actually indicate a very limited understanding or an unrealistic estimate of multicultural and global education practices.

When the questionnaire was first used in 1993, two student teachers who scored themselves high were the ones who were ranked the lowest of six student teachers when observed for their actual application of multicultural and global concepts (Brown, 1993). Their understanding of multicultural and global education seemed limited to curriculum content as provided by the cooperating teacher with little or no modification. In addition, multicultural and global concepts were not applied to the other critical elements of the classroom. For instance, both had stereotypical displays (one, an Indian feather headdress for Seminoles, and the other, sombreros for Mexicans). More important, in several incidents both student teachers showed insensitivity and actual cruelty towards students in their care (Brown, 1993).

In contrast, the student teacher who graded herself the lowest on the Self-Assessment Questionnaire actually received the highest ranking for application in the classroom. It seems that this student teacher understood the complexity of multicultural and global education issues and how much they invaded every phase of teaching. She modified the curriculum to include other perspectives, she used a variety of cooperative learning strategies, and she established a self-government system in the classroom. Most important of all, she showed sensitivity and empathy towards students whose class and ethnicity were different from hers (Brown, 1993).

Such disparity between self-assessment results and objective findings can hopefully be eliminated or minimized with an increased knowledge base of what application practices entail plus honest peer dialogue and personal reflection about what is really happening. Focusing on the process rather than scores also helps with maintaining an objective approach to assessment. This should not be viewed as a test of how many right, but a form of professional development action or research.

Think and Act

■ Note down one or two multicultural and global things that you already do from each section of the Self-Assessment. Choose one to discuss with a colleague.

■ Look at the largest discrepancies between "What Is" and "What Should Be." Make an action plan to improve one of these items.

Use of the Results

Several approaches can be taken for applying multicultural and global concepts to the classroom. First, an examination of things already done will give a baseline from which to operate. Using the Self-Assessment form has probably already brought to mind many specifics that fit under the different sections. Noting these will help to give each person a feeling of accomplishment. When that is completed, goals for improvement can be set. One way to prioritize goals is to make an action plan based on those areas that need the most work.

Another possibility involves choosing the easier possibilities first. Teachers could immediately tackle parts that require relatively small adjustments or small time investments. Perhaps, as a start, reading a few articles on another religion's basic beliefs and practices would give more insight and understanding in that area. For example, the media's portrayal of Middle Eastern terrorists leaves many people in the United States with negative attitudes toward the religion of Islam. Reading about the basic religious tenets, called "The Five Pillars of Islam," talking with a Muslim religious leader or imam, and attending services in a mosque might give a more comprehensive understanding of this religion and the range and complexity of its practices worldwide. Work here will help to modify assumptions or attitudes towards Islam and Muslims, emphasizing that, as with any religion, the fanatics of Islam do not speak for the whole of Islam. This approach would be only a beginning, but might help provide survival information until a more in-depth study could be done.

After selecting two or three areas to investigate, teachers can jot down the action steps needed to accomplish the research. If any of these areas can be accomplished almost immediately, these should be done to create a feeling of success. Other areas can be tackled by setting a timetable of several weeks for gathering, reading, and taking notes on background information. Interview appointments can be scheduled, giving enough time to read the materials but not enough time to lose interest and motivation. Thoughtful questions take careful preparation in advance, probably when the materials are being read. Asking about facts connected with the Five Pillars of Islam, for instance, might not be as rewarding as asking the reasons behind these tenets. As with any discussion related to beliefs and values, teachers have to be sensitive to others' feelings and emotions. Listening with an open mind and withholding judgment are essential multicultural and global skills that can be applied in interviews.

After a few weeks have passed, revisiting the Self-Assessment Questionnaire would be helpful. As each section is analyzed, notes about changes already accomplished can be made. Action steps for the next few weeks can be set up. In any case, keeping the steps small and manageable will be less discouraging and a reminder that developing multicultural and global perspectives takes a lifetime of effort. Trying to do too much at once discourages anyone. Having many small steps in an action plan gives teachers the chance to reward themselves for progress along the way.

Think and Act

- Choose two or three areas for quick investigations.
- Set aside time each week to do research or reading on the chosen topics.
- Set up a separate notebook with sections for research articles. Use margins, stick-it notes, or separate sheets for ways to apply learned information in the classroom.

Conclusion

Progress in this critical classroom element of teacher is also progress that will affect all the other elements. As the other five critical classroom elements of students, environment, curriculum, instruction, and assessment are explored in the next chapters, possibilities for initiating change based on multicultural and global perspectives will occur more naturally because of heightened awareness and sensitivity. Periodically returning to think about this first critical element will be beneficial in emphasizing the process component of applying multicultural and global education. Preservice and practicing teachers must constantly remind themselves of their beliefs and values, their assumptions and attitudes that must be modified if they expect their students to do likewise.

FIGURE 2.4   Self-Assessment in Multicultural and Global Education (modified from Brown, 1993, and Cooper, 1992)

Directions: In this questionnaire each statement has two answers to be recorded. The first answer for each statement is "What Is" and relates to your present experience teaching; the second answer for each statement is "What Should Be" and relates to what you believe ought to be the situation for you, given the time spent in your teaching environment. Circle the two appropriate numbers for each statement.

KEY: 1=Almost Always   2=Frequently   3=Occasionally   4=Almost Never   5=Not Applicable

A. Personal/Professional Development	What Is	What Should Be
1. I feel comfortable discussing racial issues with people of other races as well as my own.	1 2 3 4 5	1 2 3 4 5
2. I read books or articles to increase my understanding of and sensitivity to the particular aspirations and frustrations of minorities.	1 2 3 4 5	1 2 3 4 5
3. I strive to maintain personal associations which reflect racial and ethnic openness.	1 2 3 4 5	1 2 3 4 5
4. I stay informed about international events and recognize their importance in our lives.	1 2 3 4 5	1 2 3 4 5
5. I have the professional training needed to work effectively with people from diverse cultural backgrounds.	1 2 3 4 5	1 2 3 4 5
6. I use my colleagues' expertise to extend my own knowledge of and skills in multicultural and global concepts.	1 2 3 4 5	1 2 3 4 5

B. Awareness and Sensitivity	What Is	What Should Be
7. I am conscious of cultural differences in such areas as communicating with people of other cultural groups.	1 2 3 4 5	1 2 3 4 5
8. I encourage diversity of values, lifestyles, and viewpoints even when these run counter to my own preferences.	1 2 3 4 5	1 2 3 4 5
9. I take the initiative in dispelling prejudices, stereotypes, and misconceptions among students.	1 2 3 4 5	1 2 3 4 5
10. I recognize my own cultural biases and try to see issues from other viewpoints.	1 2 3 4 5	1 2 3 4 5
11. I try to prevent any prejudiced or stereotyped thinking from unfairly influencing my expectations of students.	1 2 3 4 5	1 2 3 4 5

C. Curriculum: Content	What Is	What Should Be
12. I promote conservation and ecological concern in the classroom.	1 2 3 4 5	1 2 3 4 5
13. My students are given opportunities to express, celebrate, and maintain ethnic and racial differences.	1 2 3 4 5	1 2 3 4 5
14. I use a multicultural/ global approach and the appropriate materials to teach basic skills.	1 2 3 4 5	1 2 3 4 5

15. I stress the interdependence of nations and people around   1 2 3 4 5   1 2 3 4 5
the world, relating world events to our community.

16. I develop in students the skills and values necessary for   1 2 3 4 5   1 2 3 4 5
survival in the dominant culture without denying the
existence of other values equally appropriate in minority
children.

D. Curriculum: Resources	What Is	What Should Be

17. I know where to obtain multicultural/ global materials   1 2 3 4 5   1 2 3 4 5
that are free of racial or cultural bias for use in my
classroom.

18. I have evaluated my textbooks to determine whether   1 2 3 4 5   1 2 3 4 5
they contain fair and appropriate treatment of persons
from all cultural groups (including ethnicity, sex, age,
disability, nationality).

19. The materials that I use about minorities and people of   1 2 3 4 5   1 2 3 4 5
other countries are an integral part of the curriculum
rather than attached or treated separately.

20. I regularly bring in extra multicultural/ global materials   1 2 3 4 5   1 2 3 4 5
to supplement the curriculum.

E. Instruction	What Is	What Should Be

21. I believe that my classroom conduct encourages my   1 2 3 4 5   1 2 3 4 5
students to respect one another and be open and honest
in their communications with me and with each other.

22. I search for ways to overcome the reluctance of students   1 2 3 4 5   1 2 3 4 5
to recognize and discuss racial and ethnic questions.

23. I adjust my teaching methodologies with students from   1 2 3 4 5   1 2 3 4 5
different cultural and socioeconomic backgrounds.

24. I clearly demonstrate that academic expectations are   1 2 3 4 5   1 2 3 4 5
equally high for students from all cultural backgrounds.

25. I use cooperative learning groups with planned   1 2 3 4 5   1 2 3 4 5
combinations of students of different sexes, abilities,
and ethnic groups.

26. I encourage students to interact and learn from each   1 2 3 4 5   1 2 3 4 5
other regularly during the school day.

F. Parent/Community Relations	What Is	What Should Be

27. I seek the assistance of the community in developing   1 2 3 4 5   1 2 3 4 5
multicultural and global activities.

28. I have visited and familiarized myself with the families   1 2 3 4 5   1 2 3 4 5
and communities of my students.

29. I have attended social, religious, or cultural events   1 2 3 4 5   1 2 3 4 5
held by members of my students' communities.

30. I use parents and community members from various   1 2 3 4 5   1 2 3 4 5
cultural backgrounds as classroom assistants,
occupational speakers, and visiting lecturers.

3

The Students

One of the essential multicultural and global concepts mentioned in Chapter 1 is that diversity enriches the world of the classroom and the world outside. The wide variety of students' cultural backgrounds, experiences, knowledge, and beliefs offers every classroom a great richness to be shared. Yet many teachers, either not knowing or not caring, daily ignore this wealth. Teachers who say that they care about their students too often show in their attitudes and their actions that they care only about certain aspects of their students, not the whole unique person.

Once teachers become aware of their own cultural influences, they need to think of how their students' cultural influences differ from theirs and from each other's. Searching for ways to honor these differences within the classroom then becomes a major goal of any teacher applying multicultural and global concepts. This goal entails the understanding of what accommodations must be made for successful learning to take place and who must make those accommodations. Typically, students from diverse backgrounds are pressured by individuals and institutions to become acculturated to the dominant group in order to benefit from a U.S. public school education. Nieto (2000) suggests, however, that students should not be forced to do all the accommodating. Instead, she calls for a negotiation among students, families, teachers, and schools that will create a more equitable teaching and learning environment.

This chapter reminds teachers to look more closely at their students from a variety of perspectives so that they can, by adjusting to and building on student differences, become more effective teachers. First, the cultural concept map is revisited with students in mind. Then individual learning styles are explored. Finally, cultural learning styles, orientations, and communication styles are discussed.

Using the Cultural Concept Map for Student Investigation

Sources of Information

The cultural concept map in Chapter 2 can be revisited with individual students in mind. In a sense, the following sections on cultural influences repeat some of the information found in that chapter, but the purpose here is to examine the categories again using the perspectives of students as the main focus. With teacher–student interactions a major part of teaching and learning and a major emphasis of this textbook, a minimum amount of overlap between the two chapters is inevitable, necessary, and of value when approached from different viewpoints.

Teachers have a variety of sources of cultural information available in their classrooms and schools. Some information can be gained from classroom discussions and observations. Some cultural, academic, and social behavior data will be available in the students' files. More cultural clues and family practices can be learned from conferences with the students and their parents or guardians. For teachers working on teams with the same group of students, additional information can be gathered from their colleagues.

Ways to reference the cultural information collected need to be considered as well. Elementary teachers will probably find making some sort of a classroom grid a valuable tool. Secondary teachers might consider looking at the categories as a whole and thinking about which categories might be the most influential for students, especially at-risk students. Another approach would be to center investigations on students who seem hard to reach and who have not responded to teacher initiatives. Whatever methods are chosen for data collection and organization, teachers should keep in mind the major reason for such an exercise: The more teachers can learn about their students, the more possibilities the teachers have for reaching those students and helping them to learn.

Much of the information valuable to teachers can come directly from the students themselves. Depending upon their age, they can participate in a number of different activities that involve their own cultural groups. They can construct their own cultural concept maps, choosing with the teacher which categories to discuss and which to keep private. Student assignments about themselves and their cultural heritages can also be very informative. "I search" research papers, where students do a personal investigation of their family history, give students a chance to explore many possibilities. Of course, as with all assignments related to personal backgrounds or experiences, options should be broad enough to provide for adoptive, extended, and blended families and flexible enough to offer alternatives for students with difficult situations. Some students might be uncertain of their ethnic or racial heritage or not wish to reveal it; others from diverse religious backgrounds might not want to be singled out. Certainly, few students from working-class families or families in poverty would be willing to discuss their financial struggles or make a comparison of family shopping habits.

Although historical situations and events can be painful for students and their families to investigate, sometimes the research process itself leads to a deeper understanding and appreciation for ancestral struggles and hardships. Shawna, an African American young woman with extensive family records available, was puzzled by the sudden stop of the ancestral written history. She was stunned when she realized that she had reached the time period of slavery when her ancestors were counted as nameless property rather than as human individuals. Traci, a Jewish university student, learned for the first time her grandparents' story about their emigration from Russia and immigration to the United States. Until her inquiry, the subject had been a forbidden topic between the grandparents and parents.

Dialoguing and reflecting about each other's experiences within a safe classroom environment lead to student appreciation and empathetic understanding of diversity as demonstrated by their classmates. Students like Thi, who described her family's flight from Vietnam to her preservice peers, bring the affective component along with the cognitive information into the classroom. When students find sharing their own cultural heritages too revealing, stories or vignettes from previous classes can be used very effectively to open up conversation. These can describe historical events, present personal perspectives on cultural heritages, or talk about specific incidents of discrimination depending upon the teacher purpose.

Stories borrowed from other sources can supplement missing pieces to make sure ordinarily silenced voices are heard. Members of the Gay, Lesbian, and Straight Education Network (GLSEN) of Greater Ft. Lauderdale, Florida, have several anonymous testimonies from gay high school students that work well in workshop exercises to develop understanding and empathy (Palazzo, 2000). Nicto's (2000) case studies serve to highlight issues she discusses in her text. High school students and preservice teachers can find themselves and their peers in the students' struggles to define themselves in relationship to school, family, and cultural heritage.

Stereotypes and Generalizations

Throughout the chapter, it is important to keep in mind the problem of stereotyping. The traditional definition of stereotyping has been an all-or-none characterization such as "all Asians are smart" or "all Germans are efficient." Yet Lee and colleagues found no research documenting people who believe that *all* members of any stereotyped group have any particular attribute (Lee, Jussim, & McCauley, 1995). A more sophisticated definition sees stereotyping as accepting an attribute as generally true of a group and then imposing it on an individual without questioning the assumption. Thus, "most Asians and Asian Americans are smart" becomes "this Asian American student in my class must be smart." The first statement could be based on statistics showing that certain Asian and Asian American cultures have such a high regard for education that their children usually do very well in U.S. schools. This, then, would have some validity if "smartness" were based on success in school. The second statement about the individual student depends entirely upon the individual and his and her circumstances and might or might not be true. Even positive stereotypes can do a great deal of damage. For instance, to expect a particular Japanese American or Korean American to do well in school is to impose the "model minority" stereotype on that student, ignoring that person's individual characteristics.

Although stereotypes must be avoided, generalizations can be useful tools for understanding individuals and groups. Generalizations point out trends and possibilities, giving the investigator guidelines for further study. In the next sections that discuss the cultural groups and learning and communication styles, generalizations from research studies are made to help teachers develop ways of thinking about and acting toward their students. It cannot be stressed enough, however, that teachers must focus on their individual students rather than groups of students. Each student is unique even though he or she shares certain characteristics with other students.

Think and Act

- Make a collection of stories that illustrate different cultural experiences reflecting those in your school or university. Use students' stories if possible, but change the names. Test several of the stories with peers.
- Interview a person with a different cultural heritage than yours, composing together a vignette that can be used to illustrate that specific perspective. Consider different types of culture besides ethnic and racial. Exchange vignettes with others.
- Have students write a short story about an artifact or experience that illustrates their personal cultural heritages.
- Have students conduct interviews of each other, family members, and community people about life experiences.

Race/Ethnicity

As reflections of the society around them, classrooms and schools demonstrate racial tensions and discriminatory practices. To help students gain more positive attitudes about racial differences, teachers have an obligation to address directly racial issues, sharing the responsibility for minimalizing conflicts. One way to affirm color in the classroom is to develop appropriate language to discuss differences in people of color, within cultural groups as well as among groups. Although this might seem to be a minor point, for students of color who are regularly misidentified by White teachers, it is one more example of being identified first as part of a racial group rather than an individual. Shawntay, a Black student at a predominately White college, complained, "It's not as if there are so many of us—and I don't look anything like Maria [the woman she was regularly mistaken for by students and professors]."

When living in Southeast Asia, the first author found that Whites often had difficulty visually distinguishing among Asian cultural groups or among individuals within the same group. European Americans typically start descriptions of individuals with "blond, blue eyes, ..." The emphasis on the color of hair and eyes is less useful when whole populations of people have dark hair and dark eyes. Moreover, with the growing popularity of hair coloring among young Asians and Pacific Islanders, the description of an individual's "dark hair" can be inaccurate from one month to the next. Here shades of skin coloring, types or styles of hair, or shapes of faces, eyes, noses, ears, and cheekbones are better descriptors.

Whites are not the only ones with difficulty distinguishing between groups and among members of the same group; people of color can experience the same problems when looking at other groups, including Whites. This focus on group characteristics rather than individual differences is common when people are look-ing outside of their own ethnic or racial group. An exercise involving descriptions of the faces of students or their friends can give teachers and students practice in devel-oping a working vocabulary of descriptive terms. One caution about the class exer-cise is the possible sensitivity of students, especially adolescents, to being described. The exercise could be done using adult members of the family or adult friends in-stead of students but it would make the work less personal. The use of self-portraits, drawn or photographed and then described verbally, provides students with appro-priate words. Books such as *The Girl with the Brown Crayon* (Paley, 1998), about Paley's last year teaching kindergarten and the power of stories in children, make excellent discussion starters for students and teachers alike.

"Invisible minorities" is a phrase sometimes used to describe individuals whose cultural background is different from the dominant European American one but is ignored either because of the small percentage of that cultural group in the population or because of the lack of accurate information about the group. In her case study about a Lebanese American boy, Nieto discusses the twin problems of lack of information and misinformation, such as stereotyping Arab Americans as "rich sheikhs, religious zealots, or terrorists" (Nieto, 2000, p. 168). Lebanese Americans, for instance, have the cultural heritage of the Arab World, probably still have Middle Eastern ties, but might be Christian or might be fair-skinned and light-haired. They might also be Muslims, like the vast majority of practicing Muslims, who have no ties to terrorist groups. Ignoring the diverse backgrounds and experi-ences of Arab Americans and other invisible minorities is really a way of forcing assimilation or imposing stereotypes.

At all ages, students need to see their ethnic and racial heritages as positive aspects of their lives. In the classroom, individual exploration of heritages through interviews, guest speakers, and research can be an emphasis for the initial weeks of school that is revisited throughout the year. For some European Americans, the as-signments might bring out the first conscious awareness of specific ethnic heritages. When asked on a questionnaire about their ethnicity, usually a few European Ameri-can students will write "none." These students might have had ancestors who learned to ignore their ethnicity as they tried to assimilate. Beyond that, the students were also making an assumption that they were the norm and everyone else was "ethnic" or different. Such ethnocentric behavior by students must be addressed in the classroom so that all ethnic and racial heritages can be seen as enrichments rather than deficits.

Racism between groups of color and colorism within a group of color also need to be addressed in classrooms. In the U.S. territory of Guam, teachers in a Masters of Education cohort explained how students from the outer islands of Micronesia are the ones most often targeted for discrimination in student popula-tions predominantly of Chamorros (native Guamanians), Filipinos, Japanese, Vietnamese, and other Pacific Islanders and Asians. These teachers, who regularly deal with racist issues associated with White cultural influences from the mainland United States, were surprised when asked about combating racism against

Micronesians within their own schools. In certain mainland U.S. cities, Hispanics and Blacks or Asian Americans and other cultural groups of color have had long histories of verbal attacks and aggressive behaviors toward each other.

Within a group, colorism is demonstrated when the group members discriminate among themselves according to lightness of skin, with lightness being a desirable characteristic. The excellent film "Black Is, Black Ain't" (Riggs, 1995) discusses Black colorism along with sexism, patriarchy, homophobia, and cultural nationalism. This frank coverage of Black diversity provides an in-depth discussion about Black identity from multiple perspectives. Filmmaker Marlon Riggs adds an additional insight as a Black gay man searching for self-definition and community while battling AIDS. Works like this remind teachers of the complexity of all cultural groups when viewed from inside as well as outside the group.

Think and Act

- Develop and use describing skills for the categories of skin coloring, hair, faces, eyes, noses, ears, and cheekbones.
- Ask students to describe the face of a family member or close friend. Check categories used and the order of presentation. Use pictures of people from different ethnic and racial groups to discuss how individuals within groups describe themselves.
- Observe students on the playground. What types of interracial interactions are noted? What age groups seem most prone to same race interactions?

Class

Students and families in poverty are too often treated by teachers as willing participants in their situations, as if living that way were a choice rather than a result of complex causes. The middle-school teacher who commented sarcastically about how "those students who *can't* pay can get *free* book covers" showed no understanding or empathy for his students in poverty. Schubert talks about educators interpreting educational needs and problems through their middle-class lens and without much empathy for those "on the boundaries" (Brown, Mir, & Warren, 1996, p. 348). Consistently, these students have been judged by class rather than potential and have been tracked into vocational courses or trapped in basic skills classes, leaving them inadequately prepared for middle-level business positions or higher education (Rose, 1989).

Middle-class students sometimes demonstrate their biases through teasing and harassment. A recent newspaper story described the experience of a bright teenage girl living in a trailer park and attending school with students from wealthy homes. She related incidents of harassment by classmates for wearing less fashionable and less expensive clothing. Her resulting decision not to take honors classes because she did not want to isolate herself from the other students in poverty made sense in such a hostile environment. Questions about the girl's choices and potential consequences of these choices can open up student discussions about local forms of harassment and ways teachers and students can work to eliminate them.

As mentioned earlier in the chapter, the use of student case studies or vignettes helps students to analyze difficult multicultural and global issues through individual voices of their peers. A similar approach is student writing of personal stories about lives in the inner cities of the United States and the world recommended by Schubert (in Brown et al., 1996). This type of writing does not mean the comfortable, pretty stories that avoid real issues and real concerns of students. If truthfully told, "What I Did Last Summer" might be much more revealing than teachers are prepared to handle. Yet these true experiences need to be brought into the classroom, in fiction form if nonfiction is too personal or too painful. At all grade levels, taped oral interviews of students, family members, and community people can be done (see Chapter 5, Curriculum).

Simulations involving economic decisions based on a variety of incomes are another way to expose all students to the financial realities of living below the poverty line. For students of working-class and poor families, the exercises might provide the motivation necessary to continue school if they are combined with a solid mentoring program that offers viable alternatives. Investigating wide ranges of job opportunities along with the specific qualifications necessary for these positions has become part of typical middle school curricula. In high school, school to work programs mentioned in Chapter 9 seem to offer students the best opportunities to break the poverty cycle if they are part of a comprehensive plan to prepare students with knowledge, skills, and attitudes for mainstream businesses. Realistically, however, economic options for working-class and poor students are very limited. Educational reform must involve expanding educational opportunities and large-scale, continued funding for long-term programs coupled with an economy that has meaningful jobs with decent salaries at the end of the school experience (Apple, 1996).

Think and Act

- Research articles about teenage spending habits. Have students study teen magazines and other media for commercial pressures on teens to be consumers. Keep a record of your own spending. Does it match your research?
- Read Jonathan Kozol's *Savage Inequalities* (1991). Discuss with others the savage inequalities between schools and within schools.
- Read Kozol's *Amazing Grace* (1995) for an inside look at children in the South Bronx. How, according to the book, "do greed, neglect, racism, and expedience" (book back cover) create and sustain such a ghetto?

- Show a video such as "Unequal Education" (Listening to America with Bill Moyers, 1991) or "Children in America's Schools" (1996) and discuss the consequences of vastly different educational opportunities.

Religion

Students' religious beliefs affect many aspects of school life. Even if the individual student does not practice a religion, religious influences from the family or community are often strong determinants of assumptions and attitudes. Students as well as adults see educational and societal controversies such as banned literature, abortion, and gay rights from the perspectives of their religious backgrounds.

Christian teachers often are not aware of special religious holidays of other faiths. Recently, limited concessions have been made for students of other faiths so that they will not be penalized overtly when they miss school because of religious celebrations. Although Jewish high holy days are acknowledged more now than in the past, most teachers have to be reminded not to schedule tests on those days when Jewish students are likely to be absent. Students of other religions such as Islam and Buddhism find their special holy days rarely acknowledged by teachers who often do not know even the names of the celebrations, much less their significance or requirements. During the Islamic holy month of Ramadan, for example, the schoolwork of older Muslim students could suffer from the effects of daily fasting.

Ideally, students and teachers should know the basic tenets of major world religions and any other religions practiced by students in the school. Holy days of various religions can be honored by acknowledging them in a respectful way. Family elders or religious leaders can serve as guest speakers in the classroom. Student projects can involve video or audio taping of interviews with appropriate representatives. To avoid any proselytizing, teachers can provide guidelines for any talks or interviews.

Think and Act

- Ask community religious leaders to provide you with a one- or two-page information sheet about the basic religious tenets and religious customs.
- Use a calendar that lists religious holidays of major religions, supplemented with any religious holidays celebrated by individual students. Discuss less familiar holy days in class.
- Attend religious services of various faiths. If possible, attend with a friend of that faith to act as the cultural translator. If not, contact the religious leaders in advance to explain your purpose and ask permission. Find out about customary behavior and dress for the service.

Gender

Conscious and unconscious forms of gender segregation and discrimination are practiced daily in schools. "Girls line up here; boys line up there" is a common command in elementary classrooms. Sorting students out by gender seems to be a benign behavior, but it emphasizes differences much in the same way as sorting students by race or religion would do. Other more serious forms of discrimination affect the type of learning going on in classrooms. Studies have found that teachers treated boys and girls differently, calling on boys more frequently, asking them more difficult questions, and encouraging their efforts (American Association of University Women, 1992; Sadler & Sadler, 1994). Girls have also been discouraged from entering the traditionally male fields of science and mathematics. On the other hand, boys get more negative attention in classes, especially at the elementary level. Their typically more boisterous behavior makes settling into the passive routine of many classrooms harder for them. Boys, especially those of color, get disciplined more and labeled for special needs more often than girls do.

Teachers can analyze their own behaviors by taping classes and watching for gender equity. Quantity and quality of call-ons, praise, encouragement, and reprimands can be examined. Initiatives by students such as questions, call-outs, aggressive body language, and noisy off-task behavior might reveal patterns of student behavior and teacher response. Gender concerns might relate to whose behavior is ignored and whose behavior is reprimanded. Race or color issues might also be revealed. Student-to-student exchanges also might reveal gender concerns. Typically, White middle-class boys, especially those with assertive "macho" behaviors, will control small group discussions if roles are not assigned and followed (Henkin, 1998). Encouraging all students to listen to and accept everyone's contributions is an ongoing task for teachers.

Providing girls and boys with positive female role models in nontraditional fields is one way to break down stereotypical impressions. Trade books for younger children and nonfiction literature can speak to the students about career possibilities. Literature can also be used to open up discussions about gender discrimination in the United States and elsewhere. Books such as Pipher's (1994) *Reviving Ophelia*, Orenstein's (1994) *SchoolGirls*, or Johnson's (1995) *The Girls in the Back of the Class* provide school and home problems for reading and dialoguing. For international discrimination issues, parts of textbooks such as Wing's (2000) *Global Critical Race Feminism* can be adapted for use, especially when combined with other sources such as the Internet.

Think and Act

■ Brainstorm women's issues in a small group, with each person choosing one to investigate. Consider both national and international perspectives. Questions about equal job opportunities and salaries, for instance, assume preconditions that might not be true in other countries.

- Watch a group of children at play, looking for differences in types of play activities and the physicality of the play. What patterns are you able to determine?
- Videotape a few class lessons and analyze the interactions for gender patterns: call-ons, praise and encouragement, and reprimands by the teacher; initiatives, disruptions, and verbal and nonverbal exchanges by students.

Sexual Orientation

Sexuality is an important characteristic of being human and an overriding concern of students as they mature from asexual children to sexual adults. During the adolescent years, students are trying to find out who they are, and part of their identity search is related to sexuality (Santrock, 2001). For students and teachers alike, sexuality and sexual orientation issues are fraught with social, cultural, and religious landmines. U.S. society's ambivalence about sexuality has the media's extreme emphasis on sex and sexual behavior in opposition to powerful interest groups' desire to erase sex education from the curriculum. In schools, sexual harassment alone, both same-sex and opposite-sex, attests to the necessity of teacher intervention. In a study by American Association of University Women (1993), 85 percent of eighth to eleventh grade girls and 75 percent of boys reported being often harassed. Other adolescent problems such as rape, sexually transmitted diseases, and teen pregnancy cannot be ignored, and sexual well-being must be incorporated into the overall well-being of all students.

Gay, lesbian, bisexual, and transgender students are particularly vulnerable targets for harassment and ostracism. Because of internalized feelings of worthlessness fostered by the deep-seated homophobia in many communities, gay adolescents are also very much at risk for suicide. They need to know that classrooms are safe for them as well as their heterosexual classmates.

In upper grades, frank discussions presenting multiple perspectives should be part of the sex education curriculum. Careful planning and previewing of state and district approved materials and careful following of guidelines for student absences will minimize potential problems. "Teaching Respect for All" (Caiola, 1996), a video for teachers, parents, and other concerned citizens, provides ways to address anti-gay prejudice at the secondary level. Whether or not students are excused from any discussions, they can be held responsible for their behavior toward others.

At all grade levels, teachers can combat homophobic language and behavior. "It's Elementary" (Chasnoff & Cohen, 1996) is a powerful film for elementary teachers particularly that offers classroom examples of developmentally appropriate ways to discuss issues related to sexual orientation. Elementary children already hear and begin to use harassing language like "faggot" and "dyke," and they already know that one of their classmates has two mommies. The film "That's a Family" (Chasnoff & Cohen, 2000) is a video narrated by children for elementary children. It describes a wide range of family structures including single parent, multiracial, divorced, guardian, adoptive, and gay- and lesbian-headed households. Materials like these provide students and teachers with models for talking about sensitive topics.

Helping students to be respectful of others by stopping hurtful comments and empowering students to do the same is a starting place for teachers. Making sure developmentally appropriate resources are in the library and the sex education curriculum is actually taught, arranging for faculty and staff training, and joining local and national organizations to support gay and lesbian students and family members involve more risk taking but are essential pieces of a homophobia-free school.

Think and Act

- Watch "It's Elementary: Talking about Gay Issues in School" (Chasnoff & Cohen, 1996) or "That's a Family" (Chasnoff & Cohen, 2000). Discuss which methods you would incorporate in your classroom. At the elementary level, how would you determine what is appropriate? At the secondary level, how would you incorporate related issues into your content area?
- Contact Parents and Friends of Lesbians and Gays (PFLAG) (www.pflag.org) or other gay and lesbian groups for personal and material resources in the local community. Prepare a list of consultants for students who ask.
- Check Women's Educational Media (www.womedia.org) for other films and videos on economic and social justice issues.

Ableness

Peers can be cruel to classmates who have mental, emotional, and physical disabilities, so teacher intervention is vital to establish a positive learning climate. Discussions at the beginning of the year with all students about appropriate behavior in the classroom will help to set the tone. Stories and videos about students with disabilities, disability simulation activities, panels of people speaking about their disabilities, and "dos and don'ts" lists are ways to focus on the differences. The danger is that such activities alone might result more in students' fear of being disabled and pity for those who are, thus reinforcing stereotypes (Adams et al., 1997). Discussions about oppression and plans for possible social action steps, combined with the recognition that everyone is likely to have some disability during a lifetime, can help to provide a more balanced picture.

Interactions between students with special needs and other students need to be frequent and positive. Physical proximity is a prerequisite for friendship, but it is not enough (Stainback & Stainback, 1996). Particularly helpful are teaching strategies that promote cooperative rather than competitive work, such as cooperative learning (discussed in Chapter 6, The Instruction), community circles, partner work, buddy systems, and organized activities at lunch and recess. Also valuable are classroom furniture arrangements that encourage student–student interaction and provide access to as much of the room as possible for students with physical disabilities. In every situation, students with disabilities must be able to make valued contributions to the group (Stainback & Stainback, 1996). Teachers can facilitate this by designing activities that allow for all to participate.

Teachers find that students with special emotional needs, particularly those who act out, present the greatest challenges in inclusionary classrooms. Their disruptive behavior, much of which they cannot control without teacher intervention, can result in rejection by classmates and teachers. Rejection can increase the students' feelings of hurt and anger, which in turn can lead to more disruptive behavior. Students who withdraw are also very much at risk, although their behavior is not as disruptive to the class.

Positive steps that teachers can take include viewing disruptive behavior as needs and wishes of the student or the student's perspective about the quality or appropriateness of instruction (Hitzing, 1996). Without effective and acceptable means of communication, such students choose effective but disruptive methods to get their immediate needs met. Interventions need to go beyond just stopping the specific negative behaviors to investigating reasons behind them and implementing procedures that address the underlying problems. Reducing the amount of work, offering alternatives to reach the same objectives, changing instructional strategies, and providing teacher and student encouragement can help to reduce disruptions. Specifically teaching acceptable ways to communicate needs is another possibility (Hitzing, 1996). At the same time, the teacher can also use a nonverbal private signal as a reminder to the student about expected actions.

Think and Act

- Check Norton and Norton's (1998) text for children's literature or other anthologies for books to use in the classroom about students with disabilities.
- Screen for class usage the website for children with chronic illnesses, "BandAids and Blackboards: When Chronic Illness or Some Other Medical Problem Goes to School," at funrsc.fairfield.edu/~jfleitas/contents.html.
- Observe students with special needs to see how much they are being empowered to do their own work and how much is being done for them. Brainstorm reasons why the student is unwilling or unable to do the work. What alternatives are possible?
- Observe interactions between students with special needs and other students in the classroom. Are they frequent and positive? If not, prepare an action plan listing specific teacher interventions.

Language

Linguistic diversity among students is continuing to increase in both the numbers and the varieties of languages found in districts. Most of the over 3 million limited English proficient (LEP) students are in the lower grades. Spanish is the native language of three-fourths of the students, with several Asian languages and, most recently, Russian having significant student populations. Twenty-nine different Native American languages are spoken by 2.5 percent of the LEP students (Orozco, 1998). Teachers, parents, administrators, and other stakeholders disagree on the effectiveness of the various bilingual education models selected by schools and districts. Almost everyone agrees, however, that diverse language speakers often are at risk in public schools.

Students who speak two or more languages have a distinct advantage interculturally and internationally over their monolingual peers (Ashworth, 1988). Unfortunately, this advantage is usually considered a disadvantage in U.S. schools, especially when English is not the first language of the students. Teachers and other students with English-speaking backgrounds might be impatient or unkind in their verbal or nonverbal communications. Students sometimes internalize this attitude and become ashamed of their linguistic differences, not wanting to sound different from others. This attitude can extend to embarrassment of older relatives who have limited English and strong accents, creating serious problems within families.

The issue of Standard English as compared to Ebonics, Spanglish, and other forms or combinations of English has been discussed in Chapter 2. Classroom practice needs to be clearly stated to students and the rationale clearly explained. The language position taken by the teacher must be humane to all students while supporting appropriate learning goals. General practices to help linguistically diverse students include cooperative learning strategies and buddy systems with same-language and English-language speakers for emotional comfort and clarity of procedures. Several specific strategies are discussed in Chapter 6.

Think and Act

- Attend a community event conducted in a language you do not understand or watch without interruption for over an hour a television show in a language you do not understand. Record what you have learned, what you think you missed or want explained, and your emotional reactions during the time period. How can you apply this experience to teaching LEP students?
- Ask school language consultants to provide school-related words and phrases in written form with pronunciation guides for the different languages.
- Ask family members or community leaders to give "survival vocabulary" lessons to the class in the different languages of students with limited English. Have them include a discussion of basic cultural courtesies.

Age

One cultural group that teachers are usually very aware of is that defined by age. Realizing that students at each grade level are almost all within a year's difference in age, teachers also understand that a huge difference in physical, emotional, and social maturity can be found within that same grade's grouping of students. Still, unless teachers make a conscious effort to understand the implications for students who are at different levels from their classmates, they can slip into unwarranted assumptions about individual students.

Students who develop early physically are often expected by adults and children to behave older than their chronological age. Brothers Tom, Brian, and Kevin were very tall for their age throughout their schooling. Their mother reported that the boys were often told by teachers to "act their age." The problem was, of course, that the boys were—but the adults kept forgetting that they did not look their age. Particularly at risk for harassment by other students are the girls who mature early. At the opposite end, boys and girls who mature late are often treated as if they were younger by adults and classmates. They can become targets of ridicule for exhibiting babyish behaviors.

Emotional and social maturity differences also vary greatly among students of the same academic year. In the primary grades especially, a few months can be crucial for successful emotional and social adjustment to the heavy academic pressures. Pushing kindergarten students who are not ready for the more restrictive and challenging activities of first grade can cause those students much frustration and lack of success. In British infant (primary) schools, children start school at different times of the school year, according to the months of their birth dates. In this way, the age span among children in the same class is only a few months rather than a year or more. Although that system would be very difficult to implement in the United States, paying close attention to each child's chronological, emotional, and social age and making adjustments for younger children is one more way of looking at children as individuals as well as members of a group.

Think and Act

- Visit a toy store and ask employees about the most popular toys and games. Discuss with them what makes a specific toy or game the favorite. How do these differ from what you enjoyed as a child and adolescent?
- Analyze popular children's television shows to see what elements appeal to students. Watch the advertisements to see what toys and games are being promoted.
- Research the British infant school system. What advantages and disadvantages do you see to having different starting times during the year?
- In a classroom of students, choose the individuals who seem the most mature and the least mature chronologically, physically, cognitively, and socioemotionally. On what data did you base your selections?

Regionality

Regional differences, like any cultural differences, can be divisive or enriching, depending upon the classroom climate. For high school students particularly, the contrasts between urban, suburban, and rural can become points of friction. As facilitators, teachers need to be mindful of students whose experiences do not match theirs. Middle-class teachers living in suburbs who show disdain for the urban environment of their students in poverty might condone similar behaviors from their students. Student or teacher use of expressions such as "from the sticks" or "the other side of the tracks" demonstrates an ethnocentric attitude related to living conditions and class structure.

Students from other parts of the country can be teased by other students for their different regional accents or customs. Speech patterns and the rapidity of speech also vary from region to region. A student who has moved from the Northeast to the South might be seen as abrupt or rude, while a student who has moved from the South might be seen as slow-thinking or lazy. A discussion of speech patterns and the stereotypes seen or heard in the media can help students to examine their assumptions.

Nationality

Students whose families have immigrated from other countries have a particularly difficult time of adjustment. In most cases, they struggle with both linguistic and cultural differences; some also have to overcome traumatic upheavals from their homelands. *The Inner World of the Immigrant Child* by Igoa (1995) examines the process of acculturation through the eyes of the students. Some students learn to perform in a bicultural mode, adjusting back and forth between school and home. Helping students to make adjustments without losing their own cultural identities becomes a major concern of caring teachers.

Honoring and Sharing Cultural Backgrounds

The Native American saying about walking a mile in another's moccasins reminds all educators of the need to empathize with their students. One way to honor and share cultural backgrounds is through cultural heritage projects, with the emphasis on cultural traditions passed on from the elders in the family, extended family, or community. Maureen, a high school English teacher, uses a portfolio system that combines traditional research, literature readings, oral interviews, and class presentations with various types of written work. One part of the assignment is an "I search" paper, where the student investigates some segment of his or her family's personal history. At the elementary level, parents, guardians, religious leaders, or community leaders could assist in bringing different aspects of their cultures into the classroom.

Beyond the obvious cultural customs and traditions are the less obvious cultural influences students have had. Like teachers, students need to realize that beliefs, values, assumptions, and attitudes have strong effects on ways individuals view the world. Even in the lower grades students can be made aware of different perspectives through regular exercises with concrete examples, such as questioning students after an argument with "How do you think he felt when you called him a name? Would you like to be called a name?" Literature at all ages has many possibilities for examining different world views.

In sharing different cultures, teachers and students need to understand the iceberg principle: Most of the iceberg, the most dangerous part, is hidden under water. The cultural iceberg in Figure 3.1 is similar in that the surface differences such as clothing, languages, foods, and heroes are "above the water," or visible and tangible elements of a culture. They are relatively easy to analyze and hypothesize about (Cushner, 1999; REACH Center, 1996). The much larger and less tangible cultural aspects such as beliefs, values, assumptions, and attitudes are hidden "below the water." These elements are mostly subjective and are difficult to analyze or verbalize

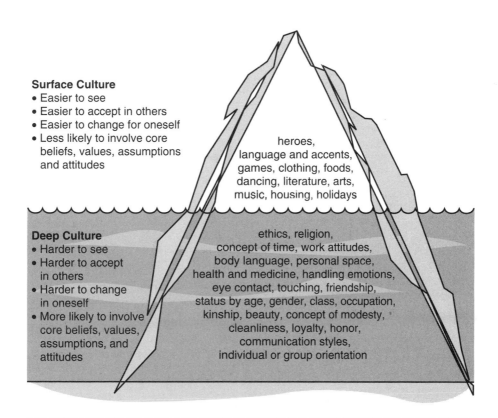

Surface Culture
- Easier to see
- Easier to accept in others
- Easier to change for oneself
- Less likely to involve core beliefs, values, assumptions and attitudes

heroes, language and accents, games, clothing, foods, dancing, literature, arts, music, housing, holidays

Deep Culture
- Harder to see
- Harder to accept in others
- Harder to change in oneself
- More likely to involve core beliefs, values, assumptions, and attitudes

ethics, religion, concept of time, work attitudes, body language, personal space, health and medicine, handling emotions, eye contact, touching, friendship, status by age, gender, class, occupation, kinship, beauty, concept of modesty, cleanliness, loyalty, honor, communication styles, individual or group orientation

FIGURE 3.1   Cultural Iceberg

about. Like the hidden part of the iceberg, these subjective elements are the most dangerous, the most likely to lead into intercultural misunderstandings if they are not taken into consideration.

Students can be made more aware of their own and others' belief systems through activities involving dialogue and reflection. One approach, used by Clark County School District (Gilluly, Jones-Mosley, & Bonar, 1996) in Nevada, is to suggest lessons across the curriculum for the less tangible elements of culture. Their brochure includes esthetics, ethics, family ties/folk myths, rewards and privileges, and rights and duties as deep culture elements. As mentioned earlier, investigating the more hidden aspects of cultures can be emotional and sometimes painful work. Thoughtless comments or statements, especially from mainstream individuals, can trigger reactions from students of oppressed cultural groups. Yet remarks such as "Girls who wear sexy clothes are just asking for it" or "I feel so sorry for anyone in a wheelchair" cannot be ignored. Sensitive teachers will minimize student blame-putting, denial, or anger by using interpersonal skills that focus on the problems not the persons.

Think and Act

■ Choose one of the more subjective areas of culture and explore the topic from the perspectives in the class. Survey individuals' understandings of manners, for instance.
■ Debate the issue of designing ceremonial masks in art. Is this disrespectful to cultures that attach sacred symbolic meaning to them? Does it compare with designing different images of the cross or the Star of David?
■ Investigate the website on international training (www.webofculture.com), particularly the sections on gestures and language. Discuss whether these are helpful or too simplistic. Imagine that you are instructing an immigrant to the United States. What gestures would you caution him or her about?

Reviewing Learning Styles

Learning styles have been defined as the preferred ways individuals process and organize information. They are the cognitive, affective, and physiological traits that individuals consistently employ when perceiving, interacting with, and responding to the learning environment (Orlich, Harder, Callahan, & Gibson, 2001). For the most part, in education the main focus is on the cognitive styles learners employ when processing information (Irvine & York, 1995). In this section, a broad interpretation of learning styles has been used to include personal traits such as brain hemispheric preferences and diverse intelligences.

Research seems to support the overall concept that individuals learn differently, but findings have been mixed about the relationship between teaching students in their preferred learning styles and student achievement (Grant, 1992; Irvine & York, 1995). Advocates for learning styles comment that teachers tend to view learning problems among culturally diverse students as problems inherent in the students themselves instead of problems caused by cultural incongruence (Nuby & Oxford, 1998). Lack of teacher understanding about learning style differences coupled with ethnocentric thought about learning can lead to negative assumptions and lower expectations for diverse students.

While learning styles theories have yet to be proven valid, learning styles research, however, has at least focused attention on the cultural context of teaching and learning. Teachers are reminded to be aware of their own instructional goals, methods, and materials as well as the personal learning styles of their students (Irvine & York, 1995). Teacher awareness of possible cultural incongruence or mismatch with diverse students is the necessary first step toward bridging the teaching–learning gap.

Learning styles research also reminds teachers of the affective side of teaching and learning. When educators fail to recognize, value, and use styles different from their own, they are in danger of not relating well to learners unlike themselves. Personal and cultural styles such as use of gestures, physical space, and body posture become significant when students' styles clash with those of their teachers. Teachers who are knowledgeable about, and responsive to, the diversity of learning styles among their students will make every effort to take responsibility in providing a more effective learning environment.

Many education textbooks mention a variety of learning styles approaches and measurements. One of the most comprehensive presentations of learning styles comes from Dunn and Dunn's Learning Styles Inventory (Dunn, Dunn, & Price, 1978). Some of the other commonly discussed learning styles approaches are Gregorc's Style Delineator (1985), Myers-Briggs Type Indicator (Myers & McCaulley, 1985), hemisphericity, and field dependence/field independence. In recent years, Howard Gardner's (1983) term *multiple intelligences* has become popularized in educational settings, especially elementary schools. Gardner (1997) has identified at least eight intelligences: linguistic, musical, logical-mathematical, spatial, bodily-kinesthetic, interpersonal, intrapersonal, and naturalist. Goleman's (1995) emotional intelligence is another aspect dealing with how individuals relate to the world and each other.

Think and Act

- Research the learning styles mentioned, looking for applications in the classroom.
- Analyze your preferred learning styles and compare the results to the instructional strategies and forms of assessment you use in the classroom. How often do you favor your own learning style preferences?

(continued)

■ For each of your preferences, make several suggestions of modifications you can make to help students with diverse preferences.

■ Analyze the learning styles of students at risk in your classroom. Do you teach to their preferred styles often, sometimes, or never?

Applying Learning Styles to the Classroom

The power of all these insights into how individuals learn is in educators' ways of looking at learning and teaching. Understanding the implications of the diversity of learning styles leads to accepting the need for diversity in teaching styles. As previously successful students, most teachers already know their preferred learning styles, either by intuitive means or through a more formal analysis. Yet unless they consciously make an effort to provide for students with diverse learning styles, teachers tend to match teaching styles to their own preferred learning styles (Adams et al., 1997).

Examining Cultural Learning Styles

Worthley (cited in Bennett, 1999) lists five cultural factors that appear to have an influence on learning styles. Findings indicate that the stronger the socialization and sociocultural tightness or the societal pressure to conform, the more field dependent the members become. Other findings indicate that the more ecological adaptation is vital for survival, the more the members have highly developed perceptual skills. Finally, the more a society is literate, the more emphasis is put on the written language, while less literate societies stress direct experience observation and modeling more.

Cultural learning styles research primarily focuses on major ethnic and racial groups in the United States. While thinking about cultural influences, teachers must keep in mind the balance between the individual as unique and the individual as a member of a cultural group. Individuals within different cultural groups vary tremendously in their ways of believing, thinking, and acting. Certain styles might be commonly found in a specific cultural group, but some individuals within that group might not have those styles at all. Other cultural influences such as gender and class also influence individual learning preferences. Thus, it is inappropriate to expect every African American student to be an expressive storyteller, although traditional African American cultural learning styles might favor auditory and kinesthetic modalities.

The styles described below are not intended to be comprehensive; the information must be understood as only a guide, not a detailed reference. The great danger of providing cultural learning styles information is that any groupings or generalizations might be used as some sort of easy checklist that leads to stereotyping (Nieto, 2000). Yet, without generalizations for guidelines, teachers may find it difficult to plan alternatives for working with culturally different students.

Work Habits

Competition is an integral part of dominant U.S. culture. As a result, this competitive spirit becomes a part of the stated and hidden curriculum in most schools. Young boys and girls are urged to do their individual best and children are praised more for their personal than for their group work. Bulletin displays such as "Star of the Week" or "Star Readers" reinforce the concept of one child or several standing out in the group.

In contrast to this dominant cultural style, other cultural groups emphasize the cooperative spirit. Children from Southeast Asian countries, for example, have grown up honoring cooperative work. Indonesia's national slogan is "work together, share together." Many African Americans, Latinos, and Native Americans have maintained cooperative practices for survival. Thus, when thrust into the competitive mode of the dominant U.S. culture in schools, these children may find difficulty succeeding in that environment.

Modalities

Visual modality (print-oriented) preference is often seen in cultures with a long history of written materials and an emphasis on being well-read or literate, such as European, European American, Northern Asian, and Asian American groups. The printed word, especially if it is a historical document, has great value. Religious documents such as the Bible or the Torah have special significance. Being able to quote printed text is a sign of an "expert" or "authority." Mainstream Americans, including teachers, tend to believe in the importance of the printed word.

Visual modality (screen-oriented) preference is related to television, movies, videos, and computer screens. Although the youth cultural group does not fit the more narrow definition of race or ethnicity, it certainly falls under the cultural category of age. Students who have been exposed to electronic equipment since birth and have had many thousands of hours of viewing time have developed different responding skills to the two-dimensional images than most of their teachers. The emphasis of electronic viewing is on movement and action. Thoughts and behavior are explicit, not implied; vulgarity and violence are commonplace and accepted.

Native American groups also tend to be visually oriented. They often use mental images rather than visually remembered words to recall concepts (Irvine & York, 1995). Storytelling, although seemingly an auditory skill, relies on visual images built around natural settings and natural events. One Onondaga storyteller describes his narrative abilities as a recounting of the images he sees on something like a flip chart of the scene.

Auditory modality preference will be found with many groups that have a history of extensive oral tradition, such as African, African American, Middle Eastern, and Southeast Asian. Here the sound and expression of words are important. Meaning might be exaggerated for effect; hyperbole, similes, and metaphors are used regularly. Speeches in Arabic, for instance, include exaggerations and flowery language; length gives the words extra power.

A well-known example of the richness of African American oral language usage is found in Martin Luther King's "I Have a Dream" speech given in 1963 (King, 1991). His use of repetition for emphasis sets a rhythm that builds excitement and anticipation. For instance, one segment comparing Lincoln's time with the time of the speech repeats the phrase "100 years later" with King adding more strength to each new repetition. In the same segment, King's poetic use of metaphors describes the African American position in contemporary society as "crippled by the manacles of segregation and the chains of discrimination" and as "a lonely island of poverty in the midst of a vast ocean of material prosperity."

African American oral tradition also includes many other stylized verbal forms such as signifying, a humorous insult or put-down, and testifying, telling the truth through story (Irvine, 1990; Smitherman, 1977). These forms allow for spontaneous creative exchanges that enrich the conversation. Because of the back and forth nature of the conversations, polychronic behavior with more than one person talking at the same time is often characteristic.

Many Native Americans are also highly auditory learners, but in a less exuberant way. They tend to be empathetic and participatory listeners, but follow the listening with private reflection. As mentioned above, traditional storytelling combines auditory and visual skills. Metaphors and descriptive pictures are part of the skills used.

Kinesthetic/tactile modality preference refers to movement and the need of a person to use movement for expression. Students whose body language mirrors their emotions might also have good coordination and graceful motion. Their need for physical activity can include the tactile aspect as well. Although young children in general have a need for kinesthetic and tactile experiences, some cultural groups— such as Africans and African Americans—seem to require more movement and convey more expression through body movement (Irvine, 1990; Shade, 1989). In the dominant U.S. culture, gender also influences early behaviors. Traditionally, boys have been allowed to be more physical in their play, while girls have been expected to be more restrained. In the classroom, these behaviors translate into boys having a tougher time settling into the more passive, quiet routine of an average classroom. Educators concerned over the labeling of children who seem hyperactive have argued that it is the traditional formal classroom, rather than the children, that displays disruptive behavior—behavior that disrupts childhood itself (Kohn, 1998).

Think and Act

■ Interview two or three good storytellers about the techniques they use to remember stories.
■ Research signifying, testifying, and other African American oral traditions. Plan lessons that use these skills.

Perceptual Styles

Field dependence, responding to information as a whole rather than as individual parts, is seen in cultures such as African, African American, Asian, Asian American, Latino, and Native American (Bennett, 1999; Irvine & York, 1995). Although European Americans in general tend to be field independent, women are more likely than men to be field dependent. Students who are field dependent tend to prefer learning information in contextual settings, focusing on people and actions rather than detailed facts (Pai & Adler, 2001). They sometimes have difficulty separating out the relevant information from the unimportant in textbooks and standardized tests, so specific contextual examples such as case studies provide them with appropriate whole and personal pictures.

Field dependent students tend to be conscious of the immediate environment and will try to organize the space around their desks. Yvonne, the only African American preservice teacher in a classroom of European Americans, seemed to take longer than the rest of the class to get started on quick in-class writing assignments. When the instructor realized what was happening, she observed her more closely. Yvonne was trying with little success to line up her text, notebook, and paper on the inadequately sized chair writing arm. Her classmates, most squished in awkward positions as they balanced books and paper, were oblivious to their own discomfort as they tackled the task. The instructor learned to forewarn the class while continuing the discussion to allow for individual organizing time before asking everyone in the class to get started.

Providing field dependent students with opportunities to organize the space around them in a classroom can help to give them physical and psychological comfort. Young students might make decorated name signs, holders for writing and coloring equipment, and other physical symbols to claim their space. Inviting students to claim individual space in this visual yet nonverbal way has the added advantage of making immigrant students and other newcomers feel more at home in an unfamiliar environment (Igoa, 1995).

In contrast, field independent students can focus in on isolated facts and isolated tasks. They more easily sort significant information from less important details, working analytically and sequentially (Pai & Adler, 2001). They often prefer to work alone, not needing as much social support as other students. Standardized multiple choice tests and the type of curriculum they tend to drive are compatible with the perceptual style of field independent students.

Think and Act

■ Observe how individual students claim their immediate territory. What kinds of physical objects do they position around them? What sort of body language do they exhibit?

■ Observe how individual students organize themselves and their belongings when given new seatwork. Are there any rituals? Are these deliberate or unconscious?

Examining Cultural Orientations

Beyond influencing ways that individuals process information as separate learners, cultural groups also have influenced ways individuals relate to each other and the environment. The classroom is an arena of countless interactions during every day. How the students act and react to each other as well as the teacher is crucial to a safe and welcoming environment. Knowing more about students' preferred orientations helps teachers provide better ways to reach students. The orientations, although expressed as dichotomies here, can also be represented by a continuum, with certain groups showing more of one orientation and others being more balanced. Again, preservice and practicing teachers must be cautioned to examine each individual's preferences carefully to avoid stereotyping.

Context

High context orientation, a term used in intercultural communication research, is the cultural equivalent of field dependence. Members of high context cultural groups such as African Americans, Asian Americans, Latinos, and Native Americans, tend to have a field dependent learning style. For some cultural groups, the context of a conversation is as important or more important than the actual words spoken. What is said is not always what is meant. Behavior is related to mutual face-saving, and individuals are expected to understand the subtleties of nonverbal communication.

Low context orientation is the cultural equivalent of the field independence learning style. Cultures such as Northern European and European American tend to have field independent members. Field independent people usually do not adapt as easily to the social context as high context people because they are less aware of nonverbal cues and the environment. They have a direct, open style and prefer explicit, careful information. They tend to interpret what is said by the words only without using the social situation to confirm or deny the verbal message. They often are goal- rather than people-oriented and tend to prefer working alone.

The cultural climate in U.S. schools generally follows the dominant European American culture with its emphasis on academic learning separate from context. This is particularly evident in secondary classrooms that emphasize factual learning, memorization, and performance on standardized multiple choice tests and that minimize the importance of the social and interpersonal context of learning. Preservice and practicing teachers, especially those who are field independent, will need to analyze the classroom situation beyond the instructional strategies to provide for the needs of field dependent students.

For high context cultural groups, the classroom is more than an academic setting; it is also the place where interconnecting relationships are played out. Students who are field dependent usually wish to know the teacher as a real person, not just the authority or expert. Teachers can share appropriate personal experiences or interests with students, allowing them to see a nonacademic side. Cecilia, a Puerto Rican professor, talked about how she administered a questionnaire to a group of Puerto Rican health practitioners. Before they would consider filling out the anonymous forms, she had to explain in detail—some twenty minutes' worth—about her position, her present objective, the future use of the questionnaire, and how all this related to them. In contrast, when Sue administered a questionnaire to European American preservice teachers she did not know, she gave an explanation of a few sentences before the students went diligently to work.

Students who are field dependent also need many opportunities to communicate with their classmates during the day. Tying conversation exchanges to instruction helps provide the needed social contact while keeping students on task. Beyond that, moments devoted to sharing of personal interests or victories help maintain a friendly, accepting classroom. Sports, music, and local current events are possibilities for pre- or post-instruction minutes. Time spent developing healthy classroom relationships is not wasted time. Working together in the arranging and running of the classroom also helps to build the personal relationships needed by all students, but especially field dependent students. Because of their need for close contact with others, field dependent students should not be disciplined by sustained periods of forced isolation (see Chapter 4, The Classroom Environment, for a discussion of this).

Think and Act

■ Compare your favorite elementary or high school teacher with your least favorite teacher. Were your emotional reactions to them connected to personal behaviors and interpersonal relationships? If so, in what ways did you feel valued or not appreciated?

(continued)

- Observe several intracultural (within the same culture) and intercultural (between cultures) interactions. Do the participants use the same types of verbal expressions, body language, and gestures?
- Select for observation a boy and girl who make frequent social contacts with other students. Keep a record of their interactions. How do they initiate them? How disruptive are the interactions? How does the teacher react?

Time

A monochronic preference relates to an understanding of time as fixed. For Northern European and European American cultures, appointment times tend to mean the time stated, with little room for flexibility. Gunilla, a Swedish woman, once explained that in winter guests invited to a home would be given arrival times a few minutes apart so that boots and coats could be removed in an orderly fashion. In contrast, other cultures would consider an arrival time for a party as approximate with no one willing to appear at the time stated. This promptness, in fact, might be a rude shock to the hosts who probably would not be ready to receive guests.

Polychronic cultures demonstrate a more elastic understanding of time. For many African and African American, Asian and Southeast Asian, Latino, and Middle Eastern cultural groups, not only are exact time schedules less important but also the sequencing of tasks is less important. In fact, several things might be going on at the same time. Conversations can have two or more people talking at the same time, the participants maintaining an interactive flow of words and responses.

Teachers who are monochronic might expect students to finish one task before beginning another or expect students to switch abruptly from one subject to another because of the time schedules. Teachers might also not recognize that some students can manage more than one task at a time. The student who seems not to be listening while he continues to do something else might well be taking everything in. Careful observation of individuals will help teachers to decide which is the case.

Sound

Polychronic cultures often have a noise orientation as well, accepting background noises as part of the fluid situation. Some cultural groups with traditional polychronic and background sound orientation are Latino, East and Southeast Asian, and Middle Eastern. Individuals develop an ability to concentrate on a conversation or quiet task while hearing a host of other sounds. During a Pakistani school show in Indonesia, the children performed their skits and dances while the audience of parents continued to carry on greetings and conversations, seemingly oblivious to the stage actions. When their own children were on stage, the respective family members and friends watched attentively but continued to chatter. No one seemed upset by the audience noise even when it all but drowned out the stage dialogues.

Modern communication and media are rapidly changing cultural noise or quiet preferences. Across the cultural groups, young people today seem to tolerate a noisy background much better than their elders. In fact, many students treat any continuous noise in the background as white noise that blocks other auditory distractions. It is not unusual to find that U.S. students, even from cultural groups preferring quieter backgrounds, prefer to study while "listening" to the television or radio.

In the classroom, students who chatter while working probably disturb the teacher more often than they disturb their classmates. Allowing on-task noises such as chattering, humming, or soft singing can again depend on the context, such as the informality of the learning situation. Playing music tapes during seatwork time, art class, or classroom clean-up times helps students who need multimodal stimulation. During more formal times, such as testing, providing soft background music can be one way to reduce the tension.

Social Dimension

The collectivist cultural preference emphasizes the group rather than the individual and is related to high-context orientation groups and field dependent individuals. Students brought up with strong family and extended family ties often are expected to work with and share with family members (Triandis, 1995). Another characteristic is recognition and respect of family obligations, even when these obligations conflict with school expectations. The Hispanic student who is chronically late to school might have the daily responsibility of seeing that her younger siblings get to their school first. Sometimes one's own desires must be sacrificed for the sake of others. Team effort rather than individual achievement is encouraged and praised. Putting oneself above others is discouraged as boastful. Tim, a Lakota Dakota/Cherokee, describes his cultural view of appropriate social behavior: "People are crabs in a bucket. When one crab tries to climb over the others to get out, the other crabs will pull it down."

In contrast to the collectivist cultures, the individualistic cultures emphasize the individual and his or her independence and accomplishments. Family members rarely feel responsible for relatives beyond the immediate or nuclear family. Students are expected to do well individually. Boys particularly are expected to be competitive and aggressive in getting ahead. U.S. schools reflect the dominant European American cultural emphasis on individual and independent achievement. The social studies curriculum has fostered the American myth of the pioneer, the rugged individual. Characters such as Johnny Appleseed and Paul Bunyan are admired for their individualistic, eccentric behavior.

Preservice and practicing teachers, predominantly European American, too often insist upon this individualistic approach to learning and classroom interactions. Although cooperative learning strategies have gained in popularity recently, some teachers still see cooperative learning as a form of student cheating and discourage sharing of answers for written seatwork. Many teachers also use classroom arrangements to discourage student interaction, emphasizing the individualistic process rather than the collaborative process of learning. Disciplinary measures involving extended periods of physical isolation can also be stressful for students with a strong need to belong. Most important is the teacher's willingness to build a community of interdependent learners. Recognizing and encouraging everyone's participation in the daily chores and sharing of the classroom is a caring teacher's role.

Think and Act

- Survey your peers or students for sound preferences. Ask them about television, radio, or compact disk use while studying.
- Test your own reactions to background noises while working. Try different types of music, talk shows, television movies, and so on. Test various volume levels.
- Analyze the pattern of a student who is chronically late to school. Are reasons given related to family obligations? What arrangements can be made to accommodate these? What process will be used to reach a comfortable compromise on both parts?

Worldview

The spiritualistic worldview has the sacredness and interconnectedness of all life as a central theme. Cultures with a spiritualistic tendency, such as Asian, Asian American, and Native American, look at the universality and the oneness of the world. Land, water, and sky should not be private possessions for personal use and misuse; they should be shared by all and treated with respect. According to this belief, the land is held in trust for the future. A Native American saying states that if a decision about the use of nature's gifts is not good for the next seven generations, it is not a wise choice.

The dominant European American culture in the United States has a materialistic orientation, which emphasizes possession and control over the natural world. Having an economically good life with many material possessions demonstrates a person's worth and position in society. According to this worldview, individuals and corporations that have control over specific resources have the right to use the resources as they see fit. In spite of a rapidly expanding world population and diminishing resources, many Americans continue to be huge consumers of wood, oil, natural gas, water, electricity, and other natural resources. Worldwide, multinational companies have expanded the same emphasis on consumerism and exploitation of resources into countries with limited financial resources or the political power to control such expansion.

The overemphasis on materialism and consumerism needs to be counteracted in the classroom as well as elsewhere. Any emphasis on accumulation of personal goods and clothing, such as expensive brand names, should be discouraged.

Teachers should be wary of management systems that are built on prizes or small gifts. They risk reinforcing the concept of possessing things as well as encouraging extrinsic rather than intrinsic motivation. An emphasis on spiritual qualities of life such as goodness, kindness, and thoughtfulness can be promoted through discussions and stories from different cultural groups.

Presenting multiple perspectives demonstrates a role model of openness and offers students other ways of examining their lives. Asian health and medical practices combining the spiritual and the physical take a more holistic approach to sickness and health. Syndromes seen from Western scientific perspectives as sicknesses to be cured by drugs and surgery are treated by some cultures as part of the whole person's state of well-being. Other cultures such as the Hmong see illnesses such as epilepsy as "the spirit catching you and you fall down"—perhaps a person specially touched by the gods (Fadiman, 1997).

Native American stories about the spiritual relationship of people to the natural world offer alternative concepts about ecology and land use. Combining the concept of the sacredness of the land with local conservation efforts would be a practical way for young children especially to think about material wastefulness. Conservation in the classroom can be encouraged with daily routines for sharing and taking care of public property. Emphasizing the proper use of furniture, books, and supplies helps to teach respect for belongings of the classroom community. Even when supplies are plentiful, teachers can encourage conserving and sharing resources by restricting amounts available at one time. Some elementary teachers provide art supplies for a group of students to share and do not allow students to have individual crayons or felt pens. Using the backs of printed sheets for writing exercises or art projects is one way to cut down on paper waste. Teachers and students together can brainstorm other creative recycling measures beyond the usual can, bottle, and paper ones.

Teachers need a good understanding of what sharing means to individual students, especially young children. Children who have collectivist cultural backgrounds with a lack of emphasis on personal belongings and children in poverty who have experienced mutual sharing out of necessity might borrow what other classmates consider as personal and private possessions. Establishing early in the year what is to be shared and what is not to be shared will minimize problems later. Insisting that any toys or games brought to school are for classroom enjoyment rather than personal use will also help cut down on possessiveness and jealousy.

Think and Act

- Read *The Spirit Catches You and You Fall Down* by Fadiman (1997) about the cultural clash of U.S. doctors and a Hmong family with a young daughter with epilepsy.
- Collect several stories about the spiritual relationship of humans to the earth. Prepare ways to use them as a mini-unit or as short activities.

(continued)

■ Visit a naturopathic store or clinic and ask for free literature about its products. How do alternative treatments and medicines relate to other worldviews? Why have they become so popular recently?

Examining Cultural Communication Styles

Research abounds in information about cross-cultural communication styles and the necessity of understanding differences for intercultural and international situations. The classroom is an intercultural workplace with numerous teacher–student and student–student interactions daily (Brown, 1993). Preservice and practicing teachers should be aware of nonverbal as well as verbal communication styles. The following are only a few of the many possibilities.

Verbal

The direct style of verbal communication is connected to low-context cultures in that the true intentions are revealed in the words themselves. The directness emphasizes values of openness, honesty, and forthrightness. "Get to the point" is a typical expression. The European American culture tends to value this direct approach to relationships with the emphasis on business objectives. The danger of this approach is that it largely ignores the personal relationships and individual feelings involved in the conversations.

Direct instructions and brusque orders and commands can be very offensive in many cultures. When U.S. companies originally expanded into certain international markets, high achievers in the U.S. mainstream business world often did not understand the importance of first building personal ties and gaining the confidence of the indigenous people. They and their companies then found the local people unwilling to work for them and resistant to any change, even when the projects would benefit them.

Exceptions to the direct form of communication for European Americans are often related to issues of controversy or embarrassment. For instance, preservice European American teachers have a very difficult time discussing racial concerns, especially when only a few people of color are present. This avoidance shows both a reluctance to offend and a lack of practice using more subtle methods of communication such as visual cues from listeners.

The indirect style of verbal communication is practiced by cultures such as many African, African American, Asian, Asian American, Latino, Middle Eastern, and Native American groups. This communication style depends on subtleties indicated by contextual cues rather than words to convey the true message. Care is taken to establish and maintain appropriate personal relationships at the same time as trying to achieve a separate objective. Face-saving is an important part of indirect verbal communication. An Indonesian might not want to embarrass someone requesting a favor, so he might halfheartedly agree, expecting the other person to sense his unwillingness and not continue with the request.

In the classroom, the teacher's position of authority and power might make it very hard for some students to disagree openly even when the teacher is requesting other perspectives. Asian cultural groups tend to hold teachers in high esteem, placing them as authority figures. Disagreeing with teachers, even in verbal arguments encouraged by the teachers, might be interpreted as a form of disrespect. Listening carefully to the tone as well as the words and watching body language will help teachers decide what students are really trying to say.

The indirect approach also shows up with the use of rich, expressive language. Arabic everyday speech contains many metaphors for effect. A simple assertive statement can be taken as having the opposite meaning because of its plainness. Cultures with long histories of oral tradition, such as African American and Native American, use many figures of speech and circular approaches to themes. When this indirect approach appears in written work, circular patterns of thought stress the harmony between the whole and its parts rather than the linear connection from section to section. Japanese writing, for instance, does not make the inferences directly but leads readers to their own conclusions.

Teachers can use the comparisons of languages to develop the understanding of multiple perspectives. Using examples of spoken and written styles from different cultures will help students with diverse backgrounds master the succinct, linear approach expected in U.S. schools. At the same time, the richness of other language styles can be used to encourage students to develop more expressive English for creative storytelling and writing. Preservice and practicing teachers themselves, especially those who have succeeded so well academically with direct, sparse English, will probably need to develop an appreciation of the subtleties offered by indirect verbal communication.

Think and Act

- Develop a file of short stories illustrating specific examples of literacy devices such as metaphors and hyperbole. Look for circular patterns of narrative. Collect stories translated from other languages.
- Check the community for local storytellers. Ask them to tell a story and then speak about the techniques they use.
- Start a storytelling tradition that encourages expressive language.

Posturing

Some cultures use their bodies assertively to convey messages of strength and status. African Americans, especially young males, tend to choose flamboyant clothing, adopt assertive standing and walking stances, move in a rhythmic manner, and act boisterously verbally and nonverbally (Hilliard, 1992; Nuby & Oxford, 1998). Such posturing, impulsive, and extroverted behaviors can cause a lack of cultural synchronization in the classroom, particularly if the teacher is White and female (Irvine, 1990). The absence of synchronization and the resulting miscommunication too often lead to disciplinary measures and even referrals for special education. The cultural conflict is further intensified by Black oppositional behavior that works against academic achievement (Ogbu, 1994). White female teachers especially have to develop skills of interpreting and responding to posturing since it so contradicts their own learned behaviors.

In contrast to posturing, some cultures and cultural groups encourage individuals, particularly women, to be more self-effacing with their body expressions. Girls in many cultures learn not to sprawl in chairs but keep themselves in a tight, contained space. Lucy spoke of her 10-year-old international daughter as being several different girls from an exuberant one when speaking Italian and English to a modest, quiet one when speaking Arabic. The dominant U.S. culture seems to accept rough-and-tough "tomboy" girls before puberty but expects more "ladylike" behavior when the girls reach their teens.

Turn-Taking

The concept of turn-taking is related to the perception of time as being fixed or flexible. Those cultures with an understanding of time as fixed tend to see talking at the same time as rude, especially if this involves interrupting someone else's narrative. An added complication is the role of status. Teachers who tell students not to interrupt them might not have any trouble interrupting students. European American interruptions often are nonsupportive of the original speaker, changing the viewpoint or even the topic. Cultures with a more fluid understanding of time see talking as more jointly participatory and accept simultaneous talking, especially among peers. Because the talking is shared, the contributions support one another. Paolo, a Cuban American, talked with his fellow doctoral students in a simultaneous dual conversation and arm patting. With his professor, however, his behavior was more restrained, indicating a respect for the professor's position.

Teachers can accommodate a variety of conversational styles by establishing different procedures for different contexts according to the objectives. Rigidly enforcing turn-taking behaviors for all occasions will probably stifle the spontaneity and interest of some students. For whole-class teacher-directed lecture and recitation, turn-taking is a more effective practice, with wait time techniques giving more students a chance to participate. For excited student-to-student discussions, however, polychronic behaviors serve to involve some children who might not get called on or whose natural enthusiasm will spark others. By setting each context before starting, using verbal reminders of procedures if necessary, teachers help students to develop a variety of communication skills for a range of situations.

Think and Act

- Observe the differences in cultural and gender groups in their stances and sitting positions. How do individual students declare their leadership or timidity?
- What is "teacher presence" in the classroom? How is it stated by posturing? How are warmth and friendliness conveyed?
- Note which students interrupt other students and why. Are their contributions supportive of the other students' conversation or ignoring others' viewpoints?

Face-Saving

This cultural preference is related to high-context orientation with its emphasis on the whole social situation. A good impression, *bella figura* in Italian, is very important. A middle-aged woman in Milan should not walk her dog in sweat pants, although designer jeans would be acceptable if coupled with quality leather boots. Beyond the physical impression, there is a psychological sensitivity to embarrassing or being embarrassed in public. In social contexts, the maintenance of polite courtesies and proper manners is essential. *Mal educato* would be said of an Italian with the lack of such manners. Students with such cultural backgrounds might be uncomfortable with certain informal practices such as calling an adult by his or her first name.

In the classroom, teachers have the responsibility to build personal as well as academic relationships with students. For some students, informal relationships with teachers would be against cultural norms. Asian immigrants, for example, might expect more formal relationships and polite courtesies between teachers and students. These students would not feel right about calling a teacher by his or her first name. Even asking questions or giving different opinions might be seen as an affront to the teacher's authority.

Students whose cultural backgrounds stress the importance of saving face are particularly sensitive to being embarrassed. They might also be very uncomfortable with any form of teasing, even if meant in a friendly way by the teacher. A teacher's thoughtless comment or action might destroy a child's chance of ever feeling comfortable in the classroom. Students with such cultural sensitivity should not be forced to speak up or perform in front of a class until they show signs of wanting to participate. The importance of understanding nonverbal communication cannot be overstressed in such cases.

Proxemics

Proxemics refers to the use of space in social situations. In some cultures, the social distance between individuals in a conversation is smaller than in other cultures. In Indonesia, for instance, a serious and private concern might be discussed up close, quietly, and with smiling and giggling (see comments about facial expressions that follow. What is one person's comfort zone can be interpreted as a threatening stance from another person's viewpoint. Yet backing away to create more personal space might be interpreted as an unwillingness to engage in discussion of the serious concern. Children might well interpret the teacher's need for more personal space as a lack of interest in them.

Think and Act

■ Think about the purpose of "little white lies" in European American culture. How do these compare to face-saving devices in other cultures?

■ Try moving into the personal space of several friends without letting them know what you are doing. Try same sex and opposite sex, close friends and casual friends. Observe their different reactions. Afterwards, measure the distance needed for comfort.

Facial Expressions

Two common areas for misunderstanding are given here. The first is the use of eye contact. European American teachers often expect students to "look them in the eye" when listening. In fact, in some cultures this is considered rude behavior, especially if the listener has lower status. As indicated in Chapter 1, Latino youngsters whose eyes are cast down might be construed to be disrespectful when, in fact, the act could be one of respect. Many Native American groups value minimal eye contact, especially with elders (Chiang, 1993). In some cultures, direct eye contact between opposite sexes is not considered acceptable and this could create problems between teachers, especially women working with adolescent boys.

Smiling is also an area of difficulty since a smile might or might not represent a happy feeling. In some cultures, a smile is a sign of embarrassment and subtle apology for this embarrassing situation. In other cultures, smiles and other facial expressions are to be restrained or concealed. Korean women, for example, might expected to cover their mouths when they are smiling. Kathleen, a European American with extensive international experience, noted her initial reaction in Korea was one of upset and anger because she thought Korean women were covering their whispers about her.

In the classroom, teachers might need to rethink assumptions about students' lack of eye contact or lack of obvious facial expressions indicating disinterest or disrespect. More subtle signs of involvement such as head or body position leaning in or away can be used to confirm or contradict the original impression.

Think and Act

- Observe the differences in male and female eye contact in public. What dominant cultural messages have females learned?
- Collect pictures of smiling faces from many cultural groups. Ask students to interpret the expressions and what might have caused them. Watch for stereotypical explanations.

Applying Cultural Styles to the Classroom

Knowledge of cultural learning and communication styles does not guarantee application. Without conscious thought and careful planning, the teachers perceive, communicate, and teach through their own preferred styles. Since teacher–student and student–student interactions are at the center of every learning situation, difficulties with interactions result in loss of learning opportunities. Too often the students are blamed for the problems when teachers must share the responsibility. At the very least teachers can work to provide a comfortable learning environment for all students by being sensitive to their students as individuals and as members of cultural groups.

The information on individual and cultural learning styles, cultural orientations, and cultural communication styles in this chapter can serve as a starting guide for developing appropriate intercultural skills. Teachers can take more time to discover each student's needs and interests academically, emotionally, and socially. Although this might seem like involving more time than teachers feel they have, especially in secondary classrooms with so many students, it should prove to be a time saver if the time spent results in better teacher–student relationships and better learning.

Time and again students of all ages report that they like teachers who like them. This sounds simple, but it involves complex relationship building. Liking students means believing in their essential goodness and treating them with respect. It means listening to their concerns and caring about them as individuals. Showing genuine interest in students' heroes, best friends, likes, and dislikes will give teachers starting topics for conversation. In order to develop strong personal relationships, however, teachers must understand how individual students perceive teacher–student relationships. For some cultures, for instance, self-disclosure in personal discussions is reserved for close friends and family members (Sue, 1995). Again, knowledge of individual and cultural learning styles, orientations, and communication styles will prove invaluable.

Teachers serve as role models for their students. The way they apply multicultural and global concepts to their relationships with students will set the pattern for all other classroom relationships. Multiple perspectives must be taught, and teachers who act as learners in their willingness to understand others set excellent examples for their students.

Conclusion

As teachers become more aware and sensitive to individual and group styles and the resulting behaviors, they can build better bridges between the dominant school culture and the various diverse cultures within the classroom. Acting as interpreters, they can explain student behaviors to other students and colleagues. They can also better explain their own behaviors to students. They, in effect, help all members of the classroom to understand and celebrate diverse ways of perceiving, communicating, and learning.

To act as mediators, preservice and practicing teachers need first to cross over cultural gaps themselves. This is done by adapting personal and professional behaviors to fit the cultural needs of individual students, especially those whose cultural influences are different from the teachers. Next, teachers can act as scaffolding to help students cross over cultural gaps, too. Such mentoring requires teacher sensitivity and solid teacher–student relationships.

Important elements in bridging cultural gaps are teacher awareness of and empathy for students' struggles with cultural conflicts. As students attempt to adjust to the dominant cultural climate of U.S. classrooms, they might encounter difficulties at home. Angie, a Vietnamese student, mentioned the tug of war between school and home. Her mother expected her to maintain the more restrictive daughter role while she was anxious to become the U.S. image of a popular girl. The more she succeeded in school socially, the harder she found her mother's restrictions. Although Angie achieved her goal of success in school with excellent grades and active social life, the cost of living in two worlds was high. Having teachers who understood what she was going through helped her realize she was not alone in her bicultural balancing struggle (Brown, personal interview, 2000).

All students must have access to the European American middle-class culture in order to take advantage of political, economic, and social possibilities in the United States. Although students are exposed to the dominant culture daily, many do not learn the ways of thinking and behaving easily. Others, like Angie, make sacrifices at home for successes in school. The goal for students should not be assimilation at the cost of their cultural heritages but an ability to live in two or more cultural worlds comfortably. Students of color, students with limited English proficiency, and students in poverty particularly have little hope of accomplishing this demanding flexibility without assistance from knowledgeable and empathetic individuals. Teachers, with thousands of personal interactions with students daily, must be the key mediators. Their awesome power requires them to accept the responsibility of mediating and navigating the diverse cultures within their classrooms.

4 The Classroom Environment

When teachers think of the environment of their students and how it has influenced them, their thoughts usually center upon the home and community outside the school. Too often, these thoughts are negative ones—what the outside environment has not done to prepare the students for school or what it is doing to prevent the students from learning in school. Chapter 8 will discuss the school environment. This chapter investigates the classroom environment and its physical, emotional, and social components. Chapter 9 will discuss the school community and ways to incorporate positive aspects of it in the classroom. Although they may have little or no influence over some aspects of the outside environment, teachers have a major responsibility for the classroom and school environments that surround students for so much of their childhood and youth.

Like the five other critical elements in the classroom, the environment is complex because it involves a good deal more than the academic side of teaching and learning. The physical, emotional, and social components play a large role in the total well-being of students. Teachers applying multicultural and global concepts to their classroom should consider the six concepts described in Chapter 1 when analyzing their own unique environment. The classroom environment must celebrate diversity, honor human rights, teach multiple perspectives, develop interconnectedness and interdependence, practice co-responsibility, and experience the global society. Co-ownership and co-responsibility of the physical arrangement and condition as well as the emotional and social climate of the classroom are essential for developing knowledge, skills, attitudes, and behaviors needed in a cooperative and collaborative classroom.

Assessing the Physical Environment

To assess the physical classroom environment objectively, teachers need to view it from multiple perspectives. Effective teachers certainly check out the space, the walls, the furniture, and perhaps the available materials to see how the lessons or class periods will work. They also think in terms of effective management, making sure that furniture and equipment placement allow for visual monitoring of students from a sitting or standing position (Stainback & Stainback, 1996). Another consideration is the travel patterns as the teacher and students go through the daily activities (Stainback & Stainback, 1996). At the same time, teachers need to consider the classroom environment from the eyes of a student or a caregiver. An objective assessment will help determine whether the room looks warm and inviting or cold and forbidding. More thought will reveal what can be changed and what cannot, or what will take only a little effort and what might take a long time and some fundamental restructuring to change.

Starting with the physical environment is practical because of the visual impact on a person entering the room. Teachers also have some control over the physical objects and their placement in the room, even if that control is limited. One way to look at the classroom is to use an assessment tool such as the Physical Environment Checklist (Figure 4.1). The checklist can be used on any classroom from prekindergarten through university. "Not Applicable" was deliberately not included on the checklist to emphasize what can be done with classrooms as opposed to what is usually done—or not done—at the upper secondary and university levels. A regular referral to the checklist will be helpful as the next parts are covered.

Organizing the Physical Environment

Student Desks and Chairs

If teachers truly believe that student discussion and dialogues are essential for optimal learning, then they must provide the means for student–student interaction to happen. Part of that preparation is the physical arrangement of student desks and chairs (Boyle-Baise & Grant, 1992). If desks are individually lined up in rows, students cannot share ideas or work together easily. Having rows of individual desks is not a successful arrangement for student interaction strategies such as cooperative learning and peer tutoring. A permanent and fixed arrangement of separate, individual desks implies that the students are not to communicate with each other unless they have the teacher as mediator. It also implies that teacher-centered whole-group lecture or lecture–recitation will be the main form of instruction since many students cannot see other classmates without turning their heads and cannot talk to one another without disturbing others. Such a permanent arrangement does not support essential multicultural and global concepts that emphasize the value of individual and group contributions.

Many elementary classrooms are arranged with groups of four or five student desks together. The groupings suggest that students share work and ideas with each other on a regular basis. Such an arrangement is a good choice for a teacher who believes that students learn from each other. The types of sharing are largely determined by the teacher, but natural interplay among students will certainly be one result of such close contact. For social and academic reasons, the groupings should be flexible. Some teachers plan a regular rotation of group members so that students get to work closely with all other classmates during the year.

FIGURE 4.1 Physical Environment Checklist

Classroom Items	*All*	*Some*	*None*
Desks and Chairs			
Are the student desks arranged to allow student–student interaction?	3	2	1
Are the student desk arrangements flexible to allow for different forms of group work?	3	2	1
Are isolated individual student desks there by student choice?	3	2	1
Is the location of the teacher's desk unobtrusive and close to students?	3	2	1
Does the teacher desktop set a friendly, orderly, and personal tone?	3	2	1
Are the main traffic patterns open enough for easy travel by everyone?	3	2	1
Walls and Ceilings			
Are walls clean, neat, in good repair, and pleasantly colored?	3	2	1
Are classroom rules few in number, positive in tone, and reflective of multicultural and global concepts?	3	2	1
Do hanging items contribute to a welcoming look without adding clutter or confusion?	3	2	1
Bulletin Boards			
Did students have input in selection of topics?	3	2	1
Did students have input in preparation?	3	2	1
Do displays of student work have something from all students?	3	2	1
Are student interests and student efforts reflected in the topics?	3	2	1
Is student achievement without student competition encouraged?	3	2	1
Cultural Pictures and Artifacts			
Do pictures show people of various cultural groups: ethnic, racial, class, gender, religion, age, language, ableness, etc.?	3	2	1
Do pictures show people wearing ordinary clothes and doing typical activities?	3	2	1
Do pictures show women, people of color, and people with disabilities in a variety of nonstereotypical situations and scenes?	3	2	1
Are pictures historically accurate and complete, avoiding stereotypical representations?	3	2	1
Are historical pictures paralleled with pictures of the same cultural groups in modern times?	3	2	1
Do pictures and artifacts show a balance of uniqueness of a cultural group and the group's similarities to other cultural groups?	3	2	1
Do pictures and artifacts show uniqueness of a cultural group without stereotyping?	3	2	1
Learning Centers, Resource Materials, and Computers			
Do students have equal access on a rotational basis to learning centers, resource materials, and computers?	3	2	1
Do materials supplement texts with multicultural and global concepts and information?	3	2	1
Are materials up-to-date and accurate?	3	2	1
Are materials free of biases and stereotypes?	3	2	1
Do materials represent multiple perspectives?	3	2	1
Are software programs free of biases and stereotypes?	3	2	1
Do software programs represent multiple perspectives?	3	2	1

Similar to the elementary level, a practical arrangement for secondary class-rooms needs to be flexible. Space is often a major issue with so many overcrowded secondary classrooms. Rows of desks might be the only practical solution spatially for a large part of the time. Yet the disadvantages mentioned above should lead teachers to consider other arrangements on a regular basis. If permanent small-group clusters present problems, at least the clusters can be created for times when group work is encouraged. Certainly, secondary students should be able to move desks and chairs with a minimum amount of time and confusion. Multicultural and global con-cepts require cooperation and collaboration among students, and clusters of desks facilitate the sharing of materials and ideas.

Another type of desk arrangement is pairing in rows. In this way students are not isolated but are able to share with only one other person. Pairs of desks in rows do not allow many students to see each other, however. A good modification of that is slanting the pairs on both ends (assuming six desks across) so that more students can see each other. Still other arrangements might involve different combinations of a U-shape. These will encourage student-to-student interaction while allowing stu-dents to face more or less frontward for parts of the lesson that are more teacher-centered.

Whatever arrangement is selected, teachers have to find their own optimum grouping allowing for frequent student–student and teacher–student communication while preventing or reducing potential management problems. Desk groupings that do not allow the teacher free access to each desk and student will not be very effec-tive in instruction and management. Too much separation of desks will severely re-strict student–student interaction and could leave students frustrated enough with being isolated to overcome that isolation by any means available.

In some elementary and secondary classrooms, individual student desks are isolated from the others for disciplinary purposes. A common student goal then be-comes that of making contact with classmates by distracting them. In many cases, pairing that student with another student helps to create a better social setup that in turn will lead to more productive work. Student isolation, whenever possible, should be the student's choice rather than the student's punishment. The former shows the student's recognition of his or her responsibility for learning while the latter only reflects the teacher's reaction to off-task student behavior.

Think and Act

■ How closely does your preferred arrangement of student desks reflect your stated phi-losophy of education?
■ If you use student desk isolation as a temporary solution to a behavior problem, do you allow the student to determine whether he or she is ready to work with others again? How soon is the student desk moved back into a grouping?

■ Ask students to plan alternative forms of desk arrangements. Select two or three using criteria presented here plus criteria suggested by the students. Try each arrangement for a week, discuss the findings, and reach a consensus on the best solution.

Teacher Desk and Storage Equipment

The location and use of the teacher's desk say a lot about individual teachers, especially if the classroom is not shared with other teachers. A teacher desk at the front of the room can indicate a teacher who wishes to be the center of attention even when students are doing seatwork. A desk at the side or back of the room removes the teacher from the front stage while offering a different viewpoint of the classroom. Even if the room is jointly used, teachers can move the teacher desk or table to other parts of the room on a regular basis. College instructors Kathleen and Sue, for instance, daily moved a table to the side of a long, narrow room for their base of operations. They found that using the front of this particular room left them feeling miles away from the students in the back. In other rooms, they regularly remove podiums from front tables and move the tables closer to the students.

The use of the desk, and its subsequent look, is another consideration. If the desk is only a depot station for papers and texts, filing shelves or containers can be arranged in a semipermanent manner. If the desk must serve as a teacher workstation as well, other furniture such as filing cabinets or bookshelves can provide extra needed space for teacher and student papers. Piles of papers and books on a desktop can create a barrier between the teacher and students whenever the teacher sits there. If sitting is rarely done, this is not a big concern; if sitting is used for paper correcting or other purposes during class time, removing that barrier will correct the feeling of distancing as well as improve the look of the desk. However the desk is placed and used, it should reflect a friendly and orderly approach to teaching. For those teachers who have their own room and desk, nonteaching desktop items such as souvenirs or a family photograph help to establish a personal relationship with students. If the classroom supports interconnectedness and interdependence, the teacher's desk must not physically or psychologically separate the teacher from the students but should serve as an extension of the teacher's belief in a learning community.

In order for students to take co-responsibility in a classroom, they need regular access to their papers, portfolios, and supplies. Providing that access is one way a teacher informs students that responsibilities for the room and its contents are to be shared. Portfolios are bulky, awkward collections that require special space arrangements. Portfolio carts are one possible solution; filing cabinet drawers are another. Classrooms with enough computers can use computer files to help solve the space problem. In these times of financial constraints and limited resources, student access to and awareness of supplies will surely provide a natural reminder about conservation of materials. Whatever solution is reached, students with access and control over their own materials and products will be more encouraged to take ownership of the classroom.

Think and Act

- How do your preferred placement and use of the teacher desk compare with different concepts of a teacher as an authority figure or a facilitator?
- Try standing in different parts of the room to check the advantages and disadvantages of the locations for the teacher desk. What different perspectives are revealed?
- What does the top of your desk reveal about you as a teacher and as a person?
- How accessible to the students are student papers, portfolios, and supplies? What rules and regulations are needed to assure equitable use of supplies?

Walls and Ceilings

If the classroom checklist results show that the walls and the ceilings are not clean, in good repair, and pleasantly colored, action steps can start here. Last year Chris, a new elementary teacher, immediately painted his room after getting hired in August. If the walls themselves cannot be repaired or changed, clever wall displays can cover up bad spots and improve the general look. If the secondary bulletin boards must contain notices of sorts, maybe areas around them can be utilized instead. Even in secondary rooms there usually is space above the blackboards for posters or other displays. Classroom rules are often located there in the front of the room. Classroom rules stated in a positive manner indicate that students are expected to maintain high standards of behavior more than rules negatively phrased in anticipation of students breaking them. Other signs or instructions should also be on a positive note.

It may seem a bit strange to be commenting on ceilings, but some teachers like to hang three-dimensional objects from light fixtures. The difficulty comes with the interference of the display items with students' behavior or work. Certain students, particularly young ones with concentration problems or students with Attention-Deficit Disorder (ADD) or Attention-Deficit/Hyperactivity Disorder (ADHD) can become distracted or disturbed by too many stimuli. A recently visited kindergarten room had so many colorful displays hanging off the walls and down from the ceiling that photos taken of the room looked like pages from *Where's Waldo?* The brightness and busyness of the room made it difficult to locate and track individual students as they went about their activities. Finding a balance between a cold, boring room and a crowded, confusing room is important.

Think and Act

- What repairs or painting can you requisition or do yourself?
- Try a few hanging items that will add color and interest to the room. Make sure they do not create a serious distraction or block anyone's view.

■ Use students to change or redo notices and posters. They can completely redesign them, illustrate them, or reframe them.

Bulletin Boards

Classroom displays need to reflect multicultural and global concepts. At all levels, the displays should be student-centered and should reflect the teacher's expectations that all students can behave and can learn. Students of all ages can and should participate in arranging the displays, with the teacher emphasizing "our" room and "our" responsibility to decorate it. Displays reflecting student interests and student efforts show that students' products are important. The best work from all students rather than only the best classroom examples indicate the teacher's interest and pride in each student's product. In the lower grades especially, students usually are delighted to have any and all of their work displayed. In the upper elementary grades, a careful choice of a variety of student efforts might minimize comparisons and competition. At the secondary level, lack of space usually prevents displaying every student's work regularly, but bulletin board presentations that include every group member's input can be utilized throughout the year.

Individual competition should not be encouraged by charts of progress displayed in the classroom. No teacher would like to look daily at a chart showing that he or she hadn't done as much work as the teacher next door had done. Even in early elementary grades, students know who are the "poor readers" and the "good readers" and they don't need stars for finished books to remind them. Such a display also emphasizes the extrinsic reward of stars rather than the intrinsic reward of enjoying a book. Another problem is created when "good readers" are singled out or labeled by teacher and classmates. Sixth-grader Mary Margaret complained that she had been chosen once again by the teacher to be the class play's narrator. Apparently, as the best reader in the class she has never been given a chance to try out for acting parts since she was "needed" for reading.

At any level, the singling out of some individuals over others, especially with visible charts or displays, can create embarrassment, resentment, and anger. Even such seemingly positive means of boosting self-esteem as "Star of the Week" need to be analyzed very carefully. Certain cultures with a strong emphasis on collective success as opposed to individual success might interpret this approach as encouraging individual bragging. An alternative procedure might be honoring a cooperative learning group for its success or improvement in working well together. In lower elementary grades, using birthday dates to form a group for special recognition is another possibility.

Bulletin boards or blackboards can also provide a degree of stability and comfort to students by displaying consistent routines and procedures. Rules and regulations for practices such as sharpening pencils or going to the bathroom can be displayed and referred to when necessary. Posting and going over the daily schedule, for instance, helps students prepare mentally and physically for future activities. Written reminders about necessary materials give them the chance to get ready with minimal verbal comments from the teacher. Posted assignments and checklists provide visual reinforcements for students of information given orally.

Think and Act

- In what creative ways can students use the bulletin boards? Brainstorm some possibilities with the students.
- Plan group projects that include interactive presentations using bulletin boards or poster boards. Set these up as learning centers for all students on a rotation basis.
- What types of group recognition can be used to encourage group cooperation and individual achievement? Which ones will not encourage competition among groups?

Pictures and Artifacts

Classroom pictures and artifacts reveal a lot about not only the topics being studied but also the perspectives of the teacher who selected them. Short-term and long-term choices can tell others whether the teacher applies multicultural and global concepts regularly in the classroom. On a long-term basis, globes, maps, and atlases are essential items to help with interconnectedness and interdependence and global society concepts (Kirkwood, 1991). Student-made time lines are valuable for providing world comparisons to particular cultural or geographical emphases in history. Including major world events, discoveries, and inventions from other subjects helps to make obvious some of the many connections among disciplinary areas as well as geographical areas.

Display choices about people in general, such as for occupations or interests, need to avoid stereotypes of any sort (see Chapter 3 for a discussion about stereotyping and generalizing). In addition, all cultural groups need to be represented as much as possible. For instance, if photographs of people in workplaces are used, they need to contain women and people of color in leadership roles as well as people with disabilities working and interacting with others. Sports themes can show a wide variety of well-known athletes, but can also include regular people of both genders, all ages, and all abilities actively participating in the sports. Similarly, pictures of children at play should contain a variety of racial and ethnic mixtures, body looks and types, and ableness. A thorough search of professional materials probably can produce examples of all types of children, not just those perceived as attractive by the publishers.

Selections of materials for specific cultural groups also must avoid different types of stereotyping such as food, clothing, and customs (Cushner et al., 1992;

Gollnick & Chinn, 1998). For instance, showing only scenes of Mexicans wearing sombreros and hitting piñatas at fiestas reinforces the stereotypical portrayal of Mexicans as fun-loving, party-giving people. If such pictures are used at all, they should be accompanied by many others of Mexicans in everyday clothes and everyday situations. Similarly, using feather headdresses and teepees as symbols for all groups of Native Americans is historically inaccurate and too often creates lifelong misunderstandings. Young children might think that Native Americans today live in teepees or that the Inuit regularly build and sleep in igloos. In South Carolina there is a wonderful working historical village explaining the political, economic, and social traditions of the Cherokee nation. Unfortunately, just outside this village are stores selling feather headdresses, tomahawks, and the like to tourists who expect and demand these inappropriate artifacts.

An appropriate display of any cultural group should show many individuals within the group living, working, and playing in a wide variety of situations. Although the curriculum might emphasize racial or ethnic cultural groups, that narrow definition of culture does not need to limit teacher choices. For example, excellent displays can be done of religious groups such as the Amish people or Muslims, age groups such as infants or the elderly, or ableness groups such as people in wheelchairs or visually impaired. Referring back to the three cultural categories of any individual—individual characteristics, cultural characteristics, and human characteristics—will help with choices of materials. The important concept here is to find a balance between uniqueness and sameness in individuals, cultural groups, and humanity.

For young children especially, historical portrayals of groups need to be balanced with present-day representations to prevent serious misconceptions. A "Then and Now" display of typical foods, homes, and clothes will give students a more realistic understanding of cultural groups. For instance, Japanese women and girls in kimonos might be shown, but pictures of Japanese adults and children in modern clothing must also be displayed at the same time. Children will then better understand that kimonos are traditional, formal clothing to be worn only on special occasions. With recent photographs of Japanese cities, children will also be learning about the interconnectedness and interdependence of groups around the world when they look at McDonald's and Burger King restaurants, apartment buildings, and people wearing Western-style suits and dresses.

Artifacts require the same scrutiny for authenticity and balance. For instance, calligraphy and painting are very important artistic elements of the Japanese culture. Yet a display of Japanese textbooks, student notebooks, and newspapers are also vital to emphasize the practical applications along with the esthetic qualities of the written language. Arising from these artifacts can be questions related to such problems as the design of computer keyboards for the Japanese language.

Careful selections of pictures and artifacts can encourage students to make comparisons and contrasts of housing, clothing, food, schooling, work, play, and other cultural expressions of living. Although the differences provide the richness of diversity, the differences need to be seen as natural and expected among humans. Pictures and artifacts often show or demonstrate the products of a culture, but rarely why or how these products came to be produced by that specific culture. Teachers applying multicultural and global concepts can help students to make the connections between a culture's location in time and place and the products of the culture. Teachers and students must try to investigate all pictures and artifacts from the culture's perspective, not from the viewpoint of outsiders. The "exotic they" approach, a heavy emphasis on seemingly strange customs, must be avoided to prevent the development and reinforcement of stereotypes.

Think and Act

- Think about your personal memories of studying other cultures. Did you build igloos, make teepees and headdresses, or dress up in kimonos? Can you remember any other unit lessons that counteracted the powerful influence of these activities? How can you resolve problems like these with your own students?
- Have students critique photographs or illustrations for omissions, marginalizing, or stereotyping (see Chapter 3 about assessing curricular materials).
- Use a display of cultural tools and implements with questions about their usage and what problems their invention solved. Have students make or modify and then use tools similar to any simple ones displayed.
- Use modern catalogues and magazines for students to identify present-day solutions of human problems of shelter, clothing, and so on.

Learning Centers and Workstations

Many resources beyond the textbook are needed to support the application of multicultural and global concepts in the classroom. One way to provide alternative materials is to set up learning centers or workstations (Kysilka & Biraimah, 1992). These arrangements should be flexible so they can be organized according to the topics being studied, but should include a wide variety of source materials such as books, magazines, articles, computer sites, and all types of artifacts.

Planning the use of extra tables, if the room has enough space, involves special consideration of curriculum and instruction. Student learning centers or workstations need to be incorporated into regular planning of instructional strategies. Providing centers or stations is of no value if students don't have the time or reason to use them. Allowing only students who finish seatwork early access to these different activities is showing favoritism to the best and/or fastest in the class. Carefully planned and posted rotation systems can make these materials available to all in an equitable way.

With time allotment, equitable does not mean equal if certain students take longer to accomplish the required tasks. Adjustments in amount of time or type and quantity of assignments can be made so every student can be successful. Another important consideration for rotation systems is the appropriate combinations of students working together. Choices about the number of students and the diversity (ethnicity, class, gender, abilities, etc.) require advance teacher planning. Using students as peer tutors with computers, for instance, can be beneficial for everyone at certain times, but these students must not dominate every small-group computer project. All students need hands-on experiences to develop the necessary skills, and the less-skilled students will need extra time. This is particularly true if certain students have home access to computers while others do not.

In elementary classrooms, a section of the room is often designated as a reading corner. A rocking chair with space around it probably indicates that reading out loud and storytelling are important activities. Low bookshelves and/or area rugs can help separate this reading area from the rest of the class. For students who prefer dimmer light, a method of blocking the overhead lights can be arranged. One innovative teacher uses a large beach umbrella with a floor lamp to create a quiet, casual reading corner. In all cases, the reading section should be inviting and comfortable to children, allowing them a chance to "get away from it all" into a book.

Secondary teachers are much less likely to arrange sections of the classroom for separate student-centered activities. Intensive scheduling can be one impetus for changing the typical whole-class arrangement. Teachers with longer class blocks will have more time per class period for student-centered work, including exploration of resource materials such as primary documents and the Internet. Thinking through the wide variety of possible instructional strategies, some of which will be discussed in Chapter 6, The Instruction, will help with the planning for individual research and/or small group investigation.

Think and Act

- What rotation systems are used for student access to learning centers, workstations, and computers? Do they allow fair access, as opposed to equal access, for all students?
- Review the placement of tables and extra equipment. What does this say about your teaching strategies? What arrangements work best for student-centered activities? Small group and cooperative learning tasks?

Special Considerations

Students who have physical disabilities should have their classroom needs met as much as possible. These accommodations are often required legally as part of the student's Individualized Education Program, but thoughtful accommodations are indicative of teachers with multicultural and global concepts. Pathways for wheelchairs can be calculated when the optimum arrangement of furniture is being considered at the start of the year or term. Students with hearing or visual impairments can be given special locations in the classroom. If students need special supplies or equipment, they or their helpers should be able to get them without disrupting the lesson. In some classrooms, the supplies can be in a special section of a bookshelf or a cupboard. In shared rooms, a note or code in the lesson plan book can be a reminder for the teacher to provide the supplies before starting the lesson. In most cases, teachers should discuss physical accommodations with the students themselves, privately and in a matter-of-fact way. If the students are too young or unable to communicate their needs, parents and school and community professionals should be consulted. In any case, special education teachers and other professionals can offer suggestions for ways to approach students about their needs. All students must be approached with care and sensitivity, but students with emotional disabilities need special consideration.

Showing thoughtfulness and consideration to students with disabilities is a priority for teachers and students in any classroom. Teachers must model appropriate behavior that demonstrates application of multiple perspectives with an attitude of empathy and understanding rather than pity. Appropriate behavior often includes modification of regular routines, so this requires constant vigilance. Martha, a college student in a wheelchair and with limited upper body mobility, mentioned how one professor always left handouts at the front of the lecture hall where she could not reach them. When she asked to have the papers put at the back, the professor would comply for that class period. The next class, the papers would show up at the front of the lecture hall again. The lack of consideration of this professor demonstrated his inability to see the learning place from Martha's viewpoint. He not only allowed a physical barrier to impede one of his students, but he also created an emotionally disturbing situation for that student.

Think and Act

- Examine the most frustrating accommodations you must make by law. Brainstorm with colleagues new and creative ways to provide these.
- Look beyond the required accommodations for other ways to facilitate learning. Consider lighting, temperature, background noise or music, and furniture (soft chairs, pillows).

Assessing the Socioemotional Environment

Although the physical environment can make a big difference in establishing a classroom climate that supports multicultural and global concepts, the socioemotional environment is even more vital. Difficult physical environments can be overcome, but threatening socioemotional environments can destroy students in even the best physical environments. Every student has a right to feel safe and se-cure in the classroom. This must be the first concern of any teacher. Beyond this, of course, teachers would like students to feel eager to enter the classroom, to look for-ward to the time they spend with them and with each other.

The term "classroom climate" is often used to refer to the socioemotional as-pect of the classroom. According to the perceptions of individuals in the classroom, the climate can be warm or cold, friendly or forbidding. Over the years the class-room climate has been evaluated by means of different types of observation instru-ments. Some of the earlier ones looked at how the teacher and students interact with each other. Flanders (Simon & Boyer, 1967), for instance, investigated teacher and student verbal exchanges while Buehler and Richmond (Simon & Boyer, 1967) were more interested in nonverbal behavior. Recently the journal *Teaching Toler-ance* conducted a survey polling hundreds of educators about use of racist, sexist, homophobic comments, or slurs against specific religions in their classrooms (Holliday, 2000).

Verbal and nonverbal behaviors between teacher and student and among stu-dents can be examined for the effect they have on the classroom climate. The class-room Socioemotional Environment Checklist in Figure 4.2 provides a method for teachers to assess the emotional and social feeling of the classroom. Regular refer-rals to the checklist will be helpful as the next chapter sections are covered. For more objective assessments using the checklist with a tally system, teachers can pair up to collect data in each other's classrooms. Aides and outside observers can also participate in data gathering. Another possibility is videotaping or audiotaping les-sons. For any self-assessment or peer assessment, caution should be taken to report factual data rather than comment in a judgmental way, even if the comments are positive. Teachers need to analyze the data and reflect on the implications without being overly influenced by emotional or defensive reactions. The emphasis must be on taking feedback and using it to improve the classroom climate.

Organizing the Socioemotional Environment

Proactive Measures

Effective teachers are proactive about establishing a healthy socioemotional envi-ronment in their classrooms. From the beginning, they make it clear that a healthy classroom climate is the co-responsibility of the teacher and students. They discuss with their students early in the school year, and throughout the year whenever needed, the establishment and maintenance of a caring, learning community in the classroom. Teachers and students can prepare class rules together and post them in an obvious spot. In every classroom, class rules should be backed up by a fair and consistent disciplinary plan of action.

Although core ethical values such as respect, responsibility, honesty, and car-ing are essential parts of cultural groups everywhere, the expressions and practices

FIGURE 4.2   Classroom Socioemotional Environment Checklist

Teacher Behaviors	*All*	*Some*	*None*
Teacher Verbal Behavior			
Acceptance of feelings expressed by students?	3	2	1
Praise or encouragement of student actions or behavior?	3	2	1
Acceptance or use of ideas of students?	3	2	1
Use of feedback rather than criticism?	3	2	1
Avoidance of reproving or disapproving remarks?	3	2	1
Avoidance of disparaging, sarcastic, or belittling remarks?	3	2	1
Avoidance of comments of racism, sexism, homophobic bias, or bias against a religion?	3	2	1
Teacher Nonverbal Behavior			
Use of expressions of approval such as smiles?	3	2	1
Use of gestures of approval such as nods, thumbs up, silent claps?	3	2	1
Use of receptive body posture such as slight leaning forward, nonrigid stance, open arms?	3	2	1
Use of gestures of comfort and acceptance such as quick touch, quick hug, light tap on shoulders? (lower grades only)	3	2	1
Avoidance of expressions of disapproval such as annoyance, disgust, or anger?	3	2	1
Avoidance of gestures of disapproval such as violent head shaking, shaking fist, threatening pointer finger?	3	2	1
Avoidance of reproving or disapproving body posture such as withdrawal, closed and rigid stance, crossed arms, and clenched fists?	3	2	1
Avoidance of confrontational body posture such as "in the face" movements or gestures?	3	2	1
Avoidance of angry touches such as pushing, grabbing arm or shoulder?	3	2	1

Student Behaviors	*All*	*Some*	*None*
Student Verbal Behavior			
Acceptance of feelings expressed by other students?	3	2	1
Praise or encouragement of other students' actions or behavior?	3	2	1
Acceptance or use of ideas of other students?	3	2	1
Use of feedback rather than criticism?	3	2	1
Avoidance of reproving or disapproving remarks?	3	2	1
Avoidance of disparaging, sarcastic, or belittling remarks?	3	2	1
Avoidance of expressions of racism, sexism, homophobic bias, or bias against a religion?	3	2	1
Student Nonverbal Behavior			
Use of expressions of approval such as smiles?	3	2	1
Use of gestures of approval such as nods, thumbs up, silent claps?	3	2	1
Use of receptive body posture such as slight leaning forward, nonrigid stance, open arms?	3	2	1
Use of gestures of comfort and acceptance such as quick touch, quick hug, light tap on shoulders?	3	2	1
Avoidance of expressions of disapproval such as annoyance, disgust, or anger?	3	2	1
Avoidance of gestures of disapproval such as violent head shaking, shaking fist?	3	2	1
Avoidance of reproving or disapproving body posture such as withdrawal, closed and rigid stance, crossed arms, and clenched fists?	3	2	1
Avoidance of confrontational body posture such as "in the face" movements or gestures?	3	2	1
Avoidance of angry touches such as pushing, grabbing arm or shoulder?	3	2	1

of these values differ greatly from group to group. These different practices, when brought into the classrooms, can be sources of conflict among students and teachers. For example, what one culture considers a form of respect can be interpreted by other groups as a form of domination. More conservative Islamic practices concerning women's clothing and women's personal freedom outside the house are interpreted by most Christians as restrictive rather than protective of women's purity. In the United States, many fundamentalist groups such as the Southern Baptist ministry have declared the man as head of the household who is owed obedience, an act considered by other Christian groups as a denial of human rights to women.

Discussions about core ethical values such as respect, responsibility, honesty, and caring are also recommended by character education proponents such as Lickona (1996, 1997). The danger of such packaged programs, however, is the tendency to emphasize one right way of thinking. Students are to be led by catchy slogan or homilies into believing as their older and wiser leaders do; students become then passive receptacles to be filled (Kohn, 1998). This type of teaching is a form of indoctrination that does not allow for multiple perspectives. The interpretation and the resulting practice of core ethical values become that of the dominant U.S. culture. Such practices as "Star of the Week" displays and certificates for good behavior are accepted without critical examination, although emphasis of the individual in opposition to the group is discouraged in many cultures.

Teachers have the very difficult role of promoting core ethical values while dealing with practices that, from their own personal perspectives, might oppose these basic values. It is not the role of teachers to convert students and their parents; it is, instead, to understand and respect multiple perspectives. At the same time, teachers have an obligation to support only those practices in the classroom that demonstrate multicultural and global concepts and lead to a democratic working environment. Any forms of intolerance and practices of discrimination that are condoned or ignored will work to destroy any healthy class climate promoting these values.

Management systems such as those advocated by Glasser and Dotson (1998) stress the importance of student responsibility and student choices along with an emphasis on teamwork and a learning community. These approaches support the multicultural and global concepts of human rights and interdependence. Establishing a safe and secure classroom environment is an essential step toward building a cooperative learning community where students feel free to express themselves and to take risks.

Think and Act

■ Check to see what the status of character education is in your school, district, and state. Does it appear in the curriculum? Under what sections and what standards? Is the model one of compliance rather than critical thinking?

(continued)

■ Review classroom rules. Do they reflect core ethical values? Are they written in positive language rather than negative? Do they demonstrate regard for self-respect and respect for others? Do they emphasize a cooperative learning community?

Respectful Interactions

Appropriate Teacher Behaviors.   Developing mutual respect in the classroom is the ongoing responsibility of teachers and students alike. Teacher demonstrations of interest in students as people can work to build the needed respect. Greeting individual students as they enter the classroom serves as both a welcome and a reminder for students to settle down. Talking to students beyond academic subjects, using their interests for conversations, expresses a concern about their concerns. Attending student events and activities shows teacher involvement in what matters to students. In addition, sharing personal anecdotes or interests reveals the teacher as a real person to the students. Developing a two-way communication through mutual sharing of personal interests works to establish the all-important bonding necessary for a healthy classroom climate.

Positive words of encouragement and a lack of sarcasm, negative labeling, or name-calling are reflective of a healthy classroom environment. Many management systems speak to the need for calm but firm and consistent teacher behavior in face of student disruptive behavior (Charles, 1996). Teachers may understand that all humans feel at risk socially sometime in their lives, but they do not always remember that the frequent, forced interactions with others in a classroom and school are particularly stressful. Teachers have no excuse for using sarcasm, belittling, or shaming of students as a disciplinary method.

Teachers must be role models for their students, trying to "see across boundaries" (Freedman, Simons, Kalnin, & Casareno, 1999, p. 227), whatever the boundaries may be, to try to understand why students acted the way they did rather than lashing out at them for their negative behaviors. When the role modeling is negative, students have little or no defense against such cruel treatment and either act out or swallow their anger as a result. In addition, expressions of anger and frustration by teachers can, in turn, lead to increased student anger or frustration, creating a very volatile situation. In one middle school classroom, the White female teacher had money stolen from her purse. She immediately assumed that the three boys of color, who had previous records of disciplinary measures, were the thieves. Her student teacher reported that the cooperating teacher had over the semester shown disrespect towards the boys by not interacting positively with them and by verbally reprimanding them first for any class disruptions. Whether the boys took the money was never established. In contrast, the stealing of students' personal worth in front of their classmates by such disrespectful treatment was painfully witnessed by the student teacher.

Teachers must carefully monitor their own behavior towards isolates and students lacking social skills or teacher appeal. Negative nonverbal communication by teachers can be a trigger for similar student behavior toward socially inept individuals. Students easily pick up on teacher dislikes even if disparaging words are not used, and young children especially will often mimic their teacher's negative behavior. Teachers who visibly respond more warmly and affectionately to some students show in their actions a bias towards others. The White student teacher in Florida who hugged White fourth-grade girls but rarely touched the other children as they all left at the end of the day might have been only responding to specific girls' affectionate gestures. The message conveyed, however, was that she and those White girls were part of an inner circle other children could not enter.

Showing students specifically what they can do to help each other is also necessary. With appropriate teacher encouragement, students will often take responsibility for making sure everyone can participate as fully as possible. At all levels, new students should have teacher-chosen peers who can act as guides and supports for the first few days. Students with limited English proficiency can benefit from careful pairing or grouping with others for help in instruction or directions. Particularly helpful in the early stages would be students who speak the same second language and who can act as translators and guides. Students with disabilities also need sensitive teacher intervention since other students probably need encouragement initially to include them. Pairing special students with helpful peers while teaching all students to be helpful to each other can be a two-pronged approach.

Students can learn to assist quietly and efficiently and to take pride in their classmate's successes. Designated helpers will make the process smoother. Some kind of rotation system is usually a good practice so that various students get a chance to practice being considerate. Helping also provides an advantage to the helpers who get to know students who might be otherwise ignored or avoided and who have different and interesting experiences to share. An effective teacher will make an effort to ensure that the interactions between pairs are positive and work to build a reciprocal relationship rather than a one-way helper–helpee partnership (Bishop, Jubala, Stainback, & Stainback, 1996).

Martha, the college student in a wheelchair mentioned earlier, had classmate Amanda who took responsibility throughout the term for note-taking and helping with papers, materials, and physical adjustments. Amanda was quietly conscious of Martha's needs and was proactive but not intrusive about providing assistance. Martha, in turn, felt comfortable enough to share her personal needs and experiences of discrimination, frustrations, and accomplishments with her peers. Her personal viewpoint gave the other preservice teachers, particularly Amanda, a tremendous learning experience. Emphasizing these mutual benefits and the interdependence for learning is part of the teacher's role. The classroom celebration of diversity is particularly important with issues of ableness when societal norms too often worship the able and super-able and see the "dis" rather than the ableness of persons with disabilities.

In every classroom, there are apt to be friends and foes, leaders and isolates. Tools such as teacher observations or sociometric surveys will help locate these individuals. One method, often used in elementary grades but valuable in secondary grades as well, is to find out each student's peer preferences for play or work through a written or oral survey. Then the teacher has the choice of placing foes together to encourage cooperation or keeping them separate to prevent possible trouble. An easily accomplished task is probably a better time for students to work on social skills, while a more difficult assignment might be the time for already established and comfortable combinations of students.

Think and Act

- Design a lesson to teach about respect directly. What different perspectives should be included? How can these perspectives be solicited to avoid a preachy, authoritarian approach Kohn (1998) warns against?
- Have regular dialogues about respect with students, their parents, and the community. What manifestations of disrespect or "dissing" are particularly offensive to students?
- Use a sociometric survey such as a sociogram to learn about interpersonal relationships in the class. Note overdominant leaders and neglected and rejected isolates. Plan interventions to help both types of students.

Active Teacher Intervention.   Beyond being a role model for students, the teacher is responsible for active intervention on the behalf of individual students. Teachers must prevent students from bullying or harassing each other; threatening behavior cannot be allowed under any circumstances. Even students with emotional disorders need to be prevented from name-calling, bullying, or picking on other students in any way.

Physical intervention by a teacher is recommended only when the teacher believes the student will do harm to other students or himself or herself. Students who punch others, throw chairs, or hit their heads against the wall must be stopped immediately. Teachers are legally in trouble, however, for the use of any physical force without due cause in most, if not all, states. Yet in certain cultures and certain regions of the country, "spare the rod and spoil the child" is an accepted philosophy and corporal punishment is an expected practice. Students who do not respond to a firm but calm voice might be conditioned to angry voices and physical retribution in home situations. One approach to try is the use of short, clipped sentences said in a stronger voice. "Sit—down—this—minute!" might work when "Would you please sit down?" has no effect. The trick is to mean business and sound very firm without losing control.

Think and Act

- Check the legal regulations about physical touching of students. Know your rights and responsibilities.

- Ask older teachers about the history of corporal punishment in the district. What were their reactions when it was discontinued? If corporal punishment is still in practice, what are the restrictions?
- Research texts and articles on management for the use of corporal punishment in schools. What are the arguments for and against it? Are the authors' positions too theoretical when teachers have to face violent students?

Controversial Content. Controversial content in the curriculum can be triggers for emotional outbursts and anger expressed against individuals or groups. Multicultural and global issues such as racism, sexism, and classism are particularly sensitive areas with multiple perspectives. These topics should not be avoided, however, since they are the very issues that need to be discussed in order for heterogeneous groups of students to work and learn together. Chapter 5, The Curriculum, discusses multicultural and global curriculum content in more depth.

In the book *Inside City Schools* (Freedman et al., 1999), teachers whose classrooms are described express the importance of conflicting student ideas and the necessity at times of some pain in order to experience growth. Yet volatile confrontations must be kept under control to prevent permanent socioemotional damage. The teachers suggest certain techniques for calming students down in the midst of arguments. For example, students can be helped to gain a certain emotional distance by stopping a heated verbal battle and writing down their perspectives and points of argument.

Social Skills Training. For isolates at any age, teachers can incorporate social skills training for them and their peers into lessons and activities. Skills such as how to accept a new member into a group and how to join a group already working together need to be taught, especially in the early years, so that children do not establish patterns of rejecting and being rejected. Strategies such as role playing and acting out prepared skits are very useful here. Policies set and enforced by teachers can include the elementary playground rule suggested by the phrase "You can't say 'You can't play'" (Paley, 1993, 1995). This rule ensures that every child gets included if he or she wishes to join and is willing to follow the already established game rules of the group.

Cooperative learning strategies combined with careful teacher intervention will help to create and maintain at least working relationships among students. For cooperative learning activities, pair and group combinations should be worked out in advance by the teacher to make sure that groups are evenly balanced by race, gender, academic ability, and temperament. Allowing student choice of partners on a regular basis is not a wise policy because student choice puts less popular classmates at risk. Cooperative work should also contain the five distinct characteristics necessary for success, especially that of having a group goal and individual responsibility (Johnson & Johnson, 1994). See Chapter 6, The Instruction, for further discussion of cooperative learning.

Think and Act

- Examine a district or university video catalogue for videos teaching social skills and cooperative learning. Preview several and decide whether you would purchase each for classroom use. Explain why.
- Read Paley's (1993) book *You Can't Say You Can't Play*. How could this be implemented in elementary classrooms and schools?
- Observe and record over several periods or a day the interactions of individual students most at risk socially. Ask an aide or volunteer to help if necessary. Which interactions were positive and which were negative? Which were initiated by the student, by the teacher, or by other students?

The Cooperative Learning Community

Students who have a difficult time academically can feel threatened by a seemingly overwhelming amount of subject material to be learned, especially at the secondary levels. Ways must be found to help these students feel successful in the classroom. Applying multicultural and global concepts to curriculum, instruction, and assessment will help in developing a happy and healthy learning environment (see Chapters 5 through 7). Making sure that activities provide for a wide range of learning styles will also help students be more successful (see Chapter 6, The Instruction).

One major way to encourage a productive and supportive class environment is to maximize cooperative practices and minimize competitive practices. Students already know at a very early age that some learn faster than others; some read better, some do math better, some remember instruction better. Knowledge of differences is natural to humans, but an emphasis on differences to the disadvantage of some is socially learned. A thoughtful teacher will not allow expressions of individual comparisons with one student putting down another. Beyond that, the teacher applying multicultural and global concepts will make curricular, instructional, and assessment choices based on cooperative principles. Cooperative learning strategies such as those discussed in Chapter 6 are particularly helpful for encouraging students to work and share together without unhealthy competition.

Teachers have a variety of choices to help students set personal goals separate from everyone else. One popular method is the use of individual portfolios, showing progress over time. Student Sharon can see her improvement in writing a clear paragraph since she tried this task a month ago. While working on paragraph construction, she does not benefit from being reminded that Karim can already compose an excellent five-paragraph critique of a story. If, instead, the teacher and Sharon's concerns center on how she sets and achieves her own goals, then Karim's achievements will matter less to her.

Think and Act

- Analyze your own personal behavior for the past week. In what ways have you shown cooperative skills and attitudes? In what ways have you shown competitive skills and attitudes?
- Analyze your classroom activities for the past week. Which ones included cooperative aspects encouraging interdependence, mutual respect, and sharing of resources?

Conclusion

The classroom environment, through its physical appearance and its emotional and social climate, influences all that goes on within the classroom. By being proactive about the desired qualities of the classroom environment, teachers can work with students to establish a healthy learning community in face of even the most discouraging outside-the-classroom environment. Making the physical environment look as warm and welcoming as possible can be the first step. The physical appearance, however, is not as important as the emotional and social climate. Teachers and students alike have the responsibility to make sure everyone is a welcome member of the community. Ongoing vigilance of verbal and nonverbal behavior by teachers and students is needed to establish and maintain positive interpersonal relationships. Key to successful relationships are the twin concepts of self-respect and respect of others. Much of the positive climate can be built through continuing emphasis on the interconnectedness and interdependence of the community members.

5

The Curriculum

Teachers' personal views of curriculum greatly influence their participation in curriculum development. If teachers view curriculum solely as the state and district written requirements, then the likelihood of their creating or even modifying curriculum becomes diminished. If, however, teachers see curriculum as organic and evolving, then in all probability they will become involved in the process of curriculum development in their classroom. Further, if they see curriculum as a social construction, as developed by individuals and groups according to their goals and objectives, then they will try to involve other stakeholders, particularly their students, in the curriculum development process. This chapter looks at how the curriculum can be made to reflect multicultural and global concepts and perspectives.

The work of curriculum development is by no means easy. Teachers who have been involved in the active construction of a curriculum know how time-consuming and mind-boggling the planning can be. For issues related to multicultural and global education, the effort is even more frustrating because these fields are filled with controversy. Every cultural category has strong advocates for a variety of stances, whether the category is a seemingly sensitive area such as race or sexual orientation or a less obvious one such as age. Furthermore, multicultural and global education materials are not always of good quality and sometimes are biased or factually inaccurate. Individual teachers, then, are left with the responsibility to sort through the quantities of materials available in order to build a culturally relevant curriculum.

Examining Multicultural and Global Education Concepts

Teachers who wish to incorporate multicultural education into their curriculum might center on ethnic and racial differences or emphasize only personal discrimination rather than institutional problems. These issues are important, especially in secondary schools where racist behaviors by students often become more blatant. Yet emphasizing only ethnic and racial issues and dealing only with the personal aspects ignore the many other areas of multicultural education, such as classism and sexism, and the way institutional discrimination and oppression affect us all. The deep understandings come from thorough exploration and application of multicultural concepts.

In a similar way, teachers might present a limited view of global education to their students. Lessons might focus on the easier, more obvious problems such as the need to recycle without attacking deep underlying causes such as an economy built on excessive consumerism and the uneven distribution of wealth and resources. Teachers might not understand the need to explore the many aspects of complex issues, but simplifying issues often leaves students with incomplete or inaccurate understandings. For instance, while protesting against shoe companies exploiting child labor in developing countries, students are often not aware of the extreme poverty in those countries and the need for all family members to work to stave off starvation. Even if they understand that, they sometimes do not see the intricate connections between global competition, cheap labor, profit for investors, and relationship to the students' own consumption patterns.

Think and Act

- Revisit the six applications of major multicultural and global concepts discussed in Chapter 1. Take a textbook from any discipline that is used in the local schools and inspect its content for these applications. With others, compare findings across disciplines and grade levels.
- Throughout the chapter, continue to investigate ways to modify or change the curriculum as represented by the textbook.
- Examine your state or district curriculum guides or standards for sections where multicultural or global concepts are emphasized. Choose one standard to examine more closely. What is the main learning objective? What activities would support this? How could the objective be transferred into everyday classroom life?

Changing the General Curriculum

Although multicultural education advocates disagree about the types of curriculum approaches being used in the field, most see the approaches in some sort of progression from superficial contributions to in-depth restructuring of the curriculum (Banks, 1994b; Grant & Sleeter, 1998). James Banks (1994b) describes four levels: (1) the Contributions Approach, offering bits such as holidays and events outside of the main curriculum; (2) the Additive Approach, adding content, concepts, issues, and perspectives without changing the basic structure or perspective of the curriculum; (3) the Transformation Approach, changing the basic curriculum to view content, concepts, and issues from the perspectives of diverse cultural groups; and (4) the Social Action Approach, going beyond the curriculum to make decisions and take actions to help solve important social issues. The different approaches are like steps along the way, with the last approach having the deepest commitment to the multicultural journey. In a similar way, global education can be seen as a progression of steps from the superficial, ethnocentric approach to an in-depth understanding and involvement in global issues.

The Contributions Approach

Contributions can be seen as outside bits and pieces that are not considered important enough to be integrated into the regular dominant curriculum. They might be tacked on during specific holidays or celebrations such as Hanukkah, Martin Luther King's Birthday, or Earth Day. Although information might be dispensed about the occasion and activities carried out to honor the day, this is separate from what is taken as the important or essential learning. Even extended periods such as Black History Month (as a Black friend cynically points out, the shortest and darkest month of the year) are rarely incorporated into the curriculum itself. Banks (1994b) sees this approach as the Heroes and Holidays one, where very little is learned about the ethnic groups other than superficial information about the holiday. Global education has been treated in a similar way by many teachers with celebrations such as Earth Day being celebrated outside of the curriculum, but not becoming an integral part of it. Serious issues such as oppression, assimilation, and discrimination are avoided and problems with stereotyping or treating ethnic and cultural groups as the exotic "theys" are often created.

One possibility for expanding and deepening any holiday or celebration is to develop a thematic unit around some multicultural or global aspect. Columbus Day, for instance, is seen as an offensive celebration by some Native American because of the ethnocentric interpretation of the historical event by European Americans. *Rethinking Columbus* (1992), an excellent special issue of Rethinking Schools, provides many excellent articles for use in elementary and secondary classrooms. Original documents, including Columbus's log, are cited and compared to the distorted information found in many textbooks and trade books. Among the many suggestions for classroom application are antistereotyping checklists and questions for critiquing books. This issue alone provides many possibilities for an inquiry unit on multiple perspectives, human rights, and cultural conflicts.

Think and Act

- Check your textbooks for surface culture information as opposed to deep culture issues. Are only topics like famous people, foods, and fiestas presented? Are cultural conflicts presented from multiple perspectives? Why are multiple perspective necessary?

- If holidays such as Columbus Day and Thanksgiving Day are celebrated in your school, how could more accurate historical and cultural information be shared with young children? What cultural perspectives and cultural conflicts are involved?
- Invite guest speakers from the cultural group being studied to talk about their perspectives. Ask them about other resources to use.

The Additive Approach

The Additive Approach refers to attempts to put some information about other ethnic or cultural groups into the curriculum without changing the dominant perspective (Banks, 1994b). Additions might be extra books or units or even smaller bits of information found in the margins or boxed off from the regular part of the text. Social studies textbooks, for the most part, have used this approach to multicultural education, including information about women and people of color in short paragraphs or even in boxes. The main story, however, is still "his story" with European and European American men as the central characters. Textbooks in other subject areas have used similar means by adding bits and pieces without significantly changing the content. Females and people of color show up in the illustrations or in the boxes or specially designated separate paragraphs. Rarely are they the main players on the textbook stage.

Although adding onto the curriculum has been criticized as an inadequate way to address multicultural and global issues, this can be a place for teachers to start. Certainly, augmenting a very limited curriculum is a positive step. The danger with using the Additive Approach for curriculum development is that teachers will stop at this level. Unfortunately, stopping here means that the main curriculum stays ethnocentric, presenting only the middle- and upper-class European American male's viewpoint. The overriding concern of who controls what goes into the curricula of the public schools in the United States is never addressed and the textbooks remain biased. As with the Contributions Approach, the Additive Approach also results in the heroine, the event, or the culture displayed and studied through ethnocentric eyes with the twin dangers of stereotyping cultures and ignoring the bigger issues of oppression and injustice.

Think and Act

- Check your textbooks for add-ons. Discuss these with your colleagues or students. Why have the authors and publishers chosen this method of including the information into the regular context?
- Look for cultural conflicts and how they are portrayed. For national issues and events, how are the voices of diverse populations represented? For international issues and events, is the dominant U.S. position ever challenged from other perspectives? Why or why not?

The Transformation Approach

According to Banks (1994b), this approach addresses the basic assumptions of the traditional curriculum by helping students see concepts, issues, themes, and problems from other perspectives. The difference in emphasis at the transformation level is that history is viewed with the understanding that all cultural groups have contributed through interactions to a common synthesized history, not that other groups have contributed bits and pieces to essentially the dominant history. Multiple perspectives, frames of reference, and content from various groups are infused throughout the curriculum. The approach fits constructivist theory in that students can begin to see knowledge as a social construction, influenced by positions of race, class, gender, and so on, of individuals and groups. Using primary sources, students can read about historical events from multiple points of view and then can analyze how certain interpretations become represented more often in secondary written sources such as textbooks.

Some schools and districts have incorporated specific units into their required curriculum. Others, such as Clark County School District (Gilluly et al., 1996), provide brochures about basic concepts with suggestions of units and activities across the curriculum. Studying the elements of deep culture through the suggested integrated, interdisciplinary approach can help students with their understanding of the beliefs, values, attitudes, and traditions that motivate people to behave the way they do. If done appropriately, the unit can also assist students in overcoming ethnocentric perspectives about ways to think and act.

Thematic units have become a popular way to present multiple perspectives of at least some events or time periods. Such interdisciplinary units have the added benefit of support from research literature, especially related to the brain, that advocates integration of the curriculum for more in-depth and lasting learning (Caine & Caine, 1997). Banks (1994b) uses the example of the "Westward Movement" and how students can be made to understand the Eurocentric choice of "westward" as opposed to the more neutral term of "The Meeting of Two Cultures" in reference to encounters between European Americans and the Lakota Sioux (p. 26). Further extensions of this thematic unit could include references to many other cultural groups, including those in Mexico and British North America (later named Canada).

Although social studies is one of the easiest disciplines to transform with multicultural and global perspectives, it is by no means the only one. The curriculum for all subject areas can and should be revised to include multiple perspectives. One example of using multiple perspectives involved the integration of literature and social studies (Bailey, 1999). During the year, eighth-grade language arts students who were also studying U.S. history chose books representing the different time periods from an extensive selection of historical fiction and nonfiction. Students wrote weekly reflection pieces and prepared creative projects such as puppets, plays, web pages, and models. Student presentations centered on their connections between literature and history. The study found that student understanding of historical events and contexts had increased. Social studies class discussions and writing assignments showed student growth particularly in comparing and contrasting information. In addition, students showed an increased awareness of various viewpoints.

To prepare an appropriate multicultural or global unit, teachers need to use primary sources as much as possible. Even in lower grades, materials can be found that are written by people representing a variety of cultural groups and perspectives. Often, but not always, authors belonging to a specific cultural group will be able to express cultural perspectives outsiders might not have. The danger here is of taking one person's viewpoint as representative of a whole cultural group. Perspectives within a group can be as varied as perspectives from outside. An obvious example would be balancing *Amos Fortune, Free Man* (Yates, 1989, c. 1950), with its portrayal of a relatively contented slave, with *Letters from a Slave Girl* (Lyons, 1992) showing an unhappy captive. Using as many sources as possible will help to give a more balanced picture. Of course, the credentials of authors of primary and secondary sources need to be checked. Internet sources particularly need close examination because, although the Internet provides many exciting opportunities for information, it also offers the danger of nonrepresentative, biased, or inaccurate data.

Think and Act

■ Choose one unit in your curriculum to develop using different voices from literature. Elementary teachers might choose math or science for the challenge. Look for fiction and nonfiction books. Include international examples whenever possible. Check libraries and Internet sources for multicultural anthologies.

■ Discuss how the change in the curriculum affects the emphasis of the unit. What have you gained from this? What will your students gain?

In the lower elementary grades, calendar events are sometimes used as themes. Unfortunately, the emphasis too often has been on Christian religious holidays as well as national ones. To infuse multicultural and global perspectives into the curriculum, this emphasis can be changed to a seasonal one: fall with harvests, winter with festivals of light, spring with rebirth of the land, and summer with growing plants and animals. Even religious holidays that have become secular, such as St. Valentine's Day, need to be considered from multiple perspectives. If some children are unable to participate in a party, then a party is not serving the needs of all children. It is not enough to provide an alternative type of entertainment for the children. Those children are still left out of the classroom event and are being discriminated against. An additional advantage of avoiding a party situation complete with sugar-infested food is that children, especially those who are obese or who have diabetes, will not be tempted by unhealthy food.

Perhaps the most effective way to ensure that multicultural and global perspectives are an integral part of a curriculum is to start from the students' perspectives. If teachers believe that students construct their own meaning using their background experiences, following constructivist theory (Brooks & Brooks, 1993), then students' out-of-school curriculum should be used as a means to bridge the gap from the known to the unknown. Schubert (Brown et al., 1996) suggests starting with the students' interests such as Nintendo and computer games. Universal themes like the mysteries of life and the human condition can still be developed by using students' personal experiences as starting points.

Mass media presents a different kind of a problem for teachers. Students today are so inundated with television, movies, videos, magazines, and the like that the overall effect is one of brainwashing. Instead of ignoring this influence, teachers can use these resources for critical thinking work. "Street Fighter" of Play Station II has stereotypical portrayals of international opponents that can be analyzed for the characters as well as its violence. Movies like Disney's "Pocahontas" distort historical events in such a powerful way that it is difficult for students not to take the entertaining presentation as a factual account. Some sort of comparison chart can be prepared by students to illustrate the changes. Discussion can center around the reasons why the movie producers might have made the changes.

International problems can be related to students' own lives in a meaningful way. The Internet offers many possibilities for study of global issues. One excellent source for children is UNICEF's Voices of Youth (www.unicef.org/voy/meeting/meethome.html). The site includes information about children's rights, dangers facing girl children in the world, and the effects of war and conflict on children. In essays and pictures, youth around the world speak out about problems such as child labor. An interactive quiz on children and work is provided. Students can add their own opinions at several places.

Other issues relating to multinational corporations and consumerism can also be made meaningful for students. Michael Apple (2000) gives an example of French fries, a poor Asian country, and a rich U.S. fast-food restaurant corporation. The country, in an attempt to import foreign capital, sold vast amounts of farming lands to the international agribusiness concern, driving off families that had lived for generations on the land without official documents. These people ended up in the cities without housing and social supports, including schools. Thus, there are more urban poor without schools in the Asian country because "so many [U.S.] folks like cheap French fries" (p. 84). Through serious study, students can come to a deep understanding of everyday realities for millions of people—"the denial of basic human rights, the destruction of the environment, the deadly conditions under which people (barely) survive, the lack of a meaningful future for the thousands of children" and the interconnected issues such as political economy and class relations (p. 84).

Think and Act

- Examine the Play Station II characters for their stereotypes. Why do they appeal to children? What alternative characters and plot could you invent that would support multicultural and global concepts such as interconnectedness and interdependence?
- Compare a movie such as "Pocahontas" with historical sources. Discuss the pros and cons of the Disney Corporation taking over a historical site.
- Use the Internet for researching other international issues related to children. Find sites to bookmark for elementary and secondary students.

The Social Action Approach

Banks (1994a) refers to this type of approach as the decision-making and social action approach. Grant and Sleeter (1998) call this approach education that is multicultural and social reconstructionist. In both cases, the authors are referring to teacher and student action that leads to social change. Although they are discussing multicultural education, the same holds true for global education. With this approach, teachers help their students to become "social critics who can make reflective decisions and implement their decisions in effective personal, social, political and economic action" (Banks, 1994b, p. 152). As informed citizens of the classroom, school, local community, or world, students then work for personal and societal change. Students are thus empowered to make curriculum decisions, to work out of the curriculum, and to go beyond it. The curriculum becomes the process, progress, and product of making a better world for all.

Content Starting Point.   The knowledge covered in a curriculum can be organized into two basic categories: content or subject matter and processes or skills (Orlich et al., 2001). The first is information students must know or understand, or the facts, concepts, and generalizations related to the subject being studied. The second is an action or process students must do, either mentally or physically. With a social action approach to multicultural and global education, both forms of knowledge are involved, since appropriate curriculum involves student knowledge, attitudes, skills, and behaviors. Depending upon teacher purpose, either content or process can be the starting point.

Often, with a social action approach, a unit or lesson will start with an emphasis on content knowledge and move to process knowledge as students learn to apply their new knowledge through social action in their classrooms, schools, and communities. Lessons on democracy, for instance, do not stop with the study of the Constitution and the three branches of government but continue on to practice democratic skills such as articulating interests, debating issues, and exercising power (Sleeter &

Grant, 1988). Students in Donna's fourth-grade class in Orlando first studied Florida's government, then organized into senators and representatives to the state legislature (Brown, 1993). The whole class made up bills that became the rules and punishments for the classroom, and then the legislative groups voted on the top ones to enact. One selected law involved punishment of classroom misbehavior such as swearing and name-calling. Donna reported that students saw the student law as a deterrent because their classmates were watching and listening carefully since they all were eager to have trials. Monitoring each other's behavior also seemed to result in more awareness of personal feelings.

Integrated units based on specific multicultural and global concepts can be starting points as well. The ongoing famine in the Sudan is one example of a persistent global problem that can be investigated through all subject areas. Math has statistics about food consumption; science has ecological issues about land use and population; social studies has cultural conflicts and governing concerns; English has news reports and narratives of events, and so on. Students can first gain awareness of the problem of famine, then learn how the problem affects them through the interconnectedness and interdependence of world systems and how their world position is privileged. Concrete applications of understanding can be demonstrated by students giving personal examples of food consumption in their own lives, making comparisons, and discussing the implications. Finally, students can organize food drives, work at community kitchens, collect for UNICEF, and get involved in numerous other projects locally, nationally, or internationally.

A unique opportunity for curriculum development using both the transformation approach and the social action approach will be presented during the bicentennial recognition in 2003–2006 of the Lewis and Clark expedition. Many materials and events are already being prepared by civic and commercial groups. Educators everywhere must take care that these events do not add to historical misinterpretation or distortion of the expedition and its consequences. The expedition bicentennial could easily become a "glitzy travel poster" sort of entertainment leading tourists down well-manicured paths or Lewis and Clark could be described as the "first eco-tourists" (Spence, 2000, p. B2). Even using Sacajawea as the main or only spokesperson for Native American viewpoints conveys a Eurocentric approach because, as Banks states, "she helped Whites to conquer Indian lands" (1994a, p. 26).

Students studying preparations for the bicentennial can support efforts by Native American groups to tell their stories. They can write these groups for more information or urge educational video companies to prepare documentaries giving different perspectives. They can search for pertinent articles in journals such as *Aboriginal Voices*, *Multicultural Perspectives*, and *Teaching Tolerance*. They can search for materials from organizations such as Rethinking Schools (www. rethinkingschools.org) and the National Association for Multicultural Education (NAME). They can become active in their own community to ensure the media hear all the voices, even those who are opposed to any celebration at all.

Think and Act

■ Plan a series of lessons around a local issue that has global connections, such as land usage or water pollution. Brainstorm ways to involve younger and older students.

■ Download several lesson plans with multicultural or global content from the Internet and critically evaluate them according to the different approaches discussed by Banks. Try to find lessons at the higher level approaches. Modify at least one to fit a specific class.

■ Design an action plan and questionnaire for interviewing school community members (students, teachers, staff, etc.) about school concerns. What steps and precautions must be taken before interviewing starts? What would you expect to learn? How could your findings be turned into plans for change?

Process Starting Point.   Another part of the social action curriculum is to teach the student-empowering processes or skills directly. For instance, human rights lessons can address racist literature or sexist advertisements but can also include lessons on how to confront and respond to racism or sexism. A wide variety of topics in the dimension that Banks (1997) calls prejudice reduction can be explored. The lessons teaching the skills directly are best as an integral part of the curriculum, but certainly can be incorporated separately at teachable moments. For instance, if racial or sexist incidents happen in a school, teachers need to help students work through the crises and develop proactive behaviors to reduce the likelihood of such incidents occurring again.

One example of student empowerment through a thinking skills curriculum is conflict resolution. After nationally publicized incidents of horrific violence, interest in conflict resolution programs in schools has become more pronounced. Although the focus has often been on violence prevention, Johnson and Johnson (1995) emphasize the need for student change of habits, attitudes, values, and perspectives. They recommend a comprehensive program including nurturing cooperative learning environments, positive and lasting friendships, and partnerships with parents and community along with conflict resolution/peer mediation training for all students.

An excellent example of a process starting point for the social action approach is found in a school within a school in Cincinnati (Hawley, 2000). Steve Hawley has set up a computer lab school with the original objective for 40 at-risk students to develop computer and other technological skills. The lab school has become much more than a place to learn technological skills, however. The students now run computer programs for the rest of the school and assist in a variety of other technological ways, including teaching teachers and other students computer skills. The selected students also use the lab for doing independent study in courses they need for credits. They are still enrolled in the high school but are finding alternative ways to complete the work they had missed in their regular classes. In addition, the students are developing useful corporate behaviors with solid possibilities of jobs when they graduate. One way Hawley has helped his students gain poise and communication skills is to have them, through multimedia presentations, tell their own stories about almost failing and then finding hope. As the students find more meaningful ways to learn and make their preferences heard, the innovative lab curriculum has begun to revitalize its urban school.

Think and Act

■ Investigate different conflict resolution or peer mediation programs using Johnson and Johnson's (1995) guidelines. Select one or two to present to colleagues, giving advantages and disadvantages.

■ Check the university or school library for textbooks that provide multicultural and global education lesson plans. Compile a list of possible books to purchase. Go online to the publishers and review each book's table of contents. Select a top few to recommend for purchase.

■ Choose one specific multicultural or global topic and build a mini-unit on it. Exchange lesson plans with two or three of your colleagues.

Working with Standards

State standards and benchmarks have become a mandatory part of most teachers' curriculum. State experts beyond the classrooms have moved from guidelines and frameworks, giving an overall view of what is to be covered in various disciplines and grades, to the much more prescriptive standards. The type of assessment based on standards and the use of the findings are serious concerns for teachers (see Chapter 7, The Assessment). The curriculum itself is also an area needing investigation because of the beliefs and values being imposed upon teachers and students. For instance, just the choice of topics covered in the standards and assessment means that a sorting of curriculum content has already been done by people outside of the individual classrooms.

Although teachers must work with these requirements, they can open up their curricula to include multicultural and global content and processes. Certain standards speak directly to multicultural and global content; others deal with processes such as perspective-taking. For instance, in Essential Academic Learning Requirements (EALRs) from Washington State Commission on Student Learning (1998), Mathematics EALR 5.2 states: "describe examples of contributions to the development of mathematics such as the contributions of women, men, and different culture" (p. 63). Science EALR 1.3 states, under "interdependence of life," that the student will "describe how an organism's behavior and ability to survive is influenced by its environment, other life forms, and availability of food and/or other resources" (p. 75). The same EALR, under "environment and resource issues," states that a student will "know humans and other living things depend on the natural environment, and can cause changes in their environment that affect their ability to survive" (p. 75). All three EALRs contain obvious components of multicultural and global education.

Standards dealing with processes also contain elements of multicultural and global concepts. Mathematics EALR 2, "the student uses mathematics to define and solve problems," contains sections such as "investigate situations, analyze information, and predict results and make inferences" that can be applied to multicultural and global issues (Washington State Commission on Student Learning, 1998, pp. 60–61). For instance, studying statistics about the consumption of natural resources can lead to rethinking of lifestyles, reducing consumption, and reusing and recycling, part of the Framework for Earth Systems Education developed by Mayer (1997). In a similar way, science EALR 2, "the student knows and applies the skills and processes of science and technology" (p. 76), can be taught from a global worldview. In fact, this standard matches nicely Understanding #3, "the development of scientific thinking and technology increases our ability to understand and utilize Earth and space," in Mayer's Framework (1997).

Think and Act

■ Search your state standards for obvious multicultural and global concepts. In which content areas did they appear? Were they content or process based?

■ Choose a standard in each elementary content area or each secondary grade level in your field and brainstorm ways to incorporate multicultural and global subject matter or concepts.

Examining Textbooks

Many teachers rely on textbooks for much of the curriculum. If the district provides a textbook for a subject, the book too often becomes the major source of information in the classroom, even at the elementary level. The major difficulty of making a textbook the curriculum is that textbooks primarily reflect the views of the dominant society, in this case the European American middle- or upper-class Christian male perspective. A very small number of textbook publishers control the market and the publishers themselves are controlled by what sells. Large states such as Texas and Florida that mandate specific textbooks as well as curriculum have additional influence in what gets printed. The result is too often a predominance of the dominant perspective and a watering down or omission of any controversial issue.

For curriculum development in multicultural and global concepts, teachers must grasp the essential concept of a text not being the curriculum itself. Once textbooks are examined with a critical eye, they seem flawed in many ways. Even mathematics and science textbooks have biases in their choices of teaching approaches and learning styles, the selections of examples, and their portrayals of "good" mathematicians and scientists. Recently, state standards and assessments might have forced teachers to develop units beyond their textbooks, but the textbook companies are rapidly incorporating standards into the textbooks in an effort to hold this extremely lucrative market captive.

Teachers can start to evaluate children's textbooks and literature using some sort of guideline like the ten checklist points developed by the Council on Interracial Books for Children (1974):

1. Check the illustrations.
2. Check the story lines.
3. Look at the lifestyles.
4. Weigh the relationships between people.
5. Note the heroes.
6. Consider the effects on a child's self-image.
7. Consider the author's or illustrator's background.
8. Check out the author's perspective.
9. Watch for loaded words.
10. Look at the copyright date.

Checkpoints 1–5 raise questions about stereotyping and marginalizing of people of color and females. Textbooks might underrepresent specific cultural groups, indicating by their selection that the contributions of other groups are of less value. The selection of events also shows a bias. The interpretation of history as wars and political decisions rather than family living and cultural expressions of the arts devalues the work of all those not in power. Relationships of individuals and groups to the dominant group need scrutiny for assumed norms or accepted assimilation. Checkpoint 6 stresses the importance of looking at the students in the classroom and how they might view the book. Of special concern is any reinforcement of negative images or lack of any positive images related to the individual children's own cultural backgrounds. Checkpoints 7 and 8 remind teachers to consider whether the author is speaking as a member of a cultural group or as an outsider about another culture. As well, teachers have to decide whether this particular voice is appropriately representative of the culture while acknowledging that many different viewpoints can be legitimate ones from the same cultural group. Checkpoint 9 deals with vocabulary such as the appropriate choice of words to refer to specific cultural groups. Gender stereotyping is also an issue, such as the use of pronouns to label or exclude. Finally, checkpoint 10 is a reminder that textbooks and trade books today must be much more sensitive to multicultural and global issues and concerns.

Think and Act

- Select several textbooks in your content area(s) and assess them using the checkpoints. Compare newer and older versions of the same textbook if possible.
- Select trade books in the library that might be used for unit resources. Check fiction and nonfiction.
- Ask the school librarian about policies regarding the sorting out of books. What happens when a book is controversial? How do parents or community members get books removed from the shelves?

Choosing Other Resources

Printed Materials

In this information age, many types of print and nonprint materials are available for teachers willing to search and sort them out. Several journals are devoted exclusively to multicultural and global issues. *Teaching Tolerance* (www. teachingtolerance.org) is a magazine published twice a year and mailed to educators at no charge. The journal deals regularly with issues of discrimination; its Spring 2000 issue has an article entitled "No Place for Bigotry." *Multicultural Perspectives,* the official journal for the National Association of Multicultural Education (www.umd.edu/NAME), and *Multicultural Education* are two other possibilities for a wide range of topics. Information pamphlets or sheets distributed by organizations representing various cultural groups can offer other perspectives. The Anti-Defamation League (www.adl.org), for instance, has developed antibias curricula and materials for students and teachers.

Screen Media

Most U.S. students today have had a wide exposure to screen materials through television, videos, and movies in addition to computers. Their interest in and familiarity with screen media make these forms good possibilities for powerful learning experiences. The Public Broadcasting Service produces many shows and videos related to controversial issues. School districts often have a large selection of educational videos that can be borrowed. Again, all videos must be previewed for poor quality content. One educational video about a school's United Nations Assembly included clips of a fourth-grade class that represented the Republic of China sporting Mandarin hats, moustaches, and hair queues. For the viewer, this racist, sexist, and anachronistic portrayal ruined any positive effects the video might have had otherwise. The sad part of this was that the teachers, the school, and the video company were all trying to present global interconnectedness and cooperation to elementary students.

The Internet offers a wide range of educational materials, but teachers need to critique Internet materials carefully, especially those that do not need to be refereed or reviewed by knowledgeable people in the discipline. ERIC (Educational Resources Information Center, www.askERIC) is one reputable teacher source for books, journal articles, and manuscripts. National teacher organizations and state and federal departments of education offer other possibilities. Thousands of other worthwhile sites can be discovered through diligent searching. As Internet users know, sorting information rather than finding information has become the major problem. Chapter 6 discusses using the computer as a learning center.

Think and Act

- Research other journal sources for multicultural and global education content. Locate international journals if possible.
- Purchase news magazines from other countries. Look for articles offering different perspectives on world issues and events.
- Modify the textbook and literature checklist to use for videos and movies. What changes did you need to make? Use the university or school district media center to locate several possible videos for a thematic unit to be taught. Preview them using your modification of the checklist.

Human Resources

Human resources are often underutilized by teachers, but they can provide very exciting classroom experiences. Starting with classroom contacts serves the dual purpose of honoring students' cultural heritages and giving the teacher and other students fresh insights into individual and group interests and behaviors. Cristina Igoa (1995) uses student stories as a way to help her immigrant students work through their uprooted lives and the difficult process of acculturation to a new country, culture, and language. One of the techniques she has developed is validating each student's culture through sharing of artifacts, music, food, dance, research information, and especially memories. The students' expressions of their traumatic experiences and culture shock show up in various student-created media forms, particularly personally made filmstrips with accompanying dialogue.

Parents, aunts, uncles, grandparents, and elders in a community might also become allies with the teacher in promoting student learning. Community centers and gathering places such as religious places might have suggestions of good spokespersons for specific cultural groups. If the leaders cannot come to the classroom, they might be willing to be interviewed and video- or audiotaped by students outside of school. Students can research and prepare appropriate questions in advance.

The Foxfire example shows how oral history can be kept alive through student journalism. Over many years students in the Southern Appalachian Mountains in Rabun County, Georgia, have interviewed their elders and prepared magazines articles to tell their stories. Producing the magazine *Foxfire,* begun in 1966, provides a real incentive for this learner-centered classroom approach that connects with the local community. The Foxfire Fund, an outgrowth of the original teaching approach, supports local cultural programs recognizing Appalachian culture (www.foxfire. org/foxfire.htm).

Schools like The Foxfire School in Yonkers, New York, have applied the philosophy to their own locations and needs—in this case, the Hudson River and its relationship to science and mathematics (www.yonkerspublicschools.org/fox.htm). More modest modifications of the Foxfire program to produce classroom newspapers or magazines can be used at any grade level and with any subject. Best examples of this type of approach can result in curricular transformation and social action in the community.

Building a curriculum around student stories brings many benefits to the classroom. First, students are naturally interested in their own lives and usually will contribute to the planning process, giving them ownership of the learning. Second, students know the content well so can use this prior knowledge as a base for curricular development in any of the disciplines or a combination of disciplines. Third, the study becomes constructivist in nature with students expanding on old knowledge and building new understandings in a learner-centered approach. Fourth, this type of exploration takes students outside of the classroom into the community, bridging the gap between schooling and home and workplaces.

Think and Act

- Interview an immigrant student about his or her experiences. Develop an action plan to incorporate that student's background into a unit already prepared. How does the inclusion of this student's perspective add to the unit?
- Choose a local monument, structure, park or community center built or contributed by a specific ethnic or racial group for a class investigation. Look for ways to integrate subject areas and incorporate state standards. Pair up with someone to develop different aspects or, at the secondary level, different subject areas.

Uncovering the Hidden Curriculum

A serious problem in schools is the hidden curriculum, or the unstated beliefs, values, assumptions, and attitudes about multicultural and global concerns. What is not said but implied can be more difficult to understand for students, especially those from diverse backgrounds, than the directly taught curriculum. Some of the hidden curriculum can involve ways of interacting in the classroom. These have to be made explicit if they are the rules and regulations expected by the teacher. Directly teaching such behaviors as turn-taking and then fairly enforcing the rules help students whose cultural experiences have taught them other ways to respond.

When the implied messages in the hidden curriculum contain biases, students are subjected to a much more subtle form of discrimination. Classroom interaction analysis might reveal, as some studies indicate, that White academically successful boys can frequently get away with calling out while girls and students of color get reprimanded for the same behavior. In efforts to survive the school culture and to fit in at school, students of oppressed groups often internalize the negative messages of the hidden curriculum. In the case of call-outs, for example, those reprimanded might stop participating.

Sometimes the hidden curriculum completely contradicts the regular curriculum. One student teacher in Orlando devoted two full weeks to a required unit on Mexico. She taught her grade two students to count to ten in Spanish, told them about sombreros and serapes, and prepared Mexican foods and a piñata for the class fiesta. One week later, the mariachi band from EPCOT gave a spectacular performance at the school. Before the show the student teacher did nothing to relate the upcoming experience to her just-finished unit on Mexico. After the performance, she did not give the students a chance to express their feelings of great excitement and their physical reactions to the music, in spite of the students' animated chatter and obvious body movements as they returned to the classroom. She did not ask the son of one of the mariachi players, a student in the classroom, about his father's occupation and about mariachi music in Mexico. Instead, she returned immediately to the spelling work that had been interrupted by the performance. This student teacher showed no respect for her students' cultural backgrounds and experiences and no recognition of their immediate needs and interests. The hidden curriculum in this class spoke much more strongly about the student teacher's lack of understanding and appreciation of multicultural and global concepts than all her preparation and implementation of the unit on Mexico (Brown, 1993).

The teacher's own lived-out behavior in the classroom can directly affect the hidden curriculum in a positive way as well. A fourth-grade student teacher in Orlando showed deep understanding of multicultural concepts during the teaching of an integrated unit on the history of Florida. First, she developed the unit at the Transformation Approach level (Banks, 1994a) by changing the curriculum content about the European arrival in Florida to the European–Native American cultural encounter. Second, she brought in contemporary issues by reading to the class *The Talking Earth* (George, 1983), a novel about a modern-day Seminole Indian girl who was sent on a quest by her elders to discover her heritage. Third, from the book the student teacher developed class discussions and cooperative learning projects about cultural conflicts, endangered species, and ecological balances. Finally, the student teacher used the Social Action Approach by encouraging the students to write community and state leaders, ecology groups, and Seminole Indian organizations about their concerns and questions. When asked why she had developed the unit using the municipal library resources, especially the book and its issues, the student teacher replied, "But you *have* to!" (Brown, 1993).

Think and Act

- Discuss the hidden curriculum from your high school experiences. What groups were privileged? What groups were not?
- Compare and contrast the high school experience to your classroom. What explicit classroom policies support fairness and equity? How are these safeguarded in daily interactions?
- Prepare a lesson plan to teach the expected rules of a specific behavior like turn-taking, asking or responding to a question, or working cooperatively in a group. Monitor teacher and student behavior for following the rules.

Conclusion

Teachers have a great deal of influence over the curriculum that they teach. Even with numerous state and local restraints, teacher decisions determine exactly what content is taught to students. Teachers applying multicultural and global concepts in their classrooms will concern themselves with all aspects of curriculum development. They will work to change their present curriculum, analyzing the content with the goals of curriculum transformation and social action in mind. They will investigate new content that directly teaches multicultural and global concepts. Teachers also will analyze all curriculum materials for appropriate content and concepts. They will seek out new sources of curriculum materials, including human resources in the community. Finally, they will research their own classroom context, checking to see that the hidden curriculum supports multicultural and global perspectives.

CHAPTER

6 The Instruction

Information about the brain and how an individual learns is exploding in this challenging time of MRIs, CAT scans, and computers. The exciting research and its implications for education include learning styles, multiple intelligences, right and left brain theory, and the like. Learning styles and related areas of information processing are directly linked to instructional strategies, since the teacher's choice of strategy provides the method by which students are expected to learn the content.

Instructional strategies and learning styles are also related to multicultural and global education. Referring back to the pie concept, we can see that each person has individual, cultural, and human characteristics. Cultural influences on a person might affect his or her learning style, while individual characteristics might reinforce or counteract those cultural influences. Past experiences and present needs and interests influence how the learner and the teacher view the content. Effective teachers use instructional strategies to tap into their learners' experiences, needs, and interests. Effective teachers are also aware of their own preferred teaching styles and recognize how these preferences can hinder learning in their classrooms. Thus, effective teachers work hard to employ a variety of strategies to facilitate learning so that all students have opportunities to succeed in the classroom.

Relating Multicultural and Global Concepts to Constructivist Instruction

Multicultural and global concepts fit well with constructivist theory. Teachers who use a constructivist approach to instruction are already applying many of the concepts. Constructivist theory sees each individual as the maker of his or her own knowledge (Brooks & Brooks, 1993; Fosnot, 1996). The honoring of the individual learner's attempts to make sense of the information presented is also the honoring of that individual, a basic multicultural and global concept (Mathison & Young, 1995). Included in recognizing the individual is deliberately bringing the student's prior experiences, cultural heritage, and learning styles as well as present needs into teaching–learning situations. Participation of the learner with other learners, exchanging ideas and viewpoints, supports constructivist theory of dialogue and the multiple perspectives concept. Thus the exploration of individual interests and needs

128

through experience, dialogue, and reflection fits both constructivist theory and multicultural and global education philosophy (Brown, Kysilka, & Warner, 1996).

Six of Brooks and Brooks' (1993) constructivist descriptors seem most applicable to instruction based on multicultural and global education concepts. A seventh descriptor, added by Brown and colleagues (1996), has also been included here.

1. Constructivist teachers encourage and accept student autonomy and initiative.
2. Constructivist teachers allow student responses to drive lessons, shift instructional strategies, and alter content.
3. Constructivist teachers use raw data and primary sources, along with manipulative, interactive, and physical materials.
4. Constructivist teachers engage students in experiences that might engender contradictions to their initial hypotheses and then encourage discussion.
5. Constructivist teachers inquire about students' understandings of concepts before sharing their own understandings of those concepts.
6. Constructivist teachers encourage students to engage in dialogue, both with the teacher and with one another.
7. Constructivist teachers encourage students to engage in reflective thinking

The following sections explain how each of these constructivist descriptors supports the application of multicultural and global concepts.

Student Autonomy and Initiative

Teachers who encourage and accept student autonomy and initiative are applying both constructivist principles and multicultural and global concepts. Student autonomy and initiative in the classroom are needed to develop the knowledge, skills, attitudes, and behaviors for participating actively in the pluralistic, interconnected, and interdependent global society. This overriding principle means teachers honor students as co-learners, encouraging students to take responsibility for their own learning. Applied to instruction, teachers can provide students with many choices of ways to learn the required content. Students practice decision making and ways to work with others, important skills in multicultural and global education.

Effective teachers use a variety of instructional strategies, from teacher-centered ones such as lecture recitation to student-centered ones such as cooperative learning. Allowing students choices of strategies adds another dimension. Choices might be based on learning styles, personal interests, or abilities. For students with special needs, alternative forms of instruction could be required by their IEPs. For all students, genuine choices help students take responsibility for their own learning. For instance, students might like to work alone, work in pairs, or work in small groups for completing a specific assignment. Being able to choose which way to work means that each student is then responsible for making sure that his or her choice is successful. Encouraging and accepting student autonomy and initiative leads to student empowerment, an important part of multicultural and global education.

Think and Act

- How does John Dewey's position that children learn best by actively engaging in experiences fit with your understanding of student autonomy and choice? What does Dewey's democratic classroom look like? What is the teacher's role?
- Analyze a unit or a week of lessons. Were choices provided in the *same* lessons for type of task or assignment? Resources and materials? Work combinations (alone, in pairs, in small groups)? Where can choices be added in areas that have not had choices before?
- Interview two or three children of different ages about their understanding of some scientific phenomena. Try something familiar like growing plants and then something more abstract like the moon's phases. How do you view their attempts at constructing knowledge?

Student Responses

Teachers who allow student responses to drive lessons, shift instructional strategies, and alter content are applying both constructivist principles and multicultural and global concepts. Multicultural and global education emphasizes the richness of diversity and the importance of multiple perspectives in the classroom. These imply that contributions from students are encouraged and valued. When students bring in comments and suggestions based on their backgrounds and experiences, effective teachers use these as scaffolding to new learning. Teachers with multicultural and global concepts in mind use students' cultural experiences not only for bridging to new material but also for developing the necessary concepts and themes.

Most teachers have heard about the "teachable moment," a time in the middle of instruction for extending or presenting a new concept or idea. Usually, a student has asked a question or made a suggestion that, if picked up by the teacher and expanded, could spark a new way of looking at whatever was being studied. Effective teachers look for teachable moments; effective teachers who wish to apply multicultural and global concepts can find those specific moments as well. One key is looking for a specific time when only one perspective is being presented by a student and seeing that other viewpoints need to be added. Another key is looking for one of the multicultural and global themes that might be illustrated by what a student said or did during the lesson. The teacher's role in either case would be to break the pattern of the lesson, letting the new perspective or concept become the driving force. Here the students' interests or needs are met through the application of multicultural and global concepts.

Doing a search in the curriculum for places to add perspectives or develop themes is a planned, organized approach (see Chapter 5, The Curriculum). With instruction, however, the teachable moment search must be a spontaneous, insightful one that the teacher grabs at that instant. One advantage to such a teachable moment in multicultural and global education is that the teacher truly becomes the learner along with the students. The teachable moment is often something unexpected and new to the teacher as well as the students. The moment, of course, could be expanded into a planned research project or mini-unit. The point is to make such insightful moments a deliberate part of instruction by being flexible and open enough to recognize the possibilities when they occur.

Another way that student responses might influence instruction is when students act as teachers. In many classrooms, teachers set aside some class time for student presentations and demonstrations. To increase the usage of students as teachers, peer tutoring can be used. One caution would be to make sure all students get to be teachers at different times. For students who are not as strong academically, tutoring younger children is a possibility. For instance, "Reading Buddies," tying upper-grade students with lower-grade students is becoming a more common practice in elementary schools. Another method involves using a cooperative learning strategy such as Jigsaw II (Johnson & Johnson, 1994) where each student in a small group becomes an expert on specific information to teach other group members.

Think and Act

- Calculate the amount of time last week that students have been the teachers for (1) student presentations or demonstrations, (2) peer tutoring in pairs or in small groups, or (3) tutoring students in other classes.
- Make a list of students who have strong technological skills. Use them as peer tutors or group leaders for Internet or multimedia assignments.
- Try similar lists of students who have specific skills such as musical, artistic, and athletic. Provide opportunities for them to be teachers.

Raw Data and Experiential Learning Materials

Teachers who use raw data and primary sources, along with manipulative, interactive, and physical materials are applying constructivist principles and multicultural and global concepts. Because of the involvement with beliefs, values, assumptions, and attitudes, multicultural and global concepts are best learned through experiential activities. As in the constructivist classroom, the teacher can provide multicultural and global conceptual learning through the use of appropriate resource people and materials. Student-centered experiential learning involves the cognitive, affective, and psychomotor domains of learning, leading to better learning conditions and possibilities even for change in beliefs and assumptions.

Pairing individuals who have diverse cultural backgrounds can be a useful way of having students experience intercultural communication. Even seemingly monocultural classrooms have many categories of diversity that should not be overlooked. Diversity such as gender, religion, or ableness can be used for the pairing as successfully as ethnicity. Another possibility would be to go outside the classroom to pair students with new immigrants or students with limited English proficiency. For preservice teachers, universities often have international students who would like one-on-one practice in English conversation. Wilson (1992) suggests setting up conversation partners, helping each partner to gain needed insight in multiple perspectives and experience in communication skills.

Although the conversation partners concept is really designed for a semester or year, it can be modified for shorter periods of time if necessary. Careful teacher guidance for any conversation partner activity is needed. Students can prepare questions in advance in order to give each conversation a focus. Taping the formal part of the interviews might be helpful for students who have difficulty taking notes while listening. Student interviewers must be willing to give something of themselves in turn for using others for research. If it is mutual sharing of cultures, equal amount of time must be spent on each partner's culture. A commitment for continued conversation beyond the project's end can be beneficial for both students. In fact, one of the hoped-for side benefits is friendship across cultural boundaries.

Guest speakers can also be powerful primary sources of information. Speakers can be from the community or even members of the class or school. In a high school gifted English class, an East Indian young woman defended her Hindu beliefs to her mostly Christian classmates. As she explained her participation in an *ashram,* a retreat for religious meditation, her openness, knowledge, and religious devotion were obvious to everyone. Her classmates gained in respect for her and her religion that was so different from their own (Brown et al., 1996).

Reading materials of all types provide a wide range of multicultural and global perspectives (Chapter 5 discusses this further). Children's literature has many fascinating first-person accounts that can be used for student-centered activity prompts. Students can act out the parts, write sequels, or illustrate settings or events. Videos of cultural groups and historical events offer the visual image so important to many students. Audiotapes of speeches or interviews can be set up as part of a classroom research center supplied with question prompts and suggestions for related research. Tapes of songs and musical instruments can also be used in relationship to a study of different cultures or a comparison of music from different places.

Think and Act

■ What primary sources have you used or observed in the past week? List resource people who could help you find primary sources for future topics.

- Arrange conversation partners inside or outside the class. Be sure questions are prepared in advance of each session.
- Plan a learning center around an audiotape of a speech or music. What kinds of different activities could you relate to the audio segment?

Contradictory Experiences

Teachers who engage students in experiences that might engender contradictions to their initial hypotheses and then encourage discussion are applying constructivist principles and multicultural and global concepts. Multicultural and global concepts require self-examination of beliefs, values, assumptions, and attitudes before any fundamental change in thinking and behavior can take place. One way to help students reassess their beliefs and assumptions is to provide classroom experiences that deliberately cause cognitive dissonance.

Using primary sources with conflicting viewpoints is one possibility. Students can research and present multiple viewpoints to controversial issues. Simulations or role plays of the different perspectives provide active learning with affective objectives. Role playing can be done collectively, with each small group representing one person, as a culmination of a cooperative learning research task. Switching roles after one round of simulations or role plays offers another way to reinforce the idea of multiple perspectives. Debriefing after an interactive and emotional session is a necessity. A combination of discussion and written reflection seems to work very well. Discussion gives everyone a chance to share cognitive and emotional learning experiences, while quiet reflection provides individual opportunity to synthesize the learning in written form.

Guest speakers can also provide different perspectives. Curtis, an African American, described his childhood experiences as a sharecropper's child in the South and the alienation he had felt when he first attended school in the North. Because he was articulate, dressed professionally, and held a master's degree and a well-paying middle-management position, his comments about institutionalized discrimination were powerfully felt by his audience of education students (Brown et al., 1996). His representation of the American myth of "Anyone can make it" combined with his documentation of cultural and institutional discrimination caused strong dissonance in the minds of the predominantly European American middle-class students.

Think and Act

- Think about the last time you heard a guest speaker. What advance organizer was used beforehand to focus your listening? How did the speaker's viewpoints influence discussion afterwards? What new perspectives were gained?

(continued)

- Invite guest speakers to present their perspectives on specific issues or events. Consider a guest debate, panel, or forum. Have research done and questions prepared in advance. Invite student guest speakers to present their perspectives. Consider a more formal format using a podium for effect.
- Look for many ways to present diverse student voices—through readings of anonymous writings, trade books with similar stories, prepared scenarios, or current events.
- Set up an eCircle for safe chat sessions within the classroom or across classes. Prepare reflection questions that encourage multiple perspectives. Ask students to comment and then respond to other students' comments.

Students' Understandings

Teachers who inquire about students' understandings of concepts before sharing their own understandings of those concepts are applying constructivist principles and multicultural and global concepts. With multicultural and global concepts, teachers must use students' perspectives as starting points. Teachers have the difficult task of balancing willingness to listen to all viewpoints with needing to provide more information, clarify points, or refute inaccurate statements. This is especially hard when students see injustices such as racial discrimination as acts by individuals and not part of the broader problem of power structures, institutional discrimination, and oppression. Ahlquist (1992), in her research on multicultural education, has recognized and addressed this dilemma as an ongoing instructional problem. The way the teacher shares information based upon years of experience and knowledge of research is crucial to maintaining the collaborative nature of the classroom.

In some cases, student opinions or statements reveal underlying biases or prejudices. Teachers then have the difficult role of speaking against such statements without judging the students. The previous establishment of classroom rules reflecting multicultural and global concepts proves to be vital. If the classroom has been declared a safe learning environment for all, any form of discrimination is unacceptable. A reference back to classroom rules makes the reprimand less personal, protecting all students and embarrassing none.

Think and Act

- Read the chapter by Ahlquist (1992) and discuss her findings. Compare these with your own classroom experiences. Analyze your own reactions to tough issues that disturb you.
- Do class rules or university mission statements specifically address respect for every individual? List two examples each of respect being honored and not honored.

■ Discuss how respect includes honoring human rights and how everyone is responsible for providing a safe and secure classroom. Brainstorm ways that giving respect can be directly taught to students.

Student Dialogue

Teachers who encourage students to engage in dialogue, both with the teacher and with one another, arc applying constructivist principles and multicultural and global concepts. Dialogue is very important with multicultural and global issues, since multiple perspectives are at the core of many, if not all, of the issues. Student–student dialogue implies types of instructional strategies that encourage student interaction. Such strategies include small group work, especially cooperative learning models with the parameters of group goal and individual accountability (Johnson & Johnson, 1994; Johnson, Johnson, & Holubec, 1992). Group investigation and social science inquiry are other possibilities (Joyce & Weil, 1996). Peer tutoring also gives students a chance to work together. Often the peer tutor learns as much or more than the person being tutored.

Role playing and simulations have the added advantage of offering students the chance to act out some of the problematic situations in their lives. One possibility here is to use "critical incidents" from the field of intercultural communications (Brislin, Cushner, Cherrie, Yong, 1986; Cushner, 1999; Paige, 1993). According to Cushner (1999), a critical incident is

> a short narrative describing a situation whereby two or more individuals from different cultural groups interact in order to achieve some goal. Differences due to cultural background, orientation, perspective, communication style, learning style, and so forth, result in some conflict or problem emerging with the situation generally going unresolved. (p. 86)

Sometimes during instructional time, situations happen that need to be addressed. For example, two students have a disagreement that erupts into an argument or fight. After the immediate crisis is handled, the teacher can use the disagreement in a scenario form to work through appropriate behaviors on the part of the students. Depending upon the circumstances, the same day and same scenario or another day with modified scenario could be used. Less dramatic but as important, a teacher sometimes notices puzzled, uncomfortable, or even hurt expressions on students' faces as a reaction to something another person said or did. Questioning the students, perhaps later privately, could get to the root of the problem. Asking other teachers, speaking with caregivers, or researching literature are other possibilities. A similar incident can then be used to help teacher and students learn new ways of communicating. See Chapter 4, The Classroom Environment, for more on classroom interactions.

Student–teacher dialogues are also vital to critical thinking, but they must be genuine, not just recitation or regurgitation of factual information. If students are empowered to contribute in a meaningful way to the conversation, both students and teacher can become learners. The classroom environment must be conducive to risk taking so that students feel free to make in-depth comments or ask probing questions. Effective teachers use questioning to push understandings, to help students reflect more deeply. Yet even competent questioners run the risk of missing key student questions or comments, especially if they are asked by students with less cultural capital in the classroom, usually girls and children of color. In "Will Plants Drink Green Water?," a scenario about a second-grade class and student questions, the teacher completely missed the title question because it did not fit the context of what she had planned and because it was asked by a timid boy (Beck & Leishman, 1996–7). When the boy's question was later validated and researched, the boy gained in peer acceptance and subsequently confidence to ask more questions.

Genuine dialogue related to multicultural and global issues leads to questioning the status quo, the institutional forms of discrimination and oppression, and one's personal involvement in social justice. Students who examine complex problems from a variety of perspectives realize alternative actions and solutions can be sought. Paulo Freire (1985) talks about a problem posing approach, and uses dialogue related to adult students' situated lives. Even young children can work to better their own local environment, whether it is the classroom, the school, or the community. Dialogue in this sense becomes critical pedagogy, since it involves critical thinking, reflection, and action (Nieto, 2000). Studying about an issue is not enough; analysis combined with action to correct injustices is essential. The Social Action Approach section in Chapter 5, The Curriculum, discusses this point more fully.

Think and Act

- Analyze the last few times whole class discussions were used in the classroom. How often did students respond to ideas or opinions offered by other students? List two or three specific ways to encourage more student–student interaction in whole class discussions.
- Prepare a collection of critical incidents from intercultural communication problems witnessed in the classroom, school, or community. Sort them by cultural category (see Chapters 2 and 3). Share and exchange your examples with others. Role play and discuss several.

Student Reflection

In addition to the six descriptors chosen from the twelve listed by Brooks and Brooks (1993), one other seems to be essential. Teachers who encourage students to engage in reflective thinking are applying constructivist principles and multicultural and global concepts. Constructivist theory supports reflective thinking as a way of working through personal experiences and beliefs that shape attitudes and behaviors (Mathison & Young, 1995). Multicultural and global education in particular demands careful reflection since "language, cultural values, and cognitive styles all influence one's behaviors, attitudes, and perceptions" (p. 9). Reflection is the essential partner of dialogue; as students expand their understandings through reading, listening to, and talking about other perspectives, they must mull over the new approaches to come to deeper interpretations.

Students need time to think about what they are learning, especially when emotions as well as thinking are involved. Teachers can provide the reflective thinking time through a variety of ways. Writing activities could include journal entries, poetry, narratives, skits, plays, critical incidents, concept maps, and outlines. Other activities could include dramatic movement, video- or audiotaping, and creating or finding art or music to fit the emotions revealed. Portfolio pieces collected during the semester or year can contain several different types of reflections. Returning to these periodically can help students see their own growth of understanding and empathy.

Think and Act

- Explain the process of dialogue and reflection in light of a school or community multicultural or global dispute. What barriers do you find that prevent the different sides from seeing each other's viewpoint? Can it be resolved? What steps are needed?
- Analyze reflective writing in the classroom during the last week or month. Did it include multiple perspectives from any of the cultural groups, including national ones?
- Think of at least one way other than journal writing that you could add a reflective thinking task to each subject area you teach or plan to teach.

Applying Learning Styles Knowledge to Instructional Strategies

Chapter 3, The Students, describes the importance of learning styles for individuals and cultural groups, providing examples and research information. This next section will give some application suggestions so teachers can take advantage of the learning styles of their students. Adapting all instruction to fit the individual preferred learning styles of students would be impractical when students' learning styles are so diverse. Most authors recommend that teachers use a wide range of instructional strategies to reach all students some time during the instructional unit (Caine & Caine, 1994; Orlich et al., 2001). When specific students are not doing well in school, however, teachers can analyze the students' learning styles to see if more of the curriculum can be presented in these preferred ways of learning.

Work Habits: Cooperative and Competitive

Students with cooperative preferences often come from families and cultural groups that stress the importance of working and playing together. Sharing the task to succeed together rather than competing for the reward is reinforced by the adult members. Students who prefer to work with others to accomplish a goal usually respond well to cooperative learning strategies.

Heterogeneous groups arranged by the teacher are typically recommended by researchers to ensure a balance of ability levels, ethnic groups, and genders. Pang and Barba (1995), however, caution teachers to be aware that different cultural groups tend to have their own concepts of group formation and interaction, preferring to choose their own leaders or work in mixed-age groups. Allowing students to select their groups occasionally provides for individual preferences while arranging groups the rest of the time minimizes the exclusion of some students by others.

Johnson and Johnson (1992) note that five distinct features are characteristic of cooperative learning strategies: (1) positive interdependence, (2) face-to-face interaction, (3) individual accountability, (4) development of social skills, and (5) group evaluation. Positive interdependence, working together for a group goal, helps everyone to be successful, while individual accountability holds each student responsible. Interdependence and development of social skills are essential multicultural and global concepts in the classroom.

A wide variety of cooperative learning strategies have been developed that range from relatively easy to apply to very complex. At all levels, the specific skills of cooperation such as thinking out loud, asking others to think out loud, and listening carefully to others must be taught by direct instruction in order to have all students succeed (Baloche, 1998). Starting simply and checking student understanding and participation along the way can assist in avoiding potential problems. For instance, Think-Pair-Share, using two instead of three to four students, would not be considered by some a cooperative learning strategy. It is, however, an easy way to introduce skills needed for more complex forms to students who have not had cooperative learning in the past. Each partner thinks and notes down ideas to the presented question or problem. Then the partners share ideas and compose an answer together.

Triads and Round Robin are examples of cooperative learning types that require a medium amount of skill from the teacher. "Triads" uses the three roles of speaker, questioner, and observer. The speaker makes statements; the questioner asks questions; the observer notes verbal and nonverbal behavior, giving feedback afterwards. The activity is repeated three times with each person playing all roles. Round Robin has each person commenting in turn on a problem or issue presented by the teacher. Each person must have the same amount of time and must talk without comments or interruptions from the other group members. After everyone in the group has spoken, a group discussion helps to organize and summarize the viewpoints. Both of these types work well for multiple perspectives.

Cooperative learning types such as Jigsaw II (Johnson & Johnson, 1994) require more organization by the teacher and more skills by the students. Jigsaw II has two sets of groups, the home and the expert. Home groups are numbered, and then expert groups with the same numbers meet. Each expert group is responsible for a different area of material from the other expert groups. The expert groups research and prepare the essentials of their material. When the experts return to their home groups, each is responsible for sharing his or her materials with the others in the group. Jigsaw II works well with review material as well as research material.

Although cooperative learning strategies fit many students, especially those from cultural groups that advocate working together, they do not work well with all students. Some students prefer individual achievement and enjoy competing with others. The dominant U.S. society reinforces competitiveness and individualism, as do most school cultures. Students who prefer to work alone should be given that option at least occasionally. These students, usually field independent, are often task-oriented and want to solve the problem by themselves. One possible accommodation would be for these students to work alone but to join a group later for discussion of solutions. Including these students in cooperative learning group work at least some of the time is essential because they need to develop social skills along with cognitive skills.

Another typical problem with cooperative learning groups is the unequal contribution of student efforts. High-achieving students can feel as if they have been left with the majority of the work, because their standards of required work are higher than their teammates or the teammates do not do their assigned share. Proactive discussions about exact requirements with written guidelines such as rubrics help with clarifying expectations. Group process rubrics, for instance, provide descriptions of what a cooperative team player should do. Individual grades for some if not all the work will also help. Necessary at all education levels is careful teacher supervision of groups and individuals in the form of progress checks such as partial-work deadlines, individual conferences, and monitoring of group meetings.

Think and Act

- Examine the last time you participated in a cooperative learning situation, either as a student or a teacher. Were all five of Johnson and Johnson's (1994) characteristics present? If so, what difficulties were still there? Were they resolved successfully? If not, did the missing characteristic(s) affect the outcome? Why or why not?
- Prepare and present a simple cooperative learning exercise using one multicultural or global concept. Have the participants assess the exercise based on the five characteristics. What observations, either about groups or individuals, did you make during the exercise? How does student assessment help students to take responsibility during instructional time?

Modalities: Visual-Print, Visual-Screen, Auditory, and Kinesthetic

Students who are visual-print-oriented often come from families or cultural groups that have a long history of literacy, such as many European American and Asian American groups. The dominant European American educational system stresses the importance of the printed page. In most classrooms, especially at the secondary level, printed text material is an essential part of the classwork and homework. Providing for students who are visual-print-oriented is usually not a problem for teachers who themselves are often visual-print-oriented. Students who are not visual-print learners have a much more difficult time achieving in most schools in the United States.

Many students today are visual-screen-oriented with thousands of hours of television and video viewing before they even start school. Effective teachers take advantage of this preference by using television, videos, and computers as tools in the classroom. Rather than just turning on the television or playing a video, however, teachers need to incorporate specific parts into lessons. Using guides provided by public television such as the journal *Cable in the Classroom*, teachers can prepare their students for what is going to be shown. Screening videos in advance not only helps with introductions to the material but gives the teachers choices in how much to show and when to stop the video for discussion. Chapter 5, The Curriculum, mentions using a modification of the textbook biases checklist for videos. Even videos with flaws can be used if one of the students' tasks is to critique the video for ethnocentrism or other biases. One caution would be to make sure the visual image does not leave a vivid impression that cannot be erased with more accurate information. Related discussions and activities before, after, and sometimes during the viewing focus students' attention on essential concepts.

Both television and videos need to be used for teaching students skills of critical thinking related to viewing. Advertisements, for instance, can be studied in the fall as part of an anticonsumerism campaign. The commercial pressure to spend on gift-giving months before Christmas exemplifies the extreme consumerism in the society. Students in poverty and students with other religious beliefs are particularly vulnerable to feeling left out. Research projects can be done analyzing the quantities and types of advertisements used to target certain audiences, especially young children. The twin problems of consumption of natural resources and consumerist societies such as the United States fit a number of multicultural and global themes.

Computers add another powerful tool to a classroom. The Internet especially provides many interactive experiences for students along with supplying a tremendous amount of information. Computer usage time, for Internet or for educational programs, must be planned by the teacher to guarantee all students fair access. Allowing students play time on the computer after their work is completed is not an adequate and equitable arrangement. Some students will rush work to get to the computer; other more careful or slower students will rarely get a chance. Thoughtful scheduling of student time on the computer is essential to avoid unequal access and possible domination by the more capable or more computer-literate students.

One use of the computer at all grade levels can be as a learning center. Bookmarked Internet sites related to topics being discussed in class can provide a wealth of information, including visuals impossible to import into the classroom by other means. Preparing Internet sites in advance will prevent wasted student time unless actual searching is the skill being developed. Teacher-selected sites can also help prevent biased or inaccurate information being used as references. Another type of computer learning center can be set up with educational software or a word processing program. However the computer is used, written instructions at the center need to include a description of the specific activity, step-by-step directions, and a self-assessment tool so students can work without teacher assistance.

Think and Act

- Use the district or county teacher resources to locate videos that support multicultural and global concepts and the classroom applications (Chapter 1). Use or have students use the textbook biases checklist in Chapter 5 to analyze the videos.
- Start a file of websites that fit thematic units taught during the year. Ask colleagues and older students for good sites related to upcoming topics.
- Build a website that can be used for current units. Plan interactive lessons linking the site to other sites.

Students with auditory modality preference often have families or cultural groups with a rich heritage of oral traditions. Storytelling in schools has grown in popularity recently, at least in the elementary grades, and should be used throughout the grades. It helps develop the flow of language with colorful descriptions. Use of similes, metaphors, and hyperboles are common in this kind of oral expression. The "I Have a Dream" speech of Martin Luther King, Jr., is an excellent example of oral tradition. The speech has the added advantage of dealing with multicultural and global themes of oppression and human rights. Of course, many selections should be made, exposing students to a wide variety of famous and not-so-famous leaders.

Along with storytelling, other oral possibilities can be explored. Student presentations and demonstrations, role playing, and skits and plays can be incorporated into every subject area. Parents and community leaders can be guest speakers and interviewees. Good examples of rap, with praise rather than put-downs by favorite artists, can be gathered and imitated. Rap techniques can be used for student writing, either for rote memorization of facts or for creative compositions. Students can tape stories of others, such as their conversation partners mentioned earlier. Students can also tape short stories, their own or others', for younger children in the school. Good speaking and listening skills can be developed with practice. Using rubrics developed in class to evaluate speeches and presentations give students guidelines in advance.

Think and Act

- Find exemplary examples of rap to share. Try creating your own using a multicultural and global concept (see Chapter 1).
- Produce a classroom version of a talk show using a multicultural or global theme. Panelist characters can be current experts or historical figures.
- Play tapes of old radio mystery or comedy shows for oral listening practice. Describe or have students describe or illustrate favorite scenes. Compare old shows to modern versions. In what ways has the language changed?

Students with kinesthetic modality preferences often have cultural influences, especially ethnicity and gender, that conflict with a school setting that demands their sitting quietly the majority of the time. Teachers, whose behaviors had allowed them to succeed in schools, sometimes have trouble teaching students who cannot and will not sit still. Effective teachers provide for these students by not expecting docile, passive learners and by using instructional strategies that incorporate the kinesthetic needs of students.

Providing interactive and manipulative materials regularly not only helps students with kinesthetic needs but also works with constructivist theory, as mentioned earlier. Although most teachers are aware of young children's needs for handling concrete objects, some teachers do not realize that this need carries far beyond the early grades. Many older children and teens, and even some adults, have not developed the ability to use abstract thinking, especially in unfamiliar or uncomfortable content areas. Most students benefit from starting new concepts with concrete or semiconcrete examples. When preservice elementary teachers are reintroduced to fractions as part of their education program, some individuals always confess that they had difficulty understanding fractions. Having them work with the same manipulatives used in classrooms helps them to relearn the concepts.

All students benefit from learning activities that include physical actions, but students with kinesthetic preferences need numerous other opportunities throughout the day. Effective teachers find legitimate ways for these students to leave their chairs and move about the room. Using students as assistants for supplies and equipment is one possibility. Having students move to different parts of the room for small-group work is another. Scheduling breaks for stretches during longer class periods is another. Teachers can watch for signals of physical restlessness, especially at key times such as before lunch, late in the afternoon, or after stressful situations such as tests.

Think and Act

■ Discuss the use of recess for punishment. Why is this practice so common even though it is contradictory to multicultural and global concepts?

■ Analyze the instructional strategies used or observed for a week, noting every time concrete objects or manipulatives were employed. How could you increase the percentage of kinesthetic experiences? What materials would be appropriate for the students' cognitive levels? What affective objectives are also involved?

■ Keep anecdotal records of students who seem to need more physical movement than their classmates do. How do they try to meet these needs? What types of activities can be incorporated in lessons and between lessons to help these students?

Perceptual Styles: Field Dependent and Field Independent

Students who are field dependent often have cultural influences with a high context orientation. Field-dependent students tend to be social, preferring to work cooperatively. Activities mentioned under cooperative work habits also suit these people. In addition, field-dependent people need structure and benefit from carefully planned activities. Examples need to be provided with rules, and concrete objects work better than abstract examples. Illustrations such as drawings, cartoons, and photographs enhance the understanding of stories or information. Case studies and scenarios help these students set the stage for analyzing the embedded concepts. High interest and meaningful materials appeal to these students. They would prefer to investigate local practices of recycling and waste disposal rather than research facts about recycling and waste disposal statewide. Role playing or acting out concepts such as multiple perspectives provides the needed context. Students can also benefit from making their own scenarios to show their understanding of abstract concepts.

Students who are field independent often have cultural influences with a low-context orientation. Field-independent students tend to be more systematic and logical and often prefer to work alone. They enjoy analyzing materials and solving problems without assistance from others. They can draw the important information from readings, sorting out important information from extraneous details and do not mind learning isolated facts such as names and dates. Rules, lists, outlines, and step-by-step directions are good tools for them. Teachers can present information in forms of word puzzles or problems to solve. Many of the written assignments in classrooms, even work sheets, appeal to the logical, analytic styles of these students.

Think and Act

■ Take a concept you are studying and create both a short outline and a web for it. Which method do you use more? Why?

■ Design several different types of graphic organizers for introducing and learning new material. Use course work if you are not teaching.

■ Analyze any worksheets used in the past week. How often were the skills practiced out of context? Which exercises did the students like or dislike? Have them rate the sheets for learning new information, practicing skills, and keeping their interest.

Multiple Intelligences

Multiple intelligences (MI) is the term Howard Gardner (1983) has used to emphasize the concept of intelligence as not one fixed cognitive ability but a collection of capacities. Gardner (1997) now states that there are at least eight intelligences: linguistic, musical, logical-mathematical, spatial, bodily-kinesthetic, interpersonal, intrapersonal, and naturalist. Although MI are not learning styles in that they are abilities connected with specific content, they also demonstrate the diversity of the ways people relate to their environment. Gardner claims that schools in the United States generally recognize and reward only the linguistic and logical-mathematical abilities of students. Including the other intelligences in classroom instruction is another way to apply multicultural and global concepts.

Possibilities for recognizing and developing different intelligences are numerous. Some teachers, particularly at elementary levels, have created thematic units that tap all eight intelligences. For instance, a thematic unit on the Amazon rain forest could include reading and writing summaries of forest facts and concepts (linguistic), listening to and singing local music (musical), calculating sizes and amounts of timber (logical-mathematical), building dioramas of forest levels (spatial), acting as various forest animals (bodily-kinesthetic), writing and producing a play about forest events (interpersonal), keeping a diary about living in the forest (intrapersonal), and visiting a local forest for comparison with the Amazon (naturalist).

The advantage of a thematic unit built around the intelligences is the deliberate planning for certain intelligences that are usually not emphasized in regular school activities. The difficulty with using this approach is finding suitable material for all eight areas. Teachers can also look at their instructional practices throughout the week to see where, if at all, the various intelligences are encouraged or taught. Adding skits and plays, playing and singing songs, or building structures on a consistent basis will take planning but could bring out student skills and talents not noticed earlier. Interpersonal skills can be developed through cooperative learning activities, especially if teachers emphasize group processing. Activities such as role playing that examine personal beliefs and feelings will help students with intrapersonal skills as well as interpersonal skills.

Think and Act

■ Keep a record for several hours of class time noting when any of the various intelligences were employed by the students. Which intelligences were never used? Which were rarely used? List different ways at least two more of the intelligences could have been included in the same lessons.

■ Observe the interactions of a small group of students when they are problem solving. How do the different students negotiate solutions? What successful and unsuccessful skills were observed?

Emotional Intelligence

A closely related concept to Gardner's (1983) multiple intelligences is Goleman's (1995) emotional intelligence, or the ability to manage emotions, empathize, and handle relationships. Goleman believes that teachers should be doing more to promote these qualities in students. Students who are socially awkward might not pick up on social cues as easily as others do. Teachers can help children become more socially adept by instructing them in how to join a group of children already playing a game, how to show different emotions in their voices, and how to read other children's body language. These skills relate directly to multiple perspectives and the interconnectedness and interdependence of people.

Providing for Linguistically Diverse Students

Suggestions for linguistically diverse students—such as pairing them with same-language or helpful classmates, incorporating their cultural heritage into the curriculum, learning and using classroom survival words in their languages, and implementing cooperative learning strategies—have been mentioned elsewhere. Specific instructional strategies for these students that are used in sheltered English classrooms are also effective in mainstream classrooms (García, 1994). Increasing wait time gives students the extra processing time needed to understand and respond to questions. Simplifying the language and emphasizing important nouns and verbs helps students concentrate on the essential parts. Using gestures and body language, showing pictures and objects, and providing manipulatives offer students visual and kinesthetic modalities along with the auditory one. Constantly correcting grammar is not recommended; instead, accepting and rephrasing of students' answers in

Standard English provides the grammatical models without embarrassing and si-
lencing students. Repeating the same explanation in a louder voice when students do
not understand is another habit to avoid. Rephrasing with simpler vocabulary is a
better choice. In studies focusing on Mexican American elementary schools, effective teachers with these linguistically diverse students also "had high expectations
and refused to consider any of their students as intellectually disadvantaged"
(García, 1994, p. 272).

Immigrant students present a special challenge for teachers because of their
experiences of being uprooted, experiencing culture shock, and adjusting to a new
world. Igoa (1995) recommends a threefold cultural/academic/psychological model
of teacher intervention. One strategy she uses is "dialogue intervention, which addresses the feelings of the child through the development of a close relationship and
continuous dialogue between the child and teacher" (p. 117). A typical example
would be the child saying that she couldn't spell and the teacher answering that she
could spell her own name. In this way, the teacher is responding in a positive way to
the fears of the child rather than trying to brush away those fears. Teachers can role
model this method for all students, encouraging them to use the same positive language with other classmates. Like other educators with linguistically diverse students, she recommends that teachers encourage peer bonding through a variety of
student–student interactions such as the buddy system, peer tutoring, and study
groups.

Providing for Students with Special Needs

As with linguistically diverse students, students with special needs require instructional strategies that fit their individual cases. Courses and texts in special education
offer specific suggestions for a wide variety of special needs students, including
those who are gifted. This section serves only as a reminder that inclusionary classrooms today are most likely to have several students who have been labeled as special needs as well as several students who have similar or other academic concerns
but have not been labeled.

As mentioned earlier, if students have been labeled and have an IEP (Individualized Education Program), then teachers are legally required to honor it. Beyond that, teachers have the moral obligation to help all students succeed. Preparing
modifications while planning lessons reminds teachers of the required adjustments
for students with IEPs along with possible alternatives for other students struggling
with the same concepts.

As with the suggestions for linguistically diverse students, many modifications are also beneficial for other students in a classroom. For instance, organizational devices such as advance organizers, graphic organizers, outlines, and partial
outlines seem to be particularly helpful to students with learning disabilities but they
also serve all students. Verbal devices such as clear directions and procedures,
modeling, explicit cues, elaboration, analogies, and metaphors all provide scaffold-

ing to help students work through a task (Monda-Amaya & Pearson, 1996: Orozco, 1998).

Depending upon the individual students, other instructional adjustments can include adjusted learning context, modified or different learning objectives, alternative tasks, levels of reading materials, and types and quantity of assignments. First, the learning context can be adjusted to meet special needs (Orozco, 1998). As mentioned in Chapter 4, the classroom environment can be checked for displays that are too colorful or too distracting. Special seating such as carrels or desks at the side or front can be arranged. Materials to help with organization such as special notebooks or clipboards and focusing devices such as line trackers can be provided. Daily agendas on the board giving visual cues about the sequence and materials needed are also useful.

Flexible learning objectives can include a common goal or general objective such as effective communication while the specific objectives differ (Stainback, Stainback, Stefanich, & Alper, 1996). Some students can write short stories while others combine illustrations and words and phrases. Still others can tape their stories or dictate them to their peers. Sometimes the same objective can be expected but the amount of work or the time to do the work can be adjusted.

Varying activities is another way to attend to individual differences. Asking all students to do some sort of final project for a unit while offering many possibilities allows for creativity and multiple intelligences. Project suggestions could be anything from Internet research to dioramas and murals to original poems and songs. Sometimes the activity can stay the same but the objectives or materials change (Orozco, 1998). Learning the names of shapes can be changed to learning colors; cutting out shapes can be modified to tracing, coloring, or cutting them with assistance.

In some situations, multiple adaptations of learning context, objectives, activities, and assessment might be necessary. A cooperative learning community will support such adaptations understanding that the goal is for all students to achieve their own learning objectives.

Think and Act

- Interview older students who are bilingual about their school experiences. What services and techniques worked for them? What didn't? What forms of discrimination did they face in and out of school?

- What kinds of provisions have you observed being made for gifted and talented students? How do these compare with what the literature recommends? Why is a gifted and talented program often hard to fund in a district?

- Check your lesson plans for modifications. What type of adaptations are used regularly? Rarely? How do you ensure that students with special needs work collaboratively with other students, contributing to the group effort?

Conclusion

Teachers can support multicultural and global concepts by the choices they make for instructional strategies. Diversity in the classroom is honored when teachers use a wide variety of instructional strategies to provide for the diverse learning styles of their students. Human rights are honored by giving students autonomy and responsibility through choices of ways to learn. Multiple perspectives are also honored when teachers show and allow many approaches to the same questions or problems. Interconnectedness and interdependence are developed whenever strategies such as cooperative learning are used in the classroom. Co-responsibility is practiced when students help each other to share, work, and learn as a community. Teachers and students together make their classroom a global society when instruction calls for the use of multicultural and global knowledge, skills, attitudes, and behaviors.

7

The Assessment

The sixth critical element in the classroom is assessment. Classroom assessment covers a wide range of processes by which information is gathered about student learning. Caring teachers look for assessments that will fairly evaluate what their students know and can do. Fairness includes offering students many opportunities to demonstrate their learning, from standardized and teacher-made tests to portfolios and performances. Using a wide variety of assessment methods before, during, and after instructional units helps teachers gain a more comprehensive picture of student learning throughout the learning cycle. This information can then be used to modify curriculum and instruction as well as inform students and parents of progress and achievement. Teachers who are aware of multicultural and global concepts will also be concerned about equity issues such as whether certain types of assessment favor certain types of learners.

Comparing Traditional and Authentic Assessment

Traditional assessment methods have been described as paper-and-pencil tests that depend to a large extent upon verbal-linguistic and/or mathematical-logical abilities. Because they are quick momentary glimpses of student learning, they have been called snapshots of students' learning. Traditional methods usually assess only discrete bits of factual information that have been memorized and reproduced on demand. They do not gauge an individual's ability to apply what has been learned to new and challenging situations so much of the learning is forgotten after the tests (Darling-Hammond, 1991; Wiggins, 1992).

In contrast to traditional assessment methods are methods that have been recently labeled authentic. According to the literature (Montgomery, 2001; Newmann, 1995), what makes an assessment authentic are the following criteria:

1. The assessment is related to real-world tasks.
2. The assessment is complex, involving process, progress, and product.
3. The assessment involves self-assessment by the learner.

Rather than the snapshots of traditional methods, these are seen as moving pictures over time.

Authentic assessment methods better complement multicultural and global concepts because the criteria allow for diversity of learning styles and abilities. Further, the methods are an integral part of the instructional unit so that students can self-assess as they work, thus taking better control of their own learning. Yet few teachers would wish to do away completely with traditional assessment methods. Just as using a variety of instructional strategies benefits students with diverse learning styles, so does using a variety of assessment methods. Teachers need to analyze how they can help students succeed with all types of assessment. First and foremost, assessment for the effective teacher applying multicultural and global concepts is a means of finding out about students' learning in order to help them learn better. As Tomlinson (1999, p. 11) states it, "Assessment always has more to do with helping students grow than with cataloging their mistakes."

Working with Traditional Assessment

Classroom Tests

Although traditional assessment methods do not suit certain types of learners, they will continue to be used in U.S. classrooms for a variety of reasons. Teachers themselves too often view paper-and-pencil tests as the real evaluation of learning, especially if they succeeded with these traditional assessment methods when they were students. They also tend to think these forms of assessment are objective, thus fair to all students. In fact, multiple choice, true-false, and matching test formats are often called "objective," as if the actual selection of material were not already showing biases on the part of the test makers.

Beyond the biases inherent in selection of material to test, the construction itself of tests can help or hinder different types of learners. Field-independent learners tend to be more successful with multiple choice, true-false, and matching test formats than field-dependent students. This type of test appeals to the students' logical, sequential style. The isolated facts do not bother them; they have little need for contextual information. Thus, even the so-called objective tests actually favor certain students, just as other forms of assessment such as essay questions or performance-based methods favor other students.

If paper-and-pencil tests continue to be used in the classrooms, teachers can help students do better on the tests by directly teaching them test-taking techniques. Field-dependent students, for instance, might need help in sorting out what is required. Reminding students to look exams over completely before starting so that they have the whole picture of what is expected is one way of helping. For essay exams, students can learn techniques such as answering questions they feel confident about first or preparing a graphic organizer before starting. For multiple choice tests, they can learn verbal cues such as avoiding "always" or "never" answers and other ways to eliminate choices.

Teachers can also work to make their test formats easier for all students. Keeping the vocabulary simple and concise is particularly important in content areas to avoid testing reading ability rather than content subject knowledge. The look of the test also matters. Leaving enough space between sections helps students sort the parts out more easily. All questions using the same format should be together, with easier questions at the start to encourage students. Divisions within complex questions such as long essays help students organize their answers. Specific criteria required for the answer can be put in outline form, providing a handy checklist. The length of the test also has to be carefully calculated so students do not feel overwhelmed and have plenty of time to finish. Whenever possible, timed tests should be avoided since they more accurately test the learner's rate of response than the learner's knowledge.

Finally, teachers need to be sensitive to students' feelings when tests are returned in class. It is hard to imagine that there are still teachers who return tests in the order of the grades received, but cases are reported regularly of just that practice. Grades should be put on the inside of the tests so students can conceal their results from classmates. Discussions of test results should be general enough that individual students' mistakes are not targeted. Scolding students for bad results might help the teacher vent his or her frustration but rarely serves the purpose of motivating students to do better next time. Reteaching any missed material is usually better saved for another day when student and teacher emotions are not so involved.

Think and Act

- Research articles or books on test-taking skills to be taught. Check to see how many of these skills you know and use when taking tests. Plan a lesson to teach one of the skills to a class or peers.
- Take a census of students' preferences for types of test items. Use old tests to have students analyze formats. Apply these findings to the next test you prepare.

Standardized Tests

Some stakeholders in education see standardized tests as the best form of accountability for schools. These summative forms of assessment are really forms of evaluation or judgment about collected information (Guild & Garger, 1998). Their purpose is to identify levels of success in order to categorize students, schools, and districts; they rank students rather than help them learn. Results of state and national standardized tests have been used to make high-stakes decisions about education. Advocates for assessment reform speak about the overuse and misuse of standardized testing. They see standardized tests as inadequate in tying assessment to curriculum and instruction, emphasizing higher level thinking and problem solving, developing lifelong learners, and reflecting local involvement in learning outcomes (Darling-Hammond, 1997). In fact, one major concern is that standardized tests are now driving curriculum and instruction.

Those educators concerned with multicultural issues have criticized the use of standardized tests as screening devices that favor European American middle-class students (Banks, 1994b). Certainly the type of information tested and the format used to test that information favor students who are field-independent learners in that the tests call for knowledge of discrete facts without contexts. The relationship of field-independent individuals to cultures that have low-context orientations supports this argument about cultural bias (see Chapter 3 about learning and cultural styles). The use of standardized tests has also resulted in students of color, low-income students, and students with limited English proficiency being overrepresented in classes for mentally retarded students and underrepresented in classes for gifted and talented students (Patton, 1992). Finally, the tests have been accused of keeping students of color and low-income students from better educational and economic opportunities (Mercer, 1989).

The present-day reality of schools and districts is that the results of standardized tests, inadequate and biased as they may be, are extremely important to administrators and teachers. When assessment conflicts with curriculum and instruction, assessment often forces changes in the curriculum and/or instruction. In Oregon and Washington, too many elementary teachers responsible for standardized testing in their grades are minimizing or eliminating entirely science and social studies from their curriculum. According to reports, the fact that their students are not tested in these areas is by far the major reason for these decisions. Science and social studies are still on the books—they even show up in teacher lesson plan books—but they are rarely given the full allotted amount of time. Some effective teachers are using multidisciplinary and interdisciplinary units to include science and social studies to some degree, but the curriculum squeeze means less content is covered. One cynical teacher in Portland, Oregon, reported that perhaps the state science and social studies standardized tests, "coming soon in a school near you," will force these subjects back into the curriculum. Standardized tests in these subject areas are likely to be similar to the others in their high emphasis on factual, superficial knowledge.

Although teachers have to live with standardized testing, outside of the classroom they can be advocates for change. They can volunteer for school, district, and state assessment review committees, especially as new state standards and benchmarks are being written and piloted in districts. Unfortunately, so-called collaborative sessions aligning assessment questions with state standards and benchmarks can end up being a form of rubber-stamping if the guidelines imposed on the participants are too rigid. In a recent summer session, participants were to prepare test questions, but the standards and benchmarks were already written and could not be revised. Thus, a question about women's roles in society in the early 1900s was eliminated because "women's rights" not "women's roles" was the terminology used in the benchmarks. As the participant discovered, the session products are then considered as resulting from the collaboration of testing experts, state officials, teachers, administrators, and university professors.

More successful methods of protest might be comments to the media. Teachers can speak against the misuse of standardized tests for discriminatory practices and for the use of alternative forms of assessment. They can urge parents and caregivers and community leaders to protest the loss of science, social studies, and other curricular essentials. Teacher organizations, both state and national, might also be vehicles for more unified and effective protests. Rethinking Schools, a Milwaukee nonprofit educational publisher of materials on school reform (www. rethinkingschools.org), is one possible source.

Inside the classroom, teachers can help students to cope with the types of standardized tests they will have to face. Most teachers already give students practice with test formats and samples of questions. The information on learning styles (Chapter 3) can give teachers further insight into ways to guide students. As suggested earlier, teaching specific test-taking skills can be very beneficial for students who need direct instruction. For instance, field-dependent students can work on visualizing specific examples or scenarios for factual recall of information. They can learn and practice succinct writing for standardized essay tests, following such formats as the five-paragraph essay. Students who have trouble with the quantity of print can devise ways of covering up parts of the page to keep focused.

Think and Act

- Read several articles on national and state standards from professional journals. Prepare a summary of advantages and disadvantages.
- Interview practicing teachers about their positions on mandated standards and benchmarks. Ask how they approached integrating the standards into what they were already teaching.
- Compare the state-mandated time for elementary subjects not tested to the actual classroom time spent teaching the subjects. Compare notes with others to check your findings.

Working with Authentic Assessment

The three authentic assessment criteria given by Newmann (1995) fit multicultural and global concepts: (1) involving real-world tasks; (2) involving process, progress, and product; and (3) involving self-assessment. The criteria allow for student diversity, require student-centered tasks of importance, and emphasize student progress and achievement rather than competition. The discussion below of the three criteria relates to the combination of authentic task and assessment. In practice, authentic assessment cannot be separated from the authentic assignment because completion of the assignment includes using the assessment (Riley & Stern, 1998).

Real-World Tasks

Authentic assessment is an integral part of doing real-world tasks in the classroom. Real-world or "authentic" tasks are those that duplicate or approximate as much as possible tasks that people use in daily living and in their occupations. For example, preservice teachers get closest to real teaching during their field experiences, especially student teaching, when they assume the full load of a practicing teacher. The authentic assessment for student teachers is directly related to the student teaching in that it evaluates how they manage the classroom and students, prepare lessons, deliver instruction, and perform the complex responsibilities of teaching.

Authentic tasks themselves apply multicultural and global concepts in that they call for the use of different types of learning styles and allow for student choices. Students who have difficulty with learning based on verbal-linguistic or mathematical-logical skills might very well have excellent success with learning that requires other abilities such as spatial or bodily-kinesthetic. Offering students choices in ways to demonstrate their learning gives teachers a better picture of student understanding.

Think and Act

- Think of a time when students had to demonstrate what they learned (plays, skits, science fairs, art shows, etc.). Can you recall a specific student who surprised you with unusual ability or talent? Jot down the details.
- What is meant by the "real world of the classroom"? Why do some educators consider the classroom not to be real? What assumptions are they making?

Process, Progress, and Product

With authentic classroom assignments, the process students undergo and the progress they make are integral parts of the task and assessment. This involvement over a period of time compares to most real-world complex tasks. For instance, working on a district committee to prepare a multicultural education program requires commitment of purpose, investment of time, interpersonal skills, organizational skills, and much more. The final evaluation is not just in the program itself but in the establishment and maintenance of the committee structure and membership as well as the development of relationships inside and outside of the committee.

Students need to understand how important the process is to the successful completion of the product. They also need to know that the skills for such complex tasks as preparing programs or writing reports were learned through practice over time. Assessing the process and the progress each individual has made is a valuable way of saying that these are vital parts of the completed work. Assessing the process and the progress along with the product fit multicultural and global concepts since such an assessment emphasizes individual students' achievements rather than deficiencies and compares the students with themselves rather than with others.

Application of the six concepts discussed in Chapter 1, Essential Multicultural and Global Concepts, requires the involvement of the process and progress along with the product of student learning. For instance, developing an understanding and appreciation of the interconnectedness and interdependence of the world requires long-term efforts from both the teacher and the students. Interpersonal and intrapersonal skills are needed in order to apply this concept to the classroom and beyond. Authentic assessment methods can look at the process of students working together and sharing limited resources. The methods can assess how individuals have improved in their understanding, attitudes, and skills concerning cooperative learning and problem solving over time. The methods can also analyze the final products of cooperative work related to assignments about the interconnectedness and interdependence of the classroom as representative of the global society.

Think and Act

- What are the advantages and disadvantages of peer assessment of individuals in a group process such as cooperative learning?
- Brainstorm ways to handle the problem of any discrepancies between individual self-assessments and peer assessments of student participation in the group process. Consider both very high and very low self-assessments. How would you deal with the individuals? Their peers?

Self-Assessment by the Learner

Preservice and practicing teachers who believe that all students can learn will provide opportunities for students to improve their performances. One way is through the frequent use of formative assessment—assessment done during the teaching of a lesson or unit. Results of individual or group formative assessment can provide information for modifying the curriculum and instruction of that lesson or unit in order to improve student learning. Frequent and detailed feedback such as written comments on assignments allow teachers to identify areas of competence as well as to suggest strategies for improvement and remediation (Banks, 1997). When the results are shared with students, the students can use the feedback to improve their own learning. Students then can modify their work before any final grades for the lesson or unit are assigned. Such teacher practices support multicultural and global concepts by encouraging student responsibility for learning and by providing many opportunities for improvement.

With authentic assessment methods, multicultural and global concepts are more fully applied because the element of student self-assessment has been included directly in the process of performing the task. As the assignment is given, the teacher provides appropriate authentic assessment instruments with guidelines and descriptive criteria so that the students know in advance what they must do to accomplish the task successfully (see rubrics and checklists later in the chapter). Instead of the teacher providing all the feedback for students to interpret in order to make improvements, the students also act as teachers and provide feedback for their own work. They also can peer teach and peer edit each other's work. Having the means to self-assess their work during the process of learning gives students the power and responsibility for making improvements. Students become co-responsible for their own learning.

Think and Act

- In what assignments is redoing the product a natural part of the process? Are all subject areas included in such assignments? If not, where can changes be made?
- How do you provide informal self-assessment of your daily responsibilities professionally? Personally? How do these methods help you to accomplish your tasks?

Examining Authentic Task and Assessment Combinations

As discussed earlier in this chapter, the combination of authentic tasks and authentic assessment methods offers the best opportunities for application of multicultural and global concepts. Many articles and books have been published recently on authentic possibilities. The ones discussed below—portfolios, performances and presentations, and projects—are some of the more common choices in the classroom.

Portfolios

Portfolios can be used in all subjects at all levels, as demonstrated by the video "Redesigning Assessment Portfolios" (American Association for Curriculum Development, 1996). Portfolios give students an opportunity to assess and demonstrate their growth over time in a specific area. The purpose of each portfolio dictates what is to be included and the criteria used for inclusion. Teachers need to think carefully about items to be included in the portfolio in order to get the most representative portfolio for that subject or unit. For instance, examples of worst work with reflective comments about problems encountered could prove as helpful to student learning as examples of best work.

Students as well as teachers can make decisions about items chosen or discarded, especially if teacher guidelines allow flexibility of choices. Reflective pieces discussing the chosen items are an essential part of a portfolio because students examine themselves as learners, assessing their past achievements and setting new goals (Porter & Cleland, 1995). An added benefit is the insight into student learning teachers can gain from the students' reflection on their process and product. Students also benefit from sharing their work with peers (Baloche, 1998). If taught skills such as listening carefully and asking clarifying and probing questions, peers can provide excellent feedback for improvement of the product as well as reflection about the product once it is finished.

Teacher support and encouragement throughout the process of creating the portfolio itself is essential. This process has to be considered separate from the actual process of creating the individual pieces. The students need to see the individual parts, whether they are writing samples or mathematical figures, as separate contributions as well as parts of a whole. Regular class discussions combined with mini-conferences will help students understand the purpose and the process of compiling a portfolio. The final assessment or grade depends upon the teacher's purpose. Some teachers give an extra grade for the finished portfolio. The use of a rubric or checklist helps provide the necessary guidelines in advance.

Think and Act

- Review your professional portfolio (if you do not have one, think of what it would contain). How are the following demonstrated: (1) your philosophy of education? (2) your management system? (3) your creativity? (4) your growth over time?
- Research Schon's (1983) definition of a reflective practitioner and then examine your portfolio or journal. What evidence do you have of your growth as a reflective practitioner?
- Watch the video "Redesigning Assessment: Portfolios" by the Association for Supervision and Curriculum Development (1996). Discuss the use of portfolios in various subjects. What would be some advantages and disadvantages of a portfolio in mathematics, for instance?

Presentations and Performances

Presentations and performances offer a wide variety of authentic assignments. Skits, plays, scenarios, role plays, simulations, demonstrations, debates, and reports are possible at all grade levels. As is fitting for an authentic task, each one of these takes preparation for a successful product. Depending upon the purpose, the preparation and performance can be simple or more involved. Concepts such as multiple perspectives benefit greatly from role plays and scenarios that make different viewpoints integral to the performance. Other multicultural and global concepts can be explored with the use of multimedia presentations. Power Point talks give students chances to use modern technology as well as develop useful presentation skills.

Plays in many U.S. elementary schools tend to be elaborate affairs involving weeks of practice, fancy costumes, and a wealth of props and background scenery. Teachers might consider adopting one British school's concept of producing more plays with much less preparation. Weekly for the last half-hour on Friday, one class performs some simple skit taken from their language arts studies. Actors use vivid make-up and student-drawn props. Class readers describe the imaginary scenes and chorus members help the main actors with the more complicated speaking parts.

Think and Act

- Why are role plays and skits so important for developing multicultural and global perspectives?
- Prepare a skit for elementary or secondary school students using one of the multicultural and global concepts. Include introductory comments and the debriefing afterwards.
- Stage a town hall meeting based on a local problem such as water pollution or land usage. Assign and research various stakeholder roles.

Projects

Projects have many possibilities for authentic tasks as well. Although projects have been particularly popular in science and art, they can be used for any subject area. They also offer excellent opportunities for interdisciplinary and thematic units. Projects give students a chance to construct objects using spatial and bodily-kinesthetic skills. Projects can be simple or complex, depending upon the teacher's objectives and the students' abilities. They provide nicely for a wide range of interests and abilities. If projects are individualized for each student or group of students, competition for the best can be lessened.

Written work can be combined with such a project but should not be the only or the primary part assessed. Taped comments or presentations can be used for the final explanation of the project. If a project involved some kind of active participation, there are many different ways to document the process. For instance, drawn illustrations can show a work in progress. For something like a cleanup campaign of a local stream, mounted photographs before and after the cleanup can provide excellent documentary evidence. Even the construction of a mural or a diorama can be photographed to show the stages of completion.

Projects, especially at the elementary level, should be done in the classroom to give all students a fair chance to succeed. Assigning complex projects for homework shows a middle-class assumption that students have a separate workplace, appropriate supplies, and adult supervision and assistance. In the past, projects for science fairs were notorious for adult involvement to the point that some parents did most or all of the work for their children.

Multicultural and global themes work very well with projects. To make change in beliefs and attitudes requires the involvement of the affective domain. Projects can bring out the passion and caring in students. Issues about human rights, for instance, can be researched on the Internet. Child labor is one topic with numerous sites, including some with children who had been forced to work telling their stories. Ecology issues also have many sites that can be investigated. Tying this type of research with personal action plans helps make the project more of a personal commitment.

Think and Act

- Plan a simple construction project such as a diorama. Note beforehand which students you think will truly get involved and show more than their usual persistence and creativity. Confirm your guesses by close observation during project time.
- Choose a unit to be taught. Develop basic criteria for any project that students might do to demonstrate their learning. Have students brainstorm ideas for individual or small group projects. Make a master list of possible projects for students to choose.

Designing Authentic Assessment Tools

The type of authentic assessment tool employed depends a good deal upon teacher purpose and student developmental level. Examples of tools for different purposes can be found in *Authentic Assessment: A Guide for Elementary Teachers* (Montgomery, 2001) or *Great Performances: Creating Classroom-Based Assessment Tasks* (Lewin & Shoemaker, 1998). One of the most popular is a *rubric,* which contains descriptive criteria with qualitative levels of achievement. Prepared by the teacher or teacher and students at the beginning of an assignment, the rubric offers students a continuous method of formative self-assessment. Students guided by the teacher can develop skills to check the progress of their work as they are preparing it.

Designing rubrics might seem difficult at first, but rubrics have many advantages well worth the effort. Rubrics can provide clear expectations, showing students where the main emphases of the particular assignments are and setting standards of excellence. Having the rubrics in advance means the students can use them as guidelines throughout the assignment time. Teachers also have a way to justify the grades students earn, especially if the criteria are detailed and clearly understood.

Rubrics fit nicely with complex authentic tasks, since they can be designed for specific teacher purposes. For instance, a rubric that assesses group process during a cooperative learning assignment on sweatshops can stress the importance of sharing ideas, listening to others, taking turns, or whatever interpersonal skills the teacher wishes to develop during that assignment. Another process rubric can emphasize parts of the research, such as quality and quantity of resources, note-taking skills, and compiling the information. A different rubric that assesses the final product can cover the presentation of the group's findings to other students.

Along with rubrics, *checklists* are handy tools that students can use for self-assessment. Although checklists do not provide descriptive criteria and qualitative levels of achievement, they have valuable information to guide students during an authentic task. Students can use them to check off required components of a portfolio, for instance. They can also refer to checklists to make sure that all the appropriate steps are followed in the correct sequence. Robin, an English teacher, supplies her students with a checklist for common composition errors they must guard against when writing.

Think and Act

- Collect several examples of rubrics used in the local schools. Try assessing students' work according to one of the rubrics. What difficulties did you have? How can you overcome them? Switch work with a colleague and compare grading results.
- Design a rubric for a performance. Include criteria for preparation and presentation. Have students peer evaluate skits and plays.
- Prepare an observation checklist or rubric to use while students work together on a project. Include criteria for sharing ideas and encouraging others.

Aligning Assessment with Curriculum and Instruction

For the critical classroom element of assessment, the application of multicultural and global concepts includes not only the method of assessment but also the curricular content of what is being assessed and the instructional process used to assess.

Close alignment of curriculum, instruction, and assessment is a goal of effective teachers, and this goal is particularly important for multicultural and global concepts. These concepts are complex; their application involves real-world situations and requires critical-thinking, decision-making, and problem-solving skills. The use of authentic assessment methods rather than traditional methods more closely aligns assessment with multicultural and global curriculum and instruction.

Applying Multicultural and Global Concepts to Assessment

The six multicultural and global concept applications described in Chapter 1 are themselves authentic tasks that require authentic assessment for evaluating those understandings. As mentioned earlier, the applications must involve process, progress, and product. The concept of celebrating diversity, for instance, does not just mean studying and being tested on isolated facts about other cultures. It also means developing an appreciation for other ways of living and solving human problems. It requires moving from an ethnocentric viewpoint toward a more multicultural and global perspective. It involves gaining skills for participating in a diverse world. All of these ways and others of celebrating diversity can be applied in the real world of the classroom as well as the real world outside the classroom. The true assessment of individual students' abilities to apply the concept of celebrating diversity, for instance, is their actual use of these understandings and skills when working and playing with classmates from diverse cultural backgrounds.

Like all authentic tasks, the application of the six concepts requires the involvement of self-assessment by students. In this case, the process involves intrapersonal analysis since the product ties behaviors to beliefs, values, assumptions, and attitudes. In a sense, self-assessment becomes self-awareness, an essential ingredient of multicultural and global education. Students need to know who they are and how they fit into different cultural groups and the larger community, national, and international societies. Awareness of one's role and responsibilities in a pluralistic society and world demands regular self-assessment of one's progress over time. While working on assignments such as those that welcome multiple perspectives, for instance, students need to be able to check themselves for understanding of and empathy for other points of view.

Conclusion

Teachers can support multicultural and global concepts by the choices they make for assessment. Recognizing that the dependence on paper-and-pencil tests for assessing student learning will benefit certain students and penalize others is the first step. Using a wide variety of assessment methods in the classroom to give all students a better opportunity of showing what they have learned becomes the next step. Including students in their own assessment throughout the process of learning is a relatively new direction for many teachers. The end result is that students can begin to take more responsibility for their own learning since they participated in the decision-making process along the way. Shared decision making and shared assessment results particularly demonstrate the concept of practicing co-responsibility in the classroom.

PART THREE

Applying Multicultural and Global Concepts beyond the Classroom

However teachers hope and plan to apply multicultural and global concepts in their classrooms, their decisions are also impacted by outside factors beyond those classrooms. Two major influencing factors are the school beyond the classroom and the communities beyond the school, nearby and farther away. Part Three, Chapters 8 and 9, examines these larger arenas and how they can influence—and be influenced by—teachers and their classrooms.

The organization and the operation of the school reflect the beliefs, values, assumptions, and attitudes of its leadership, combined with major influences from teachers, staff, students, parents, and the community the school serves. The community also has its structure and operation reflecting the beliefs, values, assumptions, and attitudes of the parents, community leaders, and other local and regional stakeholders. Sometimes the interests and goals of the school and the community are similar; other times, they are distinctly different. Both entities, in turn, are influenced by the larger communities of region, state, nation, and world. All these influences must be analyzed and incorporated into any action plan for the application of multicultural and global concepts.

The role of the school has been changing and evolving over the past few decades. It is no longer—if it ever really was—an isolated place removed from outside influences. In fact, faculty and administration in effective schools today bring in many forms of outside involvement from reading volunteers to business sponsorship. What teachers and others in the school do to encourage or discourage others has a tremendous effect on the teaching and learning that go on in the classrooms. Chapter 8 examines the school and its components in relationship to the application of multicultural and global concepts.

The roles of local and more distant communities regarding schools are also rapidly changing. New forms of communication have brought the classrooms and schools into instant contact with people and places around the world. Instant electronic contact has led to more interconnections near and far. Politics, for instance, has become more important to schools as district, state, and national groups demand increasing accountability for educational funding. Social, cultural, and economic aspects of these expanding communities are also more intertwined with schools. Effective teachers cannot afford to ignore these varied and complex influences because of the many riches as well as the complications and sometimes even dangers they pose to teaching and learning. Chapter 9 looks at the different communities and their relationships to classrooms and schools and the application of multicultural and global concepts.

CHAPTER

8   The School

Each school in the United States develops its own culture. This culture is highly influenced by the leadership of the school, by the influence parents may have on that leadership, and by the community that school serves. However, if a school is going to adequately serve the community in which it is located, then the leadership of that school must work hard to develop a culture that is open and accepting of the constituents it serves. In addition, the whole purpose of public education in the United States must not be lost in a school's attempt to gain an identity. According to John Dewey (1916) education has both democratic and societal goals. In order for schools to serve society and to promote democratic principles, they must be organized to reflect the different interests held by the individuals and groups who inhabit the school. Democratic ways of knowing can be taught in the schools if the schools themselves function in democratic ways. Society can become more understanding and supportive of diversity and differences if schools foster those goals. Geneva Gay (1994) says it well, "Creating a cohesive society out of this country's incredible diversity requires knowledge, skills and values that can, and should, be taught" (p. 93).

According to Jerome Bruner (1996), "culture in a macro sense is a system of values, rights, exchanges, obligations, opportunities and power" and in the micro sense "it examines how the demands of the 'macro' affects those who must operate within it; how the individual makes meaning out of experiences" (p. 11). School culture (micro) is often a reflection of the larger community culture (macro), and thus what happens within the environment of the school is what the students assume will happen within the broader context of society. Consequently, it is imperative that the school culture or environment is a positive, open, accepting one that models what should be in the broader social, economic, and political culture of society. Schools must not only be a reflection of, but should be a change agent for, a more pluralistic, global, tolerant, positive society.

Establishing a Welcoming Environment

Experienced educators can walk through the front door of a school and within minutes be able to assess the culture of that school. They can define the school as friendly and accessible or unwelcoming and rigid. They can define the environment as open or closed. They can describe the school as student friendly or not. These judgments can be made relatively easily. Examinations of signs and displays, directions to visitors, behaviors of the students in the hallways, and reactions of clerical staff in the main office all reflect the culture of the school. Schools speak loudly to those who enter their doors.

The first impressions a visitor has upon entering a school are crucial to the formation of a perception of the school culture. Thus, the leadership of the school must be certain that the first impressions are positive and welcoming. The following scenarios describe how visitors to two schools might form very different perceptions of the schools.

Scenario I

Upon driving on to the campus of High School X, the visitor is greeted by rows of flags of various countries. The flags line the drive to the school's main entrance, which is clearly marked and convenient to ample parking space for visitors. Along with the flags, there are signs giving directions to the main office in English, German, Spanish, and Vietnamese languages. The office personnel greet the visitor with broad smiles and a cheerful "Welcome to our school!" Signs in the office reflect pride in the school with statements like "X where learning is our primary goal," "X a great place to learn," "X the pride of the community." Students assigned to work in the office happily escort visitors to their ultimate destination, while telling the visitors about the most recent events of the school, like winning the recent girls' basketball tournament.

A tour of the school conducted by the assistant principal reveals several factors. First, the flags represent the countries of heritage of all of the students who attend the school. The student government raised the money to display the flags, which are flown daily. The languages on the signs represent the four dominant languages spoken by the students in the school. The signs were a project of the Parent Teachers Association.

The large school has its more than 3,600 students placed in four "houses" designed to decrease the negative impact of a very large school. Students in groups of 900 share the same teachers and facilities—except for the sciences, arts and music, physical education, and technologies, which have separate facilities that are shared by all students. There are seven technology laboratories spread throughout the school to accommodate technology needs of teachers and students. The four buildings or houses are connected by cheerful, bright, internal hallways filled with displays that recognize the accomplishments of students in the arts, debate, mathematics, science fairs, various sports, and a recent Special Olympics. The received message in this school is "We honor our students and their diversity."

Scenario II

Upon entering the campus of High School Z, visitors are stopped by a guard at a portable guardhouse located behind chain link fencing. The guard asks the purpose of the visit and requires visitors to sign in. Visitors are instructed to park only in visitor parking spaces located near the front of the main building. There are no directions to get to these spaces, and if visitors manage to find them, they often discover that all spaces are occupied. Another trip to the guardhouse yields the information that visitors are allowed to park on the driveway but very close to the curbing so as not to obstruct the buses or cars that use the driveways. The sign on the main office door indicates that the office is open from 7:30–3:30 and all visitors must sign in: "Violators will be prosecuted." Similar to High School X, High School Z's staff in the main office are pleasant and helpful. There are, however, no signs or displays in the main office that indicate the motto of the school, accomplishments of students, or other indicators of pride in the school.

High School Z also has a large student population, over 4,000 students, but its many buildings are spread out over two campuses, the north campus and the south campus, nearly a half-mile apart. The north campus is made up of portable classrooms, each a self-contained unit. The walkways between buildings are exterior and open to the elements except for corrugated metal coverings. There are no displays of student accomplishments, even though the school is known for both academic excellence and success in several sports. Like High School X, this school has a very diverse student population with a mix of African American, Asian American, European American, and Hispanic students speaking at least fifteen different languages. Yet there are no signs or displays honoring any of these cultural heritages. The immediate impression of the school is cold and ambivalent.

Think and Act

- Both High School X and High School Z are large, diverse schools. What factors make one school a positive environment and the other an ambivalent environment?
- If you were the administrator of High School Z, what would you do to change the image of the school?
- Think about the high school you attended. What image would it project to a visitor? Do you think all the students who attended your high school would see the same image? Why or why not?

Improving the Physical Environment

Buildings

Unless they are involved in designing a new school or modernizing an older school, school leaders are usually not able to change much of the actual structure of the buildings. Still, certain physical aspects are under their influence. Standards of cleanliness can be set so that each member of the school feels responsible for picking up after himself or herself. Minor equipment maintenance and repairs can become joint projects by skilled individuals, including students. Some painting projects can be done by teams of volunteers from within the school or community. The physical appearance of a school very much demonstrates the pride or lack of pride in the school.

Vandalism is a serious problem for many schools and districts. Studies indicate that schools are most often vandalized by students who feel rejected by the school members, either the personnel or the students and often both. One side effect of including students in the decision-making process regarding major issues about a school could very well be reduced vandalism.

Displays

One of the factors that makes a difference between High School X and High School Z is the use of displays. Each of the displays in High School X provides a story of what life is like for various individuals in the school. Displays are organized and maintained by certain members of a school; who is involved in selections says something about the philosophy of the school. Certainly, students as well as faculty and administration should have input into what types of artifacts are chosen to represent the school.

Along with seeking input from all school members, school leaders can work toward respect for diversity by using multicultural and global perspectives when setting standards for displays on bulletin boards, in hallways, or other public areas. The following guidelines, along with those found for classrooms in Chapter 4, The Classroom Environment, may help develop culturally appropriate displays.

Representative of All People Historically.   Hall posters of historical figures should include men, women, and children representing a variety of cultural groups. There are numerous sources of posters and pictures of well-known and less well-known historical figures, many of which can be found on the Internet. Selecting individuals not as well known and including information about them can provide valuable historical lessons. Sometimes famous people can be shown in a different, more personal light. For instance, posters now show Franklin Delano Roosevelt sitting in his wheelchair, an appropriate selection for outside an American history classroom. Local history can be told in the form of murals or old photographs. Men, women, and children in a variety of settings, at work and at play, can demonstrate the richness of a community's history.

Another concern about historical displays involves multiple perspectives related to historical times and events. When historical events are being celebrated, care must be taken that a balanced picture of the event is presented. Recently, a district multicultural meeting convened in the library of an elementary school in October. Throughout the meeting a Native American member of the committee had to face a book display of Columbus, his ships, and his story. Nowhere in the display was any indication of the Native American peoples Columbus and his men encountered and subsequently enslaved. A more sensitive approach to Columbus Day would be to include books that presented perspectives from Native Americans, that discussed cultural conflicts, and that questioned whether Columbus Day should be celebrated at all. Columbus did not discover America, and even young students are capable of understanding the difference between "discover" and "take" or "conquer." Perpetuating myths, even in pictorial displays, is not appropriate when the myths distort history and trivialize human suffering.

Accepting of All Faiths. This is particularly important when dealing with traditional holiday seasons. Accompanying signs of "Season's Greetings" and "Happy Holidays" accompanied with pictures of Christmas trees and Santa Claus is not an interfaith approach. Although Christmas displays are seen nearly everywhere in the United States during December, schools must be conscious of the fact that many students attending public schools are not Christians. They may be Hindu, Buddhist, Muslim, Jewish, Agnostic, or Christians who do not believe in religious decorations. These differences in beliefs must be recognized and honored. If Christmas symbols are displayed, then Hanukkah and Kwanzaa ones at least should also be included.

An even more interfaith approach would be to decorate the school throughout the year with appropriate symbols for other religious holy days, such as the Islamic month of fasting, Ramadan. Although this month is determined by a lunar calendar, recently it has been during the winter months. A school committee of adults and students could be organized to design appropriate displays, including explanations of basic tenets and symbols. A very different approach, but not likely to be popular with Christian families particularly, would be to eliminate entirely any displays with religious connotations. Whatever decision is taken, school leaders must be sensitive to the religious beliefs of all their students and staff, not just the majority of them.

Reflective of All Talents. Traditional hall displays, especially the ancient glassed exhibits, used to be trophies from sports championships. Now more recognition is being given to students who excel in academics, the arts, and vocational areas as well as the star athletes over the years. More than just the best and brightest need to be selected for places of honor, however. Different types of contributions to the school and community can be recognized, such as dedicated student and adult volunteers. Groups of students working and playing together can also be shown, supporting the school's philosophy of cooperative efforts as well as individual achievements. Cooperative learning projects and events can be commemorated in photographic displays and narratives. Along with student and school achievements, powerful displays featuring students, teachers, and other school personnel demonstrating the mission, vision, and goals of the school will help to establish a healthy environment.

Displays featuring career opportunities or vocations and avocations should be very diverse. Artists, sports figures, and business persons of all types ought to be included in displays. Again, the theme of cooperative efforts can be carried out through exhibits demonstrating teams at work rather than individuals. The local choir or orchestra, the fire department staff, or the cafeteria crew can be shown performing their coordinated duties. Images of teachers and staff working together provide role models to all who walk in the school halls.

Inclusive of All Individuals and Groups.   Frequently, schools place student work on exhibit. If this is going to be a policy of the school, then all students should have an equal opportunity to have their work put on display. Displays must not be reserved only for the best of the best. Every student in the school can accomplish something that could be put on display for all to see. Some students are good artists, others writers. Some students can solve mathematical problems and technical science questions, others can create web pages. Whatever their talents, they should have public opportunities to share with others.

Displays and photographs that show students in the school must reflect the makeup of the student population. Groups that are often marginalized in schools, such as special education teachers and students, can be given prominent places on bulletin boards. Showing pride in these students' accomplishments advertises the school as a caring, supportive environment for all its children. In contrast, a school bulletin board that supports a "Reading Buddies" program but thoughtlessly has all buddies with white faces and Caucasian features advertises a disregard for children of color in that school and elsewhere.

Students are influenced by what they see. Schools that honor achievements of all types by men, women, and children from diverse cultural heritages convey the message to students that they also have opportunities to succeed in a wide variety of ways. Schools that define success in an open and inclusive way support the position that no one talent or ability is necessarily more important than another.

Think and Act

- Inspect the public displays in a school using the criteria given in this section. Select what you consider the best and worst examples, giving reasons for your selections.
- Prepare a school bulletin board that would fit the criteria given in this section. If possible, have students participate in planning it and setting it up. Be careful to use inclusive criteria for selecting student helpers.

Improving the School Culture

The Hidden Curriculum

In Chapter 5, The Curriculum, the concept of a hidden curriculum was discussed in relationship to the classroom. The hidden curriculum, or what students learn in school through the beliefs, values, assumptions, and attitudes held by the teachers and administrators, is also a serious concern for the school itself. What school personnel, particularly the administrators, value influences decisions they make regarding the organization of their school, the activities they support, and the way they view their students and the community. Because the hidden curriculum is a powerful tool of communication, it is essential that administrators are aware of their values and beliefs and are conscious of how their values and beliefs influence decisions they make.

Like teachers, administrators must carefully examine their basic belief systems and reflect on how their values and beliefs affect what they do and say in their school. Chapter 2, The Teacher, provides guidelines that can be also used for administrators and support people. School leaders such as principals have the added responsibility of acting as main liaisons between the school and the community the school serves. Administrators therefore must present a neutral position on controversial issues while staying open to hearing all perspectives. They need to explore multiple aspects of an issue with their students and to encourage students to formulate their own positions based upon equal access to all information. The public schools are not places to exert political agendas; they are places for academic investigation, exploration, and critical thinking.

At the same time, maintaining a neutral position in face of fundamental abuses of human rights such as racist actions is not acceptable. School leaders have a moral obligation to demonstrate respectful behavior toward all school members as well as community members except when doing so demonstrates tolerance for intolerant behavior. A synagogue in upstate New York had anti-Semitic slogans painted on its driveways. One fourth-grade teacher in the nearby elementary school organized her students into a task force that helped repaint the driveways. The principal, very supportive of the teacher's and students' actions, made sure that the local newspaper and television station reported not only the racist incident but also the students' efforts. In this way, he demonstrated his position against discriminatory acts.

The organization of the school—what extracurricular activities are allowed, what plays are produced, what field trips are encouraged, what music is heard—also speaks to the hidden curriculum of the school. Through extracurricular activities, schools can accommodate a great variety of interests of its students. For some students the opportunity to participate in extracurricular activities is the highlight of their days spent in school. Frequently, these activities serve as a motivator for students to remain in school and to complete their studies. The extracurricular activities may help students define goals for themselves and give them the encouragement to pursue those goals. They may provide students with the opportunity to assume leadership roles in school. In other cases, extracurricular activities are simply enjoyable activities in which to participate.

Whatever activities are provided, administrators must take care that the school activities are as inclusive as possible. Clubs must be open to all interested students and should encourage regular participation by all club members. For instance, any students interested in speaking Spanish should be urged to join the Spanish club, whether their level of speaking is beginning or advanced. Sports also can be inclusive, with intramural sports teams formed that accept anyone willing to practice and play.

Unfortunately, high school administrators and faculty all too often take a very competitive approach to sports because of their popularity in the community. When the star athletes of a school are allowed to ignore homework assignments or are given passing grades when they have not earned them, the hidden curriculum speaks of privileged groups and unfair practices, not of democracy and equal treatment for all. Teachers against such practices can band together to eliminate or minimize them. Making sure class expectations and grading methods are clearly stated in writing at the start and fairly implemented during the year will give teachers a more solid base to insist on equitable practices throughout the school. Contracts signed by students and parents and increased publicity to community members about high expectations can serve the dual purpose of warning student athletes and preparing community fans if tough decisions about eligibility have to be made.

Think and Act

- Discuss how the fourth-grade teacher and her class demonstrated the Social Action Approach to curriculum (see Chapter 5, The Curriculum).
- Visit a school and examine the extracurricular activities offered by the school. What can you conclude about the school and its encouragement of diversity?
- Interview several college students about their high school impressions of favored and not favored groups. Who had privileges granted by the administration?

School Personnel

Discussion of schools is not complete without examining the staffing issue of the school: teachers, administrators, and nonteaching staff, including cafeteria workers, janitors, maintenance and office personnel. Although it is desirable to have a staff that is representative of the ethnicity within a community, care must be taken not to give the wrong message to the students, families, and visitors to the school. If all the lower paying, nonteaching positions at a school are filled by people of color while most of the top administrative positions are held by White men, then the message conveyed is that of race and gender privileges. This message is particularly disturbing when the school has a preponderance of White teachers and administrators working with large numbers of students of color.

Hiring, encouraging, and mentoring teachers and other school personnel of color should be important objectives for administrators. Unfortunately, the percentage of teachers of color is decreasing rather than increasing, so the placement of teachers in classes becomes even more crucial. The administration's sensitivity to the necessity for a variety of role models for all students is revealed by whether teachers of color have advanced classes and college preparatory classes or are relegated to noncollege required classes, vocational classes, remedial classes, alternative education classes, or specialty areas like ESL. The makeup of the administrative team of a school also must be examined. If administrators of color are not in strategic curriculum positions but are only the school disciplinarians, a negative message about their value as educators might be conveyed to the students and families.

The diversity of the teaching, administrative, and support staff of a school is an important consideration. Many schools and districts in the United States are facing a shortage of teachers, however, and they have a critical shortage of teachers of color. In addition, there is a decreasing pool of prospective administrators, particularly persons of color who aspire to leadership roles. Given the increasing difficulty to find qualified teachers and administrators and even more difficulty to find qualified people of color to fill these vacancies, schools will continue struggling to provide ethnically diverse role models for all students.

Students will respond positively to caring and nurturing teachers and administrators regardless of their ethnicity or race. If school personnel can honestly convey to students that they care and that they understand and appreciate the diversity that exists in the school, they can connect with the majority of students. But the students must truly believe that these adults have the students' best interests in mind as they make decisions that affect all aspects of school. In previous chapters, six critical elements of a classroom have been addressed in regard to applying multicultural and global concepts. Administrators as well as teachers must also be familiar with these elements in order to provide educational equity and excellence for all students. School personnel must be students of learners' differences in ethnicity and race, class, religion, gender, and so forth.

Research on teacher attitudes and expectations (Good & Brophy, 1994) indicates that teachers are highly influential in affecting student achievement by holding high expectations for students and demonstrating personal acceptance of their students. Students of all colors, gender, race, religion, and socioeconomic class are entitled to teachers' respect, to teachers' expectations of high performance, and teachers' acceptance of them as human beings. This holds true for other school personnel as well. There is no place in any school for adults to transmit negative attitudes toward or low expectations of students simply because the students are not like them. All individuals who choose to work in schools with young people must think of their students as individuals who want to learn, who want to be successful in school, and who want to be respected.

A recent study involving nine urban elementary schools with impressive academic results (Charles A. Dana Center, 1999) makes several specific recommendations for school leaders including the following:

- Focusing on service to students rather than conflicts among adults in the school
- Getting resources and training that teachers felt they needed
- Winning the support of the parents
- Creating a shared sense of responsibility among school members

Collectively, the recommendations define a focused administration willing to provide strong leadership yet wanting true collaborative decision making. This type of leadership also fits with multicultural and global concepts because it recognizes the rights and responsibilities of all the school members and works to improve the learning environment of all students.

Think and Act

- Check the demographics of the school personnel against the demographics of the students in your school. What groups of students do not have role models of their ethnicity or race in prominent positions?
- Find out about the in-service training provided for school personnel about multicultural and global issues. Has the school district taken a proactive position or a reactive position (responding only in times of crisis)?

Students

Just as school personnel are expected to model positive attitudes and to hold high expectations for student performance, students must also be able to think of themselves as being able to succeed in school and maintain strong self-concepts. Part of developing a strong self-concept is having a strong understanding of one's ethnic identity. Most students, regardless of their ethnicity, do not possess a strong understanding of who they are. For example, European American students may feel superior to other students because that is what they have learned without ever questioning what that means and whether there is any truth in that perception. Other ethnic groups may be embarrassed by or ashamed of their ethnicity because of the negative publicity their groups receive in the media. Muslims, for example, may be sensitive to their public image in the United States, since they are often portrayed as violent terrorists in the news.

Many cultural perceptions held by students are not accurate and can manifest negative behaviors towards other ethnic groups. Thus, it is imperative that students have the opportunity to explore their ethnicity and their understanding of their ethnic identity in the safety of the school environment. Research by Gay (1985), Streitmatter (1989), and Tatum (1992) indicates that as students become more aware of their own ethnic identity, they become more accepting of ethnic differences; more self-accepting; and more competent in academic endeavors, social interactions, and interpersonal relations. Helping students to building positive ethnic identities will also help a school develop an environment that is accepting and respectful of differences.

Beyond working with students to develop their sense of ethnic identity, school leaders have an obligation to help students feel a part of the school community. One way to do this is to give students genuine responsibility in the organization and operation of the school. Students' contributions must be recognized in more than a superficial way. If student government groups are not allowed to make any important decisions, or if their decisions are overruled by the administration, then any pretense to support a democratic school is negated. A new principal in an upstate New York high school announced to the community that he was going to "take the school back from the kids." Indeed, he did just that, establishing an autocratic leadership that increased administration, faculty, and student divisions and contributed nothing to the easing of class and racial tensions.

Programs such as conflict resolution and peer mediation support the concept of co-responsibility for developing a community of learners. Successful programs reduce the incidents of violence or discriminatory acts by encouraging selected students to work with students before situations get out of control. Some new programs advocate training in conflict resolution and peer mediation for all students, teaching them to use appropriate strategies for finding solutions in everyday confrontations. Administrators and teachers must be sure that any students designated as peer mediators receive adequate training in their roles. Part of the training should include how to recognize the levels of violence created and to take corresponding actions.

As part of a new awareness of diversity issues, schools are beginning to sponsor student groups such as multicultural committees. Just as administration, staff, and teachers in many districts have experienced workshops or training sessions about multicultural issues, students can participate in similar programs that focus on childhood or adolescent issues about multicultural and global education. One active training program, REACH (Respecting Ethnic and Cultural Heritage) from Seattle, tailors workshops specifically for secondary students. The nonprofit organization, headed by Gary Howard (author of *We Can't Teach What We Don't Know*, 1999), provides a wide variety of materials including multicultural and global education units for grades K–12.

A basic concern about any kind of limited training program is that the program not be taken as the solution or end project. Individuals might become more aware of multicultural or global issues but they rarely change their beliefs, values, assumptions, or attitudes without deep and enduring self-reflection. In spite of the need for systematic change over time, shorter programs can raise awareness levels and can encourage more open discussions among participants. From such awareness training, students can then become active in developing or supporting initiatives in the school or community. Some secondary students have asked different representatives of cultural groups to be guest speakers, while others have become speakers themselves. Some have contributed to multicultural displays in the schools, while others have worked with mediation teams to reduce racial tension.

Think and Act

■ What suggestions do you have for school activities to help students understand their ethnicity and the ethnicities of others? Think beyond the typical ethnic or international foods and fairs.

■ Interview officers or class representatives of the school government. How do they perceive their roles? Where do they see that they have the most influence on administration, faculty, or students?

■ Research articles on peer mediation to share with your colleagues. How do these compare to what you have seen in local schools?

Collaborating with Parents and Caregivers

Traditional Contacts

Most teachers recognize the need to have collaborative working relationships with the parents, caregivers, and families of their students in order to ensure success of those students in school. However, how teachers define collaboration may be very different from what should occur between teachers and parents or caregivers. Too often in our schools this so-called collaboration becomes more of a one-way informing activity on the part of the teacher than a sharing activity with both groups contributing. Almost all schools have some type of parent–teacher association meetings or open houses to which parents are invited to meet the teachers and find out what is happening at the school. Typically at these meetings, parents are herded into classrooms where the teacher explains the curriculum and the activities of his or her room and perhaps reviews the rules of the school. Parents in high schools or with more than one child shuffle from class to class accompanied by ringing bells, never getting a chance to talk personally with the teachers. When the schedule is completed, punch and cookies are served in the cafeteria and everyone goes home.

These meetings are rarely satisfying to either the teachers or the parents and caregivers. The short time devoted to the activity does not provide enough opportunity for teachers to meet and discuss concerns, progress, and successes of students with their respective adults. In addition, parents and caregivers with whom the teacher really needs to speak rarely show up for a variety of reasons. Their own discomfort in a school setting, often based on personal negative experiences as students, could make entering a school difficult. Their work schedules could be in conflict with the times of conferences. They might not be able to afford transportation and babysitting.

Cultural attitudes about the roles of teachers and people in authority can be a strong factor in the noninvolvement of parents and caregivers. For instance, according to Peña (1999), Mexican American parents and caregivers may feel they do not have the right to question what is happening in school, especially in such an open setting. Mexican Americans believe that home and school should not interfere with each other and that families should maintain a respectful distance from the education system. To increase their participation, Peña recommends that schools help parents learn about how the education system works. Until their fears and concerns are alleviated, parents and caretakers will not participate actively even if a variety of opportunities is provided.

Some teachers are very perfunctory in their presentations and interactions with the parents. On a tight schedule, they skip courtesies such as inquiring about the well-being of various members of the family. This businesslike approach of dominant culture teachers is a cultural mismatch with many people of color and can be interpreted as cold and unfriendly. Some teachers also act as the experts and do not consult with or encourage parents and caregivers to share their ideas about school programs and activities. These meetings are teacher-dominated and teacher-oriented; they are not parent or student friendly. The process leaves much to be desired.

In addition to the PTA nights and open houses, many schools have developed newsletters to be sent home to the parents or caregivers. These are either prepared by the principal or grade level teachers or, in secondary schools, by individual teachers or guidance counselors. They are again designed to inform families about the happenings at the school. The newsletters are often well written and are sometimes very attractive; however, they do not encourage dialogue. They offer only one-way communication from the school to the families. Sometimes, not even that is accomplished if the language spoken at home is not used for the newsletters. Even if all communications are printed in the home language, adults with very little education can be overwhelmed by information sheets and newsletters.

Teachers and administrators are also expected to contact parents or caregivers when students get into trouble, whether that trouble is behavioral or academic. Rarely do teachers or administrators contact family members when students are doing exactly what is expected of them or when they excel in their activities at school. Communication initiated by the teacher is almost always seen as an indication of some sort of trouble. Parents and caregivers could dread hearing negative reports about the children they feel they cannot help academically.

Think and Act

- Select a school in your community. Ask about its publications, such as information pamphlets. Find out about its demographics.
- What types of events does the school hold for its families? How are they advertised? Who attends them?
- Observe the types of parents and caregivers who visit the school during the day. If possible, find out their purposes for visiting. Keep track of the visitors' demographics: ethnicity, class, gender, and age. What conclusions can you draw from your observations?

Involvement and Dialogue

All of the preceding strategies used to involve parents and caregivers in schools are one-way communications that preclude real success in engaging adults responsible for the children and youth in their students' education. Several other types of strategies can be developed, however, to open up the dialogue between teachers and parents or caregivers. Group information sessions are not collaborative sessions and do not encourage involvement and dialogue. They should be used for the dispensing of information only, such as explaining the new state-mandated testing systems. Smaller, more focused sessions dealing with one or two specific school problems, such as racist or sexist incidents, are better for engaging parents and caregivers in schools. Knowing the parents and caregivers, who they are, what their backgrounds are, what their interests are, would help administrators organize such focus groups.

Asking parents and caregivers to volunteer in school activities is another way to encourage two-way communication. Such solicitations should be done on a more personal level than an announcement in the newsletter or at an open house. A phone call or a personalized letter can persuade individuals better than a general request. Parents who work during school hours can be asked to contribute at other times, such as after school for helping with materials preparations or other class and school tasks. Other more creative ways to solicit family participation should be investigated. For instance, having family or community members discuss traditions, demonstrate cultural arts, or display cultural artifacts involves the students' families while providing powerful learning opportunities for students and teacher.

Teachers and administrators must be aware that many parents and caregivers feel uncomfortable in the school setting. If parents were not particularly successful in school, they probably find returning to the site of their failure very disconcerting. Consequently, in order to get some parents involved, teachers and administrators need to reach out to them. Volunteering to meet in students' homes has proved successful for many teachers, especially those working with very young children. Some kindergarten programs plan for teachers to spend weeks before school starts visiting the different homes. Finding a neutral ground like the public library, a nearby park, an inexpensive restaurant, or a church hall might prove more fruitful in getting parents to meet with the principal and/or teachers.

Time as well as location is an important consideration. Parents and caregivers should not be penalized at their jobs because their children need help in school. Setting up meetings early in the morning or after parents' work hours may also help. Perhaps the school could arrange to have parent–teacher conferences in the evenings once a month on different weekdays or offer other flexible times for the parents, including weekends if necessary. Hassles of the working day can interfere with good communication, so searching for more advantageous times might be beneficial to all.

Think and Act

- Find out how the school communicates with the parents and caregivers. Develop a parental involvement scale and rate the school with respect to that scale. Note possible ways to raise the involvement.
- Interview several teachers and ask them how they communicate with families. Identify what works best and why.

Respectful Treatment

When teachers meet with parents and caregivers, they must show respect for them and their role as their children's first teachers. The nuclear family of a father, mother, and children is not the reality for many students today. The wide range of other possibilities includes single-parent households typically, but not always, headed by women; gay or lesbian couples; and blended families with combinations of his, her, and their children. Teenagers raising children without financial or emotional support are far too common, as are older relatives forced into the role of parenting again when their own children have been unwilling or incapable of managing. Teachers need to be conscious of how they can work with all parents and caregivers to help the children and youth.

As teachers talk with parents and caregivers, they should use clearly understood phrases and explanations. Most adults have learned how to raise children by observation and personal experience. They are not often familiar with the theories of child development and appropriate parenting. As in most professions, education has developed its own jargon along with an alphabet collection of acronyms. Unless parents are educators themselves, they probably do not understand the specialized language. Rather than question what a teacher may be saying, some adults will nod their heads in agreement even though they are completely perplexed. For example, a teacher might say, "Eric is developmentally delayed. He demonstrates socially inappropriate behaviors that get him into trouble." The terms "developmentally delayed" and "socially inappropriate behaviors" have not been explained, so the caregivers are left frustrated about the unclear information.

A further concern, and a more important one, is the attitude of the teacher. If teachers act superior, impatient, or angry with the very adults who are the students' caregivers, all the good intentions and helpful suggestions are likely to be taken as unwanted interference. In the scenario about Eric above, teachers as authority figures would say, "You need to help him at home to improve his behavior in school." Here blame-putting words tell caregivers to "fix" Eric. Instead of finding ways to help the Erics in classrooms, the teachers are stating that they are not responsible for the behaviors and are further implying that they will not take the responsibility to assist the students in modifying these inappropriate behaviors in school. As authority figures with all the answers, they also show an unwillingness to find out if those same behaviors ever show up at home. This seeming lack of empathy for the caregivers' position will probably defeat any good intentions of the teacher.

Much needed information and support can be gathered when a true two-way conversation is held. Learning about the lives of students outside the school is a vital part of helping students. It also conveys respect to the significant adults in their lives. A sensitive teacher might rephrase the information in the paragraph above to make it understandable and respectful: "Most children of Eric's age can play and work together without hitting or becoming angry if they don't get their way. They know how to take turns and share. Eric got angry several times and hit another child once last week. Have you observed similar behavior at home? Do you have any suggestions of ways I can help Eric at school?" Now the teacher is explaining Eric's problems in school and is suggesting that the parents and teacher work together to find a solution to help Eric improve his behavior. This latter scenario speaks to collaborative work between teacher and caregiver. It also makes clear that parents and caregivers have a lot to contribute to the dialogue. Teachers might wish to educate the parents as well as the children but they should not lose sight of that fact that they, too, have a great deal to learn from the parents.

Some teachers and schools hold student-led family conferences, asking even young children to be active participants in the process. Using portfolios of work carefully selected from different subjects, students can talk about the progress they have made over the marking period and the goals they will set for the next weeks (see Chapter 7, The Assessment, for more on portfolios). Similar records can be exhibited for social and emotional behavior. If a student is on a behavior contract, for instance, he or she can be encouraged to lead as much as possible the discussion about collected anecdotes and other data. This approach, with portfolio or data presentation by students, empowers students to take responsibility for their own learning, academic or social. It also gives everyone an objective base for discussions about goals reached and improvements needed. A further advantage of such a three-way conference is the emphasis on individual work and progress rather than class norms.

Think and Act

■ In trying to meet with parents and caregivers, what strategies would you feel most comfortable with and why?

■ Research the literature about student-led conferences. What are the advantages and the cautions?

■ Read Vivian Paley's (1995) *Kwanzaa and Me: A White Teacher's Story* for insights from a White teacher communicating with and learning from parents of color.

Using the School as a Community Center

Across the United States, public schools have become community centers, providing a wide range of services not thought of years ago. Subsidized breakfasts and lunches for children whose families qualify are commonplace. Most schools keep their buildings open for community meetings and continuing education courses. Some schools offer basic medical and dental services. Many elementary schools provide before and after school programs for children of parents who work. Even in the summer, schools are kept open for summer school or other activities. When a school is seen as a community center, the natural ties between community members and school personnel can be strengthened. Teachers have extra opportunities to meet and work with families and community leaders through these services and activities.

One possibility for schools that seems to offer promising results is the extension of computer lab services to the community. Andrew Jackson Elementary School in Indio, California, has a team of teachers who keep the computer lab open after school and on Saturdays, thanks to federally funded grants (Butler, 2001). Students, older students, and parents may use the computers for Internet, educational software, or personal writing. A class for parents who wish to earn a Microsoft Office Users Certificate has been started. As one of the teachers stated, "We want to be sure they [parents] can get across the digital divide, too" (p. 9). The main use of the computers is by the students, however. A side effect of this after-school assistance to the students and their families has been a large jump in the school's California achievement test results.

For the most part, school personnel, particularly principals, are the primary leaders and supervisors of the school community center. They exercise a large degree of control over program choices and school usage. Another broader conceptual approach to school and/or school personnel involvement in community education programs will be discussed in Chapter 9.

Think and Act

- Contact the local school district for information about community education centers in schools. Examine their literature for the range of academic and vocational classes in English and in other languages. Find out how the classes are advertised, how well they are attended, and how much they cost.
- Visit two or three after-school daycare programs in the school. What criteria would you use to rate the quality of the care?

Conclusion

All members of a school contribute to its character as a center for learning. Who gets recognized and who gets marginalized depend very much upon the complex interactions and interconnectedness of administrators, faculty, staff, and students. Explicit decisions such as what extracurricular programs are supported and implicit decisions such as what privileges are given to sports stars contribute to the composite picture of a school and its culture. Many schools today have mission and vision statements. Whether a school actually lives up to these ideals depends upon the individuals and groups within it.

CHAPTER

9   The Community

The application of multicultural and global concepts within classrooms and schools cannot be adequately addressed by teachers unless they also understand how these same issues and concerns relate to the communities where the schools are located. What makes multicultural and global concepts imperative for every classroom also affects each community and how it views its schools.

In the past decades many communities have faced changing demographics. Population changes might be related to increasing numbers of immigrants, particularly Latinos, Asians and Pacific Islanders, and Eastern Europeans. Changes could also been related to economic shifts, as industries particularly in the North continue to downsize while companies in the Sunbelt regions are established or expanded. Areas such as the Silicon Valley have seen such phenomenal growth that the cost of living has skyrocketed, driving out working class and poor families. Whatever the reason, the population in the United States has shown many shifts and new trends over the past few decades.

These changing demographics and the resultant interests and needs of each community are reflected in the ways schools are viewed and operated. Changing demographics, increased interaction among cultural groups, the interconnectedness and interdependence of all participants in the local and the global village—these concerns and many others are part of everyday life in even the most isolated U.S. community.

Examining Community Concerns

Teachers must be seen by the community as responsible adults who are working to improve educational opportunities of all children. They do not deserve to be treated as second-class citizens by the parents or community leaders. Their opinions and ideas should be valued, not dismissed. To create positive impressions and change negative ones, teachers have to be intimately involved in the decision making about what happens in schools and to students. Schools, according to Sarason (1990) "must be coequally accommodating to the development of teachers and students" (pp. 146–147). Consequently, how teachers interact with community members becomes very important.

183

Since demographics strongly impact schools, it is imperative for school personnel to study the demographics of their community. Knowledge of who is in the community can help teachers and administrators understand what they need to do to meet the needs of all their students along with serving the interests of the community.

Think and Act

- Contact the local Chamber of Commerce about the demographics of your community. Compare today's demographics with those of ten years ago. What differences are there? What do they mean for the schools?
- Travel throughout your community, making note of neighborhoods composed of specific ethnic or racial groups. Interview a long-time resident about the changes in the community over the years.
- Analyze the demographics of a school's Parents Advisory Board or a district's School Board. Is the board reflective of the community as a whole? How might its composition influence the advice given to the school or district?

Curriculum Issues

Some parents or other community adults can object to part of the curriculum adopted by the local school, whether it is a reading program, a mathematics series, or even extracurricular activities. They find certain books the students are expected to read or the sequence of the mathematics curriculum or the lack of certain extra-curricular activities as not satisfactory. The reasons for parental objections may be related to their own schooling experiences, what they value as appropriate education, or personal religious beliefs. For instance, some Hispanic parents protest against bilingual programs for their children, believing that the children will learn English better if they are put in immersion programs.

For religious reasons, some parents object to having their children read certain books, say the Pledge of Allegiance, or participate in musical, theatrical, or sports events at a school. Often the science curriculum is a target for certain religious groups that oppose the teaching of controversial topics such as reproduction or evolution. The insistence by several conservative Christian organizations to present arguments for creationism along with or in place of evolution has influenced curricular choices and textbook content across the nation. Other religious groups have protested the Christian orientation of the school calendar. Attendance policies have been changed in many schools to accommodate absences of students participating in religious observances, and some spring and winter breaks have been altered to be more sensitive to non-Christians within communities.

The increased mobility of individuals and groups has resulted in a growing demand for some sort of standardized curriculum. Without at least a standardized year-by-year curriculum for core subjects in the middle and high school, students who move from another state, district, or even school might end up repeating and/or skipping huge blocks of content. For example, by eleventh grade Jennifer, author Brown's daughter, had experienced three years of ancient civilizations and no modern European history. Nationally, some citizens support the idea of students everywhere receiving the same basic education as part of being American. The difficulty, of course, is getting districts and states to agree on what this basic curriculum should be. Historically, individual communities have had a great deal of influence in what is taught in their district schools.

Parents or caregivers might also be looking for subjects they were taught, such as geography and spelling, and for the same instructional methods they had experienced. They do not always recognize or appreciate developmentally appropriate learning such as hands-on activities and integrated thematic units, seeing them as frivolous playing rather than studious work. When they find the programs different, concerned adults might try to influence the schools to change.

Financial Issues

Community members may not support tax increases needed to improve facilities or programs for the students. This may be particularly true with the high percentage of retirees in a community. Many retirees move to an area because the tax structure is more conducive to persons on limited income. Some resent having to pay higher taxes for services they feel they do not need. Although this was more common in the past twenty years than today, it can still pose a problem for the schools.

Responding to Community Concerns

Knowing potential areas of contention within the community and the major concerns of community stakeholders gives school administrators and teachers the opportunity to respond in a variety of ways. Proactively, information can be provided explaining potentially confusing or controversial curricular and instructional issues. School focus groups and open forums can be held before plans are put into action. Reactively, meetings of all types can be called immediately when situations become volatile. In a Pennsylvania district, panel discussions on racial tensions that led to specific action plan steps worked to defuse an irate crowd and eventually to improve racial relationships.

Beyond studying the community, teachers need to become involved in the community, contributing to the community as a concerned citizen and a spokesperson for school improvement. Meeting local leaders and attending local events is one way to get involved. Another way is to become active in community projects or organizations as a volunteer. For preservice teachers, such volunteering provides valuable community background information not available through the typical classroom field experiences.

Think and Act

- Check the education sections of the local newspapers for controversial curriculum issues in the past months. Were these resolved? How? Were all stakeholders satisfied? What alternative solutions can you offer?
- Attend a community forum or public meeting about a local issue. Take notes to compare your perspective to newspaper reports. Interview several audience members after the meeting.

Finding Community Support

The community in which the school is located must be nurtured in order to engage community members in school activities and education goals. If the school is already being used as a community center, then some ties with the community have already been established (see Chapter 8). Beyond that, teachers and administrators must become proactive in gaining community support for the schools. They must reach out to the community and ask them for their help and support. This places teachers and administrators in roles they have not necessarily been trained for—entrepreneurs. Communities have a richness of support for schools. They have both financial and personnel resources that can be used to enhance learning and activities at schools.

Most often financial resources have already been tapped with respect to athletic events. The local hamburger hangouts, the grocery stores, or an insurance agency advertise in the athletic bulletin or program, buy lights for the athletic field or the scoreboard, or supply uniforms for the students. Sometimes musical or theatrical events find sponsors within the community. Getting local businesses and organizations involved in charitable donations for the school is only a start, however.

Until recently, community people have usually not been tapped to support academic programs. Perhaps in the past administrators, school boards, and teachers thought it unwise to let the community know that they were in need of resources for their academic programs. Today there should be no hesitancy if educators truly believe in having everyone support the educational goals of the school and community. With the increased understanding on the part of educators in the important roles played by parents, caregivers, families, and other community members in students' success or failure in schools, there must be increased encouragement and even pursuit of support outside the school.

The requests can start small, such as asking persons to serve as tutors to young people, helping students to learn to read or do math. Other possibilities are using some of the expertise within the community to help teach some classes, particularly specialized classes in some of the vocational programs or the highly skilled subjects. Local university professors might be willing to set up special afterschool interest groups in areas such as photography and communications, computer skills, advanced mathematics, art, dance, or theater production. Maybe developing a volunteer group who can serve as assistants or even substitutes for teachers would be a way to get community people involved.

Connecting with Community Expertise and Leadership

Community leaders can be welcomed assets to any school or they can become a major stumbling block in making schools successful. To have them work positively with the schools is preferable to having them work against the schools. Treating these leaders as valuable resources for helping schools do their jobs is an important consideration for teachers.

Teachers should think of community leaders as their allies and as valuable resources to use in their classrooms. They need to know when and how to most effectively use these individuals in their programs and classes. For example, a teacher may ask persons from the various ethnic groups to speak to the class about their cultures and beliefs, their interests and goals, and their hopes and expectations for the future. The guests may be asked how these beliefs affect their perceptions of some major issue within the community, such as the implementation of the death penalty for capital crimes in the state, the taxing of liquor and cigarettes for school improvement, or a state lottery for education funding. These sharing sessions should not provide any individual a platform for preaching or indoctrination but should be used to inform and to help students understand how different people view issues through different lenses.

Religious Groups

Schools are allowed to teach about religion, but not to teach a religion. In order to build understanding, however, students should be exposed to the various religious practices within their community. These religious beliefs and customs can be studied where students work daily with individuals of other faiths. Religious leaders could be asked to form a panel discussion for a social studies class or for a school assembly. Having an open meeting in the evenings inviting parents might be appropriate. Knowledge is a powerful tool to change behavior and attitude. The schools are a place where knowledge should be explored and understood.

One teacher in a middle school in Central Florida used religious leaders, doctors, and parents to help her understand how she could effectively teach the Sunshine State Standards on Health Education to her students. She was particularly concerned about offending the students or their parents since some of the content touched on highly sensitive issues with respect to sexually transmitted diseases, reproduction, and nutrition. The community in which she was teaching had large numbers of African Americans, Muslims, and Hispanics. She asked religious leaders, doctors, and parents from each of the ethnic groups to come to separate focus group meetings to help her with her teaching. At these meetings, which were held in locations they had suggested, the participants discussed what they thought health education ought to be in middle school and shared their ideas with respect to the required state curriculum. Most of the participants did not disagree with the topics, but provided suggestions to the teacher on how to handle the topics in the classroom. Some of the suggestions were separating boys and girls when certain topics were to be discussed; explaining dietary restrictions with respect to religious beliefs; and adding some categories to those already part of the curriculum, specifically diseases such as high blood pressure, high cholesterol, diabetes, sickle cell anemia, alcoholism, and stress. The groups were very supportive of the teacher and were appreciative of her asking for their input. They were pleased that she was searching for ways to teach the curriculum without compromising the religious and cultural beliefs of her students (Albright, 1999).

Think and Act

- In a small team, talk to a religious leader whose beliefs are different from yours and ask him or her about issues such as teenage pregnancy, abortion, divorce, HIV/AIDS, etc. and how to deal with these issues in a public school setting.
- Compare findings with other teams who interviewed leaders of other faiths.
- Research religious community centers, finding out what services they provide for their members.

Ethnic/Racial Groups

Ethnic and racial groups with a fairly substantial presence in the community often have either a community center or leaders who are active locally and nationally. For instance, NAACP (the National Association for the Advancement of Colored People), a long-standing institution, has chapters in virtually every town, city, or district with a Black population. Contacts through school parents, social service organizations, or religious leaders can reach groups that are not so well known. Fruitful meetings with the elders and other leaders to share information or concerns will show a willingness to listen and take advice. Attending recommended meetings or events is another way to demonstrate genuine interest.

Think and Act

- Prepare a calendar of local ethnic and racial meetings and events. Plan with a small group to attend one listing a month. Compare notes on what is learned.
- Discuss the findings with your contact people to verify the information.

Social Services

Social service organizations in towns, cities, or districts have other possibilities for expertise to be shared. Generally speaking, these groups have an obligation to publicize their services. Often a telephone call to the local organizations will result in a wealth of free brochures, booklets, and other materials. Visits to or speakers from the organizations can sometimes be arranged.

Other Special Interest Groups

Leaders of local special interest groups or branches of larger nonprofit organizations offer excellent sources of information and experiences to students. Most common national groups also have Internet sites that can be explored. The American Diabetes Association and the Juvenile Diabetes Foundation, for instance, have walkathons in the fall to support their research. Teams of students can recruit participants and donors in the area. Spokespersons from the organizations can be invited to the school to explain the disease, the research, and the specialized medical equipment such as the insulin pump. Spokespersons for the hearing impaired or visually impaired can provide multiple perspectives related to living and learning in the community.

Other independent organizations with local branches provide students with opportunities for community involvement. For example, Charles Schulz, cartoonist of the famous "Peanuts," was very supportive of a program called Canine Companions for Independence (CCI). This group trains dogs, mostly golden retrievers and Labradors, to become assistance dogs for persons with disabilities. Having a puppy trainer with the puppy in training demonstrate to children how these dogs are trained to help persons in daily living tasks can make a tremendous impression. Children learn cognitively about modern methods of coping with disabilities while they experience affectively the relationships of dogs and people. Children can become enthusiastic about the program, sharing with their parents what they experienced. In some cases, children might encourage their parents to become puppy trainers. The caring so evident in the puppy trainers transfers readily to children.

Although controversial in many schools, afterschool groups for teenage lesbians and gays are appearing as extracurricular activities. In some communities, the local gay/lesbian community rather than teachers in the school sponsor these groups. The intention, contrary to what the opponents of these groups would want people to believe, is not to promote gay/lesbian activity, but to help young teenagers who proclaim to be gay or lesbian deal with the challenges of having an alternative lifestyle. Forming groups in high schools to deal with sexual orientation issues may prove helpful to children and adults alike in understanding differences in people.

Community leaders can be very helpful in sensitizing students to the needs and interests of others such as the elderly. Having secondary students participate in programs such as Meals on Wheels and Respite Care will help them develop a better appreciation for the contributions the elderly have made to their community. Spokespersons from groups such as the AARP or the Veterans of Foreign Wars

(VFW) might meet with students and share with them some of their adventures, successes, and failures. These personal historical glimpses can give students valuable lessons of how the privileges they often take for granted were developed and fought for over the years.

Think and Act

- Examine the social service resources within your community to determine who can be helpful to you in developing an understanding of the diversity within your community.
- What do you know about alternative lifestyles within your community? Do any support groups exist? If so, interview an officer or member about the challenges faced in the community.
- Volunteer to work in a setting where you are interacting with a special needs person (disabled, elderly, second-language learner, etc.). Keep a journal about what you learned from that person.

Considering School–Business Connections

Strong influences on schools in many communities today are the local businesses. What is taught or not taught can be affected through a variety of arrangements such as partnerships that businesses establish with schools. In some cases, business employers are looking for ready employees and want students to graduate from high school with specific training in skills the businesses need, thus enabling companies to hire the students without having to train them. In other cases, businesses want students to graduate from high school with excellent reading, writing, and mathematics skills and are not as concerned about specific vocational skills. They would prefer to train the students to the specifics of their company. Regardless of their specific employee needs, businesses are now realizing the importance of their own involvement in the local schools.

Partnerships can be developed for the purpose of supplying material goods to the schools. Many businesses frequently replace current technologies with new technologies. In some communities, schools profit from these upgrades by being the recipients of the computers and other technologies the businesses no longer need. Giving computers to schools works positively for both the schools and the businesses. The businesses get a tax advantage and the schools get equipment they perhaps could not afford. With new equipment also comes the opportunity for adult and student training.

In one community in Central Florida, local businesses and industries donate unused office supplies to an organization called "A Gift for Teachers." This organization was started by a local business person who realized that companies were throwing away usable supplies. It collects the materials and makes them available for teachers from schools in low socioeconomic areas. Teachers of those schools get a day at the organization's store to pick up materials they need for their children. Some businesses have also purchased materials for "A Gift for Teachers" to help schools provide supplies to the children who cannot afford to purchase them.

Partnerships can also involve the volunteering of personnel to help the school. Businesses more and more are asking their personnel to volunteer in local organizations, including schools. Using individuals as reading buddies or as big brothers and sisters to students needing extra adult attention is one possibility. Businesses can be also encouraged to participate in Career Days and give advice to students about job opportunities and required training for those jobs. Perhaps job shadowing can be arranged or apprenticeships offered to help students decide what they want to be when they grow up.

One excellent model for school–business partnerships is the Corporate Internship Program operating in Cleveland, Ohio, and now being developed in Portland, Oregon. Students in an urban Catholic high school are expected to work at a local corporation one full day a week as entry-level employees. A team of five students receives for the school the salary of the one employee they replace. The money pays for the costs of the program and the financing of the students' tuition. Students benefit from the job experience, learning the specific skills of the position along with the more subtle understanding of corporate culture.

One caution that must be addressed by teachers and administrators is exactly what influence businesses have on the schools. Companies that contribute computers to a school, for instance, often expect to get free advertising in school publications or on school walls. Sometimes companies promise equipment for receipts of purchased goods. Certain corporations provide lesson plans using their materials or food goods. Crayola and M & M experiments are commonplace in elementary classrooms. The extreme emphasis on consumerism, as exemplified by the U.S. market economy and business interests, contrasts with global concepts such as conserving natural resources. Schools must be careful not to buy into the mentality of such business interests just because they are given equipment or volunteers. In many ways, obvious and not so obvious, the economic power of local businesses in a community can affect decisions made in schools.

Think and Act

- Select a school within your community. Find out what type of business partnerships exist at that school, if any. What is the purpose of the partnership and how effective is the partnership in meeting that purpose?
- Speak to some local business people and see how interested they may be in forming something like "A Gift for Teachers" in their community. What do they see to be the advantages and disadvantages of such a program?
- Hold a debate or panel discussion about business influence in the schools.
- Inspect the school for business advertising or logos. How can teachers counteract any pervasive influence of business interests?

Becoming Politically Active

Schools can be overgoverned by federal, state, and local hegemonies. Asking local and state government officials to participate in school programs, however, serves as an information strategy that will, at least, guide some of their decision making with respect to the schools. As Seymour Sarason (1990) indicated in *The Predictable Failure of Educational Reform*, business executives and governmental officials believe that if good business management and organizational strategies are applied to the schools, then schools can improve to meet the expectations of the government and the public. This business model assumes many false similarities between business and schools, with students becoming some sort of factory product to be finished off.

Often business people and government officials have no idea of the complexity of education or how schools operate and within what parameters they must operate. Before the business leaders can positively engage in school improvement, they need to have intensive instruction in public education. They need to know and understand the challenges faced by the teachers and the students on a daily basis. The same holds true for most politicians, as they usually arise from the corporate world, not the educational world, and the rules are different when it comes to public education.

Educators need to become politically active. This is a new role for them, one previously frowned upon as inappropriate; after all, educators were expected to be neutral in the political arena. Today, being neutral is asking for disaster to happen. In order to educate the politicians, educators can hold town hall meetings where teachers, parents, administrators, and students can share their concerns and issues. Individual invitations need to be made to the local politicians encouraging them to attend the meetings. Failure of the local politicians to attend such information sessions in this age of education would be proof that educational issues are not a major concern of the politician. Working with the media is one way to make sure politicians get recognized for their participation or nonparticipation in meetings about educational issues.

Some schools and school districts do not want their problems aired in public. Without the information being publicly available, however, there is no way to keep everyone informed of the problems until the schools get a failing "report card." For example, in some school districts, there has not been enough money to maintain the schools. All monies are already spent on teachers' salaries, textbooks, administrative salaries, transportation costs, and so on, and no monies are now available to keep computers operational, to keep classrooms or bathrooms clean, to keep cafeteria equipment fixed, or other such needs. Materials for so-called extras such as music classes and art classes are nonexistent. The only people who learned about this drastic situation were the parents whose children attend those schools.

If teachers and principals cannot make their case before state legislators, they cannot expect to get things changed. Governors and legislators like to tinker with education. They like to be associated with being the supporters of education, but they rarely understand how their uninformed decisions affect the very schools they vow to improve. Particularly in this time of shrinking public responsibility, educators must speak out and must become activists for the schools and the children who attend them. Educators must nurture, inform, and direct legislators at all levels about the realities of teaching in today's schools.

Teachers accepting the moral responsibility to protect all their students might be forced to become more politically active than they wish. For example, to defend the rights of gays, lesbians, and bisexuals in schools, even to ensure the fundamental right of safety for these individuals, might make some teachers uncomfortable. Yet it is their responsibility to make schools safe havens for every student, not just those with mainstream lifestyles.

In the 2000 elections, Oregon voters very narrowly defeated Measure 9, a measure to prohibit the instruction in the schools of any alternative lifestyles. The measure was so vaguely written that passage of such a ruling could have meant teachers and school personnel were legally restricted from talking about AIDS, welcoming gay parents into the school, or even counseling gay students. Many educators had no idea how close this measure was to passing or what the implications might have meant to their roles as supportive adults for all students. Yet most teachers realize that harassment of gay students is commonplace, to the point that the term "fag" can be regularly heard on even elementary playgrounds. Fortunately, some teachers' groups did participate in fighting against the measure.

Other political action can take the form of civic work. The Clean River Plan from the Environmental Services in the city of Portland, Oregon, is an example of a municipal project for improving a river and its neighborhoods. A leaflet about the Community Benefit Opportunity calls for proposals from individual citizens and citizen groups, listing proposal criteria such as "enhances community livability and protects the environment" and "helps solve an identified community problem" (Environmental Services City of Portland, 2000). Classes and schools could brainstorm ideas, then put together and submit several proposals fitting the criteria. If projects are not currently in progress, classes could develop their own. For instance, one fourth-grade class in New York investigated the pollution of the town river and its recreational riverbank lands. They tested the water for pollutants, checked the local usage of the surrounding lands, and organized community cleanup days for the riverbanks.

Think and Act

■ Prepare an outline of the major points you would like to share with local legislators about your school. Which of these points do you think would be new or startling information?

(continued)

- Ask a local legislator to talk to you about what is and is not working in the local schools. How much does he or she know about the challenges the schools are facing with respect to achievement of students? How accurate are his or her perceptions?
- Investigate district, state, and national teacher organizations. Find out about their positions toward candidates and issues of the 2000 elections. How active were these groups in promoting their political stands?
- Contact Southern Poverty Law Center (1999) (www.splcenter.org) for its brochure, *Ten Ways to Fight Hate.*

Helping to Transform the Community

New Concept of Community Education

The new concept of community education goes beyond the use of the school as a community center such as mentioned in Chapter 8. The broader concept deals with community empowerment to cause social change. The school might or might not be used as the center of the action, but school personnel often serve as catalysts attempting community improvement in addition to school improvement (Minzey & LeTarte, 1994). Some of the concepts behind this type of program involve community empowerment, community problem solving, and community lifelong learning (Denton, 1998; Mathews, 1996).

If the community education program is indeed broader than the typical school as community center plan, then a wide range of services and activities can be incorporated under its umbrella. The initiatives might involve local health needs such as a clinic, dentistry services, eye care, and prenatal and postnatal classes along with the more traditional daycare and before and after school supervision. There can be activities for children and youth including teen clubs, day camps, and youth leadership training programs that lead to summer employment placements. There can be ongoing multiage activities such as dance, choir, art, and gardening. There can also be academic courses, such as those helping adults to achieve a GED. The possibilities depend upon the interests and the needs of the community.

The Tangelo Park Pilot Project in Florida is a unique example of a combined partnership between a hotelier, a public school system, a local university, a local hospital, a public television station, the YMCA, the civic association, and a local church. With the help of Harris Rosen, the hotelier, the project was developed providing a safety net for the community deemed "at risk." Through Rosen's efforts, every 2-, 3-, and 4-year-old will have an opportunity to attend preschool at no cost. The parents and caregivers of these children will have the chance to take parenting and vocational classes while their children are at school at no cost. Every Tangelo Park student graduating from high school who is accepted by a vocational school, community college, or university will be provided tuition, room and board, and living expenses at no cost.

Mr. Rosen also provides support by organizing several agencies for the community. An avid fund raiser, he solicits support and program assistance from the Orlando private sector. Monthly, he works directly with the public schools, the university and the hospital, the YMCA, and other groups to plan for the community. An interactive shared decision-making model is used to develop programs and solve problems within the community.

With the impetus from the mothers in the community, drug trafficking and criminal activities have diminished. The Y has become the hub of the community. The Urban Teaching Residency program was started in Tangelo Park Elementary School and its recipient school, Dr. Phillips High School. Teachers in these schools work directly with university faculty members (including the second author) to become effective urban teachers. Parent Leadership Training has been provided by the university to help the parents learn how to be effective parents and to learn how to fight for their children. Daycare centers have also been established in private homes, helped by the elementary school to ensure proper early childhood education.

Although few communities are lucky enough to find a Mr. Rosen, his gift of financial support is only one part of what he does. He is truly a catalyst, bringing together many communities services and leaders and persuading them to act on the behalf of the community members. Once revitalized, the various agencies have taken responsibility for a wide range of programs directly affecting the children and their families.

New Role for Teachers

This new approach to school–community involvement means a transformation in the way many teachers look at community concerns. Too often teachers have viewed such problems as individual responsibilities; that is, the persons involved are the main contributors to their disadvantaged situations. From this approach, teachers then see the problems as solvable through clinical casework rehabilitating the individual adults and families. The new approach emphasizes the environmental and social aspects of the problems; that is, social and political policies and practices are main contributors to the situations. From this second approach, teachers then see the importance of civic action. They can work at the causes rather than the symptoms; they can treat the clients as victims of circumstances; and they can encourage long-term solutions.

With such a community education program, teachers have a dual responsibility. Within the school, they need to rethink their attitude toward the social workers, counselors, nurses, and psychologists as part of the preventive team for planning and decision making rather than as the support staff to be called in times of crises. Collaborative work is necessary. Teachers have to be open to sharing their classrooms and their schools more equitably to meet the needs of their students.

Outside of the school, teachers must be ready to work with community leaders beyond the traditional leaders of the past. If they believe that involving others from outside the school only leads to conflict and confusion, then they are going to be resistant to change (Kowalski, 1997). They need to recognize and support individuals willing to act positively, even if these individuals seem to them to have limited leadership skills, less education, or fewer resources. In essence, this participation is a form of critical pedagogy.

Teachers can serve as facilitators by sharing their leadership and organizational expertise. They also can serve as advisors for students who wish to do service learning projects in the community. Above all, they can serve as encouragers of other community members, empowering them to take active roles in projects and programs. In *The Politics of Education* and numerous other works, Paulo Freire (1985) stresses the importance of meaningful dialogue for change making. For adult literacy programs, he suggests that initial words be those directly related to the lived experiences of the oppressed people. Thus, while they discuss reading and language they also talk about their social, economic, and political realities: "What is important is that the person learning words be consistently engaged in a critical analysis of the social framework in which men exist" (p. 57). At the same time, Freire recommends that those who see people in poverty as "marginal, intrinsically wicked and inferior" have the

> profitable experience of discussing the slum situation with slum dwellers themselves. . . . They might even end up realizing that if intrinsic evil exists it is part of the structures, and that it is the structures that need to be transformed. (p. 56)

In essence, both groups need to learn from each other—the one, skills that will empower, and the other, understanding that will enlighten and activate. Community members gain from what teachers offer as expertise in pedagogy and leadership, but teachers gain new perspectives on the institution of education and the need for true reform. The application of multicultural and global education at this level shows the transformative power of its vision.

Think and Act

- Read one of Paulo Freire's books or several of his articles. How does what he advocates fit in with Banks's transformative curriculum?
- Research the new concept of community education programs. Compare these to what is being done in local communities. Check for models and examples nationally.
- Investigate community centers and services. Volunteer to work on a program or project of special interest to you.
- Help to organize a service learning project for your classmates or your students. Work with community leaders to make the project more than a one-day or short-term involvement.

Exploring Larger Communities

The Interconnected World

Although this chapter focuses primarily on the school community, the larger communities of state, region, nation, and the world deserve mention as well. Today, even the most isolated communities in the United States do not escape the influence of the greater world around them. Already established community connections with state, regional, national, and international individuals and institutions offer exciting learning opportunities for students and teachers. With the expansion of Internet usage in the schools, new links have opened up huge sources for information and communication. Student benefits from active involvement with other peoples directly relate to all multicultural and global applications, especially understanding and experiencing the global society and its interrelatedness and interdependence.

For a person-to-person approach, contacts can be made and extended with individuals living around the world. One initial contact method could be through the extended families of students in the class or school. This activity has the added benefit of honoring the families and heritages of the students, especially if other locations and countries are involved. Studies of those locations can be based on information provided by the sources. Other possibilities might be found through such organizations as Global TeachNet, a professional development network for K–12 global educators started by the National Peace Corps Association (www.rpcv. org/globaled). One intriguing example of a correspondence between a truck driver and a geography class reported how the students tracked Buddy's travels and how Buddy urged his "Buddies" to finish their education even though he had not (Freedman et al., 1999). In the elementary grades especially, thematic interdisciplinary units can be built around personal contacts.

At the secondary level, more complex and controversial issues challenge students and teachers to wrestle with real-life global connections and concerns. For example, students could research the African Ancestry website to debate controversies such as GNA-based testing for African Americans to trace their heritages back to regions in Africa or the buying-back of slaves movement sponsored by Christian Solidarity International (www.africanancestry.com; www.BET.com).

The simple sharing of information and artifacts with other locations is another method of developing an understanding of how interconnected the world really is. Some U.S. towns and cities have paired or twinned with other places nationally or internationally. Natural connections such as size, main industries, geographic location (near a river, for instance), or name might be the inspiration for the pairing. If the community already has arranged such a pairing, students can explore ways to extend and strengthen the bonds. If not, students might approach community officials asking them to consider the possibilities. Related activities could involve preparing a proposal for twinning, establishing criteria for selection, and then researching and nominating potential candidates.

Think and Act

■ Obtain a copy of *Cable in the Classroom*, then select and tape a program related to a multicultural or global issue. If copies are not already provided free to the district schools by the local cable company, research and prepare a proposal for the school board and the cable company.

■ Search the Yellow Pages for local businesses that most likely have national and international contacts. Write letters asking the companies for preliminary information.

■ Collect names and addresses of worldwide contacts maintained by class members and their families. Prepare a class newsletter explaining the project and asking for short stories, photographs of families and surroundings, or small artifacts. Develop a class website with an e-mail link so contacts can use this option.

■ Check with municipal officials about the possibility of your community pairing with another community. Plan action steps for the project.

The Interdependent World

One common introduction lesson to exploring locally examples of worldwide interdependence is a class search of the places of origins of local consumer goods. Simple projects can be checking the tags of students' clothing and supplies. More extended projects can include writing letters to local manufacturers and their suppliers, interviewing the personnel responsible for purchasing materials, mapping the routes of raw and finished products, and making production timelines. Local business people could be invaluable sources for manufacturing, wholesale, and retail data. Small businesses especially might reveal more personal worldwide contacts, such as relatives in home countries who supply goods imported into the United States.

A more theoretical approach initially could be the selection of a world problem such as famine, drought, or child labor for intensive research. In the elementary grades, typical units include types of pollution and the destruction of forests worldwide. These can also be studied from a local community viewpoint, providing more concrete examples needed for younger children. For instance, elementary children can investigate and problem-solve the littering of their school grounds or a neighborhood playground as an example of thinking globally and acting locally. Older students also benefit from relating more intricate world problems to their own lives, so global concerns such as the spread of the Sahara Desert can be tied to more community related concerns like urban sprawl and the destruction of agricultural land.

Another approach is to look for a concrete event connected to a persistent global problem. For instance, students can study the Seattle protest of the meeting of the World Trade Organization (WTO). Students can research several websites, including that of WTO (www.wto.org), the International Forum on Globalization (www.ifg.org), and the Third World Network (www.twnside.org.sg). One curriculum (www.washington.edu/wto/classroom) recommended by Wayne Au (2000) in *Rethinking Schools* provides lesson plans with multiple perspectives on WTO.

Having students research and interview the different stakeholders of local controversial issues also helps to give insight into similar problems faced worldwide. For instance, in Oregon the damming or undamming of rivers could incorporate spokespeople and promotional materials from the lumber and fishing industries, construction companies, conservation groups, Native American populations, state and national park services, and all levels of governments. Parallels can be drawn to the Republic of China's recent decision to dam the Yangtze River at the historical and scenic Three Gorges or to the United Arab Republic's 1960 decision to dam the Nile River and flood its historical Aswan site. Students seeing similar crucial decisions being made in other countries over the years will develop an enriched understanding of the difficulties facing their community and communities worldwide.

As mentioned earlier in Chapter 5, The Curriculum, care must be taken to investigate all problems from a wide variety of perspectives. If the examples they study are concrete and meaningful enough, even young children can understand that solutions to complex problems are not easy to find. *Global Perspectives for Educators* (Diaz et al., 1999) and *Preparing Teachers to Teach Global Perspectives* (Merryfield et al., 1997) are excellent references for teachers who need more specific information about issues and examples. Chapter 5 provides other suggestions for exploring the larger communities through the curriculum.

Finally, state, regional, national, and international organizations for teachers and students have personal contacts, professional journals and newsletters, and curriculum materials available. One of the most valuable resources for teachers and students interested in multicultural and global education is the National Association for Multicultural Education. Members are primarily educators, but membership is not limited to the public and private schools and universities. Multicultural education trainers for corporations and institutions also attend and participate in regional and national conferences. Membership includes NAME's official journal, *Multicultural Perspectives*.

Think and Act

- Tour the local grocery store or specialty food store for international products. Ask the produce department manager about arrangements for selections and deliveries. Ask about price comparisons of the same product from local, national, and international sources.
- Look for local water or land usage arguments and research parallels worldwide.
- Research NAME website (http://www.umd.edu/NAME) for general information about the organization. Check out its definitions, mission statement, and special interest strands. What information is available on global education?

Conclusion

Teachers have wonderful resources available in their local communities and beyond. Working with individuals and groups to develop these resources can be time-consuming, but the rewards are well worth the effort. Teachers and schools can no longer afford to be isolated from their local and greater communities. The world of today reaches into the classroom even if the teacher has tried to close the door. Effective teachers realize the importance of allies in educating their students. They understand that they alone cannot possibly provide all the resources and information necessary to lead their students toward active participation in the local and global societies. In this information age, collaboration is vital.

REFERENCES

Adams, M., Bell, L., & Griffin, P. (1997). *Teaching for diversity and social justice.* New York: Routledge.

Ahlquist, R. (1992). Manifestations of inequality: Overcoming resistance in a multicultural foundations course. In C. Grant (Ed.), *Research and multicultural education: From the margins to the mainstream* (pp. 89–105). London: Falmer.

Albright, A. (1999). *School health education: Perceptions of African Americans, Hispanics, and Muslims.* Unpublished doctoral dissertation, The University of Central Florida, Orlando.

American Association of University Women (AAUW). (1992). *How schools shortchange girls.* Washington, DC: Author.

———. (1993). *Hostile hallways: The AAUW survey on sexual harassment in America's schools.* Washington, DC: Author.

Apple, M. W. (1996). *Cultural politics and education.* New York: Teachers College Press.

———. (2000). Remembering capital: On the connections between French fries and education. In F. W. Parkay & G. Hass (Eds.), *Curriculum planning: A contemporary approach* (7th ed., pp. 77–85). Boston: Allyn and Bacon.

Ashworth, M. (1988). *Blessed with bilingual brains.* Vancouver, Canada: The Pacific Educational Press.

Association for Supervision and Curriculum Development. (1996). *Redesigning assessment portfolios* [Video]. ASCD.

Au, W. (2000). Teaching about the WTO. *Rethinking Schools, 14*(3): 4–5.

Bailey, L. (1999). Exploring the integration of historical fiction and U.S. history in the eighth grade curriculum. *Curriculum and Teaching Dialogue, 1* (1), 3–9.

Baloche, L. A. (1998). *The cooperative classroom: Empowering learning.* Upper Saddle River, NJ: Prentice Hall.

Banks, J. A. (1991). *Teaching strategies for ethnic studies.* Boston: Allyn and Bacon.

———. (1994a). *An introduction to multicultural education.* Boston: Allyn and Bacon.

———. (1994b). *Multiethnic education: Theory and practice* (3rd ed.). Boston: Allyn and Bacon.

———. (1997). *Educating citizens in a multicultural society.* New York: Teachers College Press.

Beck, T., & Leishman, E. (1996–7). Will plants drink green water? *Educational Leadership, 54* (4): 56–59.

Bennett, C. I. (1999). *Comprehensive multicultural education: Theory and practice* (4th ed.). Boston: Allyn and Bacon.

Bishop, K. D., Jubala, K. A., Stainback, W., & Stainback, S. (1996). Facilitating friendships. In S. Stainback & W. Stainback (Eds.), *Inclusion: A guide for educators* (pp. 155–69). Baltimore, MD: Paul H. Brookes Publishing.

Boyle-Baise, M., & Grant, C. A. (1992). Multicultural teacher education: A proposal for change. In H. Waxman, J. de Felix, J. Anderson, & H. Baptiste, Jr. (Eds.), *Students at risk in at-risk schools: Improving environments for learning.* Newbury Park, CA: Corwin Press.

Brislin, R. W., Cushner, K., Cherrie, C., & Yong, M. (1986). *Intercultural interactions: A practical guide.* Newbury Park, CA: Sage.

Brooks, J., & Brooks, M. (1993). *In search of understanding: The case for constructivist classrooms.* Alexandria, VA: Association for Supervision and Curriculum Development.

Brown, S. C. (1993). *Application of multicultural and global concepts in senior elementary interns' classrooms.* Unpublished doctoral dissertation, University of Central Florida, Orlando.

Brown, S. C., Kysilka, M. L., & Warner, M. J. (1996). Applying constructivist theory to multicultural education content. In M. Kompf, R. Bond, D. Dworet, & R. T. Boak (Eds.), *Changing research and practice: Teachers' professionalism, identities and knowledge* (pp. 167–174). Washington, DC: Falmer Press.

Brown, S. C., Mir, C., & Warner, M. (1996). Improving teacher practice utilizing curriculum theory: A conversation with William Schubert. *The Educational Forum, 60*(4): 343–348.

Bruner, J. (1996). *The culture of education*. Cambridge, MA: Harvard University Press.

Butler, T. P. (2001). Bridging the digital divide. *Cable in the Classroom, 11*(1): 6–9.

Caine, R., & Caine, G. (1994). *Making connections: Teaching and the human brain*. Reading, MA: Addison-Wesley.

———. (1997). *Education on the edge of possibility*. Alexandria, VA: Association for Supervision and Curriculum Development.

Caiola, J. (1996). *Teaching respect for all* [video]. (Available from GLSTN, 122 W. 26th St., Suite 1100, New York, NY 10001)

Charles A. Dana Center. (1999). Hope for urban education: A study of nine high-performing, high poverty, urban elementary schools (executive summary). Austin, TX. Available on Internet at ed.gov/pubs/urbanhope/.

Charles, C. M. (1996). *Building classroom discipline* (5th ed.). White Plains, NY: Longman.

Chasnoff, D., & Cohen, H. S. (Producers). (1996). *It's elementary* [video]. (Available from Women's Educational Media, 2180 Bryant St., Suite 203, San Francisco, CA 94110)

———. (2000). *That's a family* [video]. (Available from Women's Educational Media, 2180 Bryant St., Suite 203, San Francisco, CA 94110)

Chiang, L. (1993). *Beyond the language: Native Americans' nonverbal communication*. (ERIC Document Reproduction Service No. ED368540)

Children in America's schools with Bill Moyers. (Sept. 13, 1996). PBS Special. Columbia, SC: SCETV.

Cole, D. J. (1984, Spring). Multicultural education and global education. A possible merger. *Theory into Practice, 23*(2), 151–154.

Cooper, A. (1992 Feb). *Student teacher self-assessment in multicultural education*. Paper presented at the annual conference of the National Association for Multicultural Education, Orlando.

Council on Interracial Books for Children. (1974). *10 quick ways to analyze children's books for racism and sexism*. New York: Council on Interracial Books for Children. (ERIC Document Reproduction Service No. ED 188 852)

Cushner, K. (1999). *Human diversity in action: Developing multicultural competencies for the classroom*. Boston: McGraw-Hill.

Cushner, K., McClelland, A., & Safford, P. (1992). *Human diversity in education: An integrative approach*. New York: McGraw-Hill.

Darling-Hammond, L. (1991). The implications of testing policy for quality and equity. *Phi Delta Kappan, 73*(3): 220–225.

———. (1997). *The right to learn: A blueprint for creating schools that work*. San Francisco: Jossey-Bass.

de Anda, D. (1997). *Controversial issues in multiculturalism*. Boston: Allyn and Bacon.

Delpit, L. (1995). *Other people's children: Cultural conflict in the classroom*. New York: The New Press.

Denton, W. (1998). Community education: On the forefront of educational reform? Part 1: The evolution of the movement. *Community Education Journal, 26*(1& 2): 28–34.

Dewey, J. (1916). *Democracy and education: An introduction to the philosophy of education*. New York: Macmillan.

Diaz, C. F., Massialas, B. G., & Xanthopoulos, J. A. (1999). *Global perspectives for educators*. Boston: Allyn and Bacon.

Dunn, R., Dunn, K., & Price, G. E. (1978). *Learning style inventory*. Lawrence, KS: Price Systems.

Environmental Services City of Portland. (2000). *Willamette River projects: Reducing combined sewer overflows*. PL 0025 revised 12–2000. Portland, Oregon: Environmental Services City of Portland.

Fadiman, A. (1997). *The spirit catches you and you fall down*. New York: The Noonday Press.

Fosnot, C. T. (Ed.). (1996). *Constructivism: Theory, perspectives, and practice*. New York: Teachers College Press.

Foxfire Fund. www.foxfire.org/foxfire.htm

Freedman, S. W., Simons, E. R., Kalnin, J. S., & Casareno, A. (1999). *Inside city schools: Investigating literacy in multicultural classrooms*. New York: Teachers College Press.

Freire, P. (1985). *The politics of education: Culture, power, and liberation*. New York: Bergin & Garvey.

————. (1998). *Teachers as cultural workers: Letters to those who dare to teach.* Boulder, CO: Westview Press.

García, E. (1994). *Understanding and meeting the challenge of student cultural diversity.* Boston: Houghton Mifflin.

Gardner, H. (1983). *Frames of mind: The theory of multiple intelligences.* New York: Basic Books.

————. (1997). *Beyond multiple intelligences.* Keynote speech at the annual meeting of the Association for Supervision and Curriculum Development, San Antonio, March 22–25.

Gay, G. (1985). Implications of selected models of ethnic identity development for educators. *Journal of Negro Education, 54:* 43–44.

————. (1994). *At the essence of learning: Multicultural education.* West Lafayette, IN: Kappa Delta Pi.

————. (2000). *Culturally responsive teaching: Theory, research, and practice.* New York: Teachers College Press.

George, J. C. (1983). *The talking earth.* New York: HarperCollins.

Gilluly, B., Jones-Mosley, S., & Bonar, S. (1996). *Deep cultural approach to multicultural education.* Brochure produced by Clark County School District, NV.

Giroux, H. A. (1996). *Fugitive cultures: race, violence, and youth.* New York: Routledge.

Glasser, W., & Dotson, K. L. (1998). *Choice theory in the classroom.* New York: HarperCollins.

Goleman, D. (1995). *Emotional intelligence: Why it can matter more than IQ for character, health, and lifelong achievement.* New York: Bantam.

Gollnick, D. M., & Chinn, P. C. (1998). *Multicultural education in a pluralistic society* (5th ed.). Upper Saddle River, NJ: Prentice Hall.

Gonzalez, R., Brusca-Vega, R., & Yawkey, T. (1997). *Assessment and instruction of culturally and linguistically diverse students with or at-risk of learning problems.* Boston: Allyn and Bacon.

Good, G., & Brophy, J. (1994). *Looking into classrooms* (6th ed.). New York: Harper & Row.

Grant, C. (Ed.) (1992). *Research and multicultural education: From the margins to the mainstream.* Washington, DC: Falmer Press.

Grant, C., & Sleeter, C. (1998). *Turning on learning: Five approaches for multicultural teaching plans for race, class, gender, and disability* (2nd ed.). New York: Macmillan.

Gregersen, H. B., & Black, J. S. (1990). A multifaceted approach to expatriate retention in international assignments. *Group and Organization Studies, 15*(4): 461–485.

Gregorc, A. (1985). *Gregorc style lineator.* Maynard, MA: Gabriel Systems.

Guild, P. B., & Garger, S. (1998). *Marching to different drummers* (2nd ed.). Alexandria, VA: Association for Supervision and Curriculum Development.

Hall, P. H., & Gudykunst, W. B. (1989). The relationship of perceived ethnocentrism in corporate cultures to the selection, training, and success of international employees. *International Journal of Intercultural Relations, 13:* 183–201.

Hanvey, R. (1976). *An attainable global perspective.* Denver, CO: Center for Teaching International Relations.

Hawley, S. (2000). *Revitalizing urban education.* Unpublished paper presentation at the annual meeting of the American Association for Teaching and Curriculum, October 5–7, in Alexandria, VA.

Henkin, R. (1998). *Who's invited to share? Using literacy to teach for equity and social justice.* Portsmouth, NH: Heinemann.

Hernández, H. (1997). *Teaching in multilingual classrooms: A teacher's guide to context, process, and content.* Upper Saddle River, NJ: Prentice Hall.

Hilliard, A. (1992). Behavioral style, culture, and teaching. *Journal of Negro Education, 61*(3): 370–77.

Hitzing, W. (1996) Support and positive teaching strategies. In S. Stainback & W. Stainback (Eds.), *Inclusion: A guide for educators* (pp. 313–326). Baltimore, MD: Paul E. Brookes Publishing.

Holliday, J. R. (2000). Survey says? *Teaching Tolerance, 17:* 50–51.

Howard, G. (1999). *We can't teach what we don't know: White teachers, multicultural schools.* New York: Teachers College Press.

Igoa, C. (1995). *The inner world of the immigrant child.* New York: St. Martin's Press.

Irvine, J. J. (1990). *Black students and school failure.* New York: Greenwood Press.

Irvine, J. J., & York, D. E. (1995). Learning styles and culturally diverse students: A literature review. In

J. Banks & C. Banks (Eds.), *Handbook of research on multicultural education* (pp. 484–497). New York: Macmillan.

Johnson, D., & Johnson, R. (1992). What to say to advocates for the gifted. *Educational Leadership, 50*(2): 44–47.

———. (1994). *Learning together and alone.* Boston: Allyn and Bacon.

———. (1995). *Reducing school violence through conflict resolution.* Alexandria, VA: Association for Supervision and Curriculum Development.

Johnson, D., Johnson, R., & Holubec, E. (1992). *Advanced cooperative learning.* Edina, MN: Interaction Books.

Johnson, L. (1995). *The girls in the back of the class.* New York: St. Martin's Press.

Joyce, B., & Weil, M. (1996). *Models of teaching* (5th ed). Boston: Allyn and Bacon.

King, M. L., Jr. (1991) I have a dream. In G. Skene (producer), *Great speeches of the 20th century* [cassette series]. Santa Monica, CA: Fhino Records, Inc.

Kirkwood, T. F. (1990). Global education as an agent for school change. In K. A. Tye (Ed.), *Global education: From thought to action* (pp. 142–56). Alexandria, VA: Association for Supervision and Curriculum Development.

———. (1991). *Implementation of global/cross-cultural awareness and understanding checklist.* Miami, FL: Dade County Public Schools.

Kniep, W. (1986). Defining a global education by its content. *Social Education, 50*(10): 137–66.

Kohn, A. (1998). *What to look for in a classroom . . . and other essays.* San Francisco: Jossey Bass.

Kowalski, T. J. (1997). School reform, community education, and the problem of institutional culture. *Community Education Journal, 25*(3 & 4): 5–8.

Kozol, J. (1991). *Savage inequalities: Children in America's schools.* New York: Crown.

———. (1995). *Amazing grace: The lives of children and the conscience of a nation.* New York: Crown Publishers.

Kysilka, M. L., & Biraimah, K. L. (1992). *The thinking teacher: Ideas for effective learning.* New York: McGraw-Hill.

Lee, Y., Jussim, L., & McCauley, C. (1995). *Stereotype accuracy: Toward appreciating group differences.* Washington, DC: American Psychological Association.

Lewin, L., & Shoemaker, B. J. (1998). *Great performance: Creating classroom-based assessment tasks.* Alexandria, VA: Association for Supervision and Curriculum Development.

Lickona, T (1996). *Character education: Restoring respect and responsibility in our schools.* [video]. National Professional Resources.

———. (1997). The teacher's role in character education. *Journal of Education, 179*(2): 63–80.

Lynch, J. (1992). *Education for citizenship in a multicultural society.* London, England: Cassell.

Lyons, E. (1992). *Letters from a slave girl: The story of Harriet Jacobs.* New York: Atheneum.

Marzano, R. J. (1993–1994). When two worldviews collide. *Educational Leadership, 51*(4): 6–11.

Mathews, D. (1996). Why we need to change our concept of community leadership. *Community Education Journal, 23*(1–2): 9–18.

Mathison, C., & Young, R. (1995). Constructivism and multicultural education: A mighty pedagogical merger. *Multicultural Education, 2*(4): 7–11.

Mayer, V. J. (1997) Earth systems education: A case study of a globally oriented science education program. In M. M. Merryfield, E. Jarchow, & S. Pickert (Eds.), *Preparing teachers to teach global perspectives* (pp. 25–54). Thousand Oaks, CA: Sage.

Mercer, J. (1989). Alternate paradigms for assessment in a pluralistic society. In J. Banks & C. Banks (Eds.), *Multicultural education: Issues and perspectives* (pp. 289–304). New York: Macmillan.

Merryfield, M. (1994). *Teacher education in global and international education.* Washington, DC: American Association of Colleges for Teacher Education.

Merryfield, M. M., Jarchow, E., & Pickert, S. (Eds.). (1997). *Preparing teachers to teach global perspectives.* Thousand Oaks, CA: Corwin Press.

Minzey, J., & LeTarte, C. (1994). *Reforming public schools through community education.* Dubuque: Kendall/Hunt.

Molnar, A. (1993–1994). Fundamental differences? *Educational Leadership, 51*(4): 4–5.

Monda-Amaya, L. E., & Pearson, P. D. (1996). Toward a responsible pedagogy for teaching and learning literacy. In M. C. Pugach & C. L. Warger (Eds.), *Curriculum trends, special education, and reform: Refocusing the conversation* (pp. 143–163). New York: Teachers College.

Montgomery, K. (2001). *Authentic assessment: A guide for elementary teachers.* New York: Longman.

Moyers, B. (1991). *Listening to America with Bill Moyers: Unequal education* [Film]. (Available from Films for the Humanities and Sciences)

Myers, I., & McCaulley, M. H. (1985). *Manual: A guide to the development and use of the Myers-Briggs Type Indicator.* Palo Alto, CA: Consulting Psychologists Press.

National Council for the Social Studies (NCSS). (1982). *Position statement on global education.* Washington, DC: Author.

Newmann, F. M. (1995). *Authentic pedagogy: Standards that boost student performance.* (ERIC Document Reproduction Service No. ED 390 906)

Nieto, S. (2000). *Affirming diversity: The sociopolitical context of multicultural education* (3rd ed.). New York: Longman.

Norton, D. E., & Norton, S. E. (1998). *Through the eyes of a child: An introduction to children's literature* (5th ed.). Upper Saddle River, NJ: Prentice Hall.

Nuby, J. F., & Oxford, R. L. (1998). Learning style preferences of Native American and African American secondary students. *Journal of Psychological Type, 44*: 5–19.

Ogbu, J. (1994). Racial stratification and education in the United States: Why inequality persists. *Teachers College Record, 96*(2): 264–298.

Orenstein, P. (1994). *SchoolGirls: Young women, self esteem, and the confidence gap.* New York. Doubleday.

Orlich, D. C., Harder, R. J., Callahan, R. C., & Gibson, H. W. (2001). *Teaching strategies: A guide to better instruction* (6th ed.). Boston: Houghton Mifflin.

Orozco, L. (Ed.). (1998). *Perspectives: Educating diverse populations.* Boulder, CO: Coursewise Publishing.

Pai, Y., & Adler, S. A. (2001). *Cultural foundations of education* (3rd ed.). Upper Saddle River, NJ: Merrill Prentice Hall.

Paige, R. M. (1993). *Education for the intercultural experience.* Yarmouth, ME: Intercultural Press.

Palazzo, D. (2000). *Silent no more: Concrete strategies for bringing lesbian, gay, bisexual and transgender content to school policy, curricula and programs.* Workshop at the annual conference of the National Association for Multicultural Education, November 17–19, Orlando.

Paley, V. G. (1993). *You can't say you can't play.* Cambridge, MA: Harvard University Press.

———. (1995). *Kwanzaa and me: A white teacher's story.* Cambridge, MA: Harvard University Press.

———. (1998). *The girl with the brown crayon.* Cambridge, MA: Harvard University Press.

Pang, V. O., & Barba, R. H. (1995). The power of culture: Building culturally affirming instruction. In C. A. Grant (Ed.), *Educating for diversity: An anthology of multicultural voices* (pp. 341–58). Boston: Allyn and Bacon.

Patton, J. (1992). Assessment and identification of African-American learners with gifts and talents. *Exceptional Children, 59*(2): 150–159

Peña, D. C. (1999). Mexican-American family involvement. *Kappa Delti Pi Record, 35*(4): 166–169.

Pipher, M. (1994). *Reviving Ophelia: Saving the selves of adolescent girls.* New York: Ballantine Books.

Porter, C., & Cleland, J. (1995). *The portfolio as a learning strategy.* Portsmouth, NH: Heinemann.

Ravitch, D. (1990). Multiculturalism: E pluribus plures. *The American Scholar, 59*(3): 337–354.

REACH Center. (1996). *Training of trainers manual.* (Available from REACH Center, 180 Nickerson St., Ste. 212, Seattle, WA 98109)

Rethinking Columbus. (1992). Special issue published by Rethinking Schools, Inc., 1001 E. Keefe Ave., Milwaukee, WI 53212 (800) 669-4192, www.rethinkingschools.org.

Riggs, M. (Producer). (1995). *Black is . . . Black ain't* [Video]. (87 minutes). Available from California Newsreel, 149 Ninth St., San Francisco, CA 94103.

Riley, K. L., & Stern, B. S. (1998). Using authentic assessment and qualitative methodology to bridge theory and practice. *Educational Forum, 62*(2): 178–185.

Rose, M. (1989). *Lives on the boundary: The struggles and achievements of America's underprepared.* New York: Macmillan.

Rossi, R. J. (Ed.). (1994). *Schools and students at risk.* New York: Teachers College.

Sadler, M., & Sadler, D. (1994). *Failing at fairness: How our schools cheat girls*. New York: Simon & Schuster.

Santrock, J. W. (1997). *Life-span development* (7th ed.). Boston: McGraw Hill.

———. (2001). *Adolescence* (8th ed.). Boston: McGraw Hill.

Sarason, S. (1990). *The predictable failure of educational reform*. San Francisco, CA: Jossey-Bass.

Schon, D. (1983). *The reflective practitioner: How professionals think in action*. New York: Basic Books.

Shade, B. J. (1989). Creating a culturally compatible classroom. In B. J. Shade (Ed.), *Culture, style, and the educative process*. Springfield, IL: Charles C. Thomas, Publisher.

Simon, A., & Boyer, E. G. (1967). *Mirrors for behavior: An anthology of classroom observation instruments*. Philadelphia: Research for Better Schools.

Sleeter, C. (1995). An analysis of the critiques of multicultural education. In J. Banks & C. Banks (Eds.), *Handbook of research on multicultural education* (pp. 81–94). New York: Macmillan.

Sleeter, C., & Grant, C. (1988). *Making choices for multicultural education: Five approaches to race, class, and gender*. Columbus, OH: Merrill.

Sleeter, C. E., & McLaren, P. L. (1995). Introduction: Exploring connections to build a critical multiculturalism. In C. E. Sleeter & P. L. McLaren (Eds.), *Multicultural education, critical pedagogy, and the politics of difference* (pp. 5–32). Albany: State University of New York.

Smitherman, G. (1977). *Talkin and testifyin: The language of Black America*. Detroit: Wayne State University.

Southern Poverty Law Center. (1999). *Ten ways to fight hate*. Montgomery, AL: Author.

Spence, M. (2000). Selling out Lewis and Clark. *The Sunday Oregonian*, May 14, pp. B1–2.

Stainback, S., & Stainback, W. (1996). *Inclusion: A guide for educators*. Baltimore, MD: Paul E. Brookes Publishing.

Stainback, W., Stainback, S., Stefanich, G., & Alper, S. (1996). Learning in inclusive classrooms. In S. Stainback & W. Stainback (Eds.), *Inclusion: A guide for educators* (pp. 209–219). Baltimore, MD: Paul E. Brookes Publishing.

Streitmatter, J. (1989). Identity development and academic achievement in early adolescence. *Journal of Early Adolescence, 9*: 99–116.

Sue, D. W. (1995). Toward a theory of multicultural counseling and therapy. In J. Banks & C. Banks (Eds.), *Handbook of research on multicultural education* (pp. 647–659). New York: Macmillan.

Tatum, B. (1992). Talking about race, learning about racism: The application of racial identity development theory in the classroom. *Harvard Educational Review 62* (1): 1–24.

The Foxfire School (www.yonkerspublicschools.org/fox.htm)

Tomlinson, C. A. (1999). *The differentiated classroom: Responding to the needs of all learners*. Alexandria, VA: Association for Supervision and Curriculum Development.

Triandis, H. (1995). *Individualism and collectivism*. Boulder, CO: Westview Press.

Washington State Commission on Student Learning. (1998). *Essential academic learning requirements: Technical manual*. Olympia, WA: Author.

Wellesley Center for Research on Women. (1992). *How schools shortchange girls*. Washington, DC: American Association of University Women Educational Foundation.

Wiggins, G. (1992). Creating tests worth taking. *Educational Leadership, 49*(8): 26–33.

Wilson, A. (1982). Cross-cultural experimental learning for teachers. *Theory into Practice, 21*(3): 184–92.

———. (1992). *To live in a multicultural world*. (ERIC Document Reproduction Service No. ED 369 668)

Wing, A. K. (Ed.). (2000). *Global critical race feminism*. New York: New York University Press.

Yates, E. (1989, c. 1950). *Amos Fortune, free man*. New York: Puffin.

Zimpher, N. L. (1989). The RATE project: A profile of teacher education students. *Journal of Teacher Education, 40*(6): 27–30.

INDEX